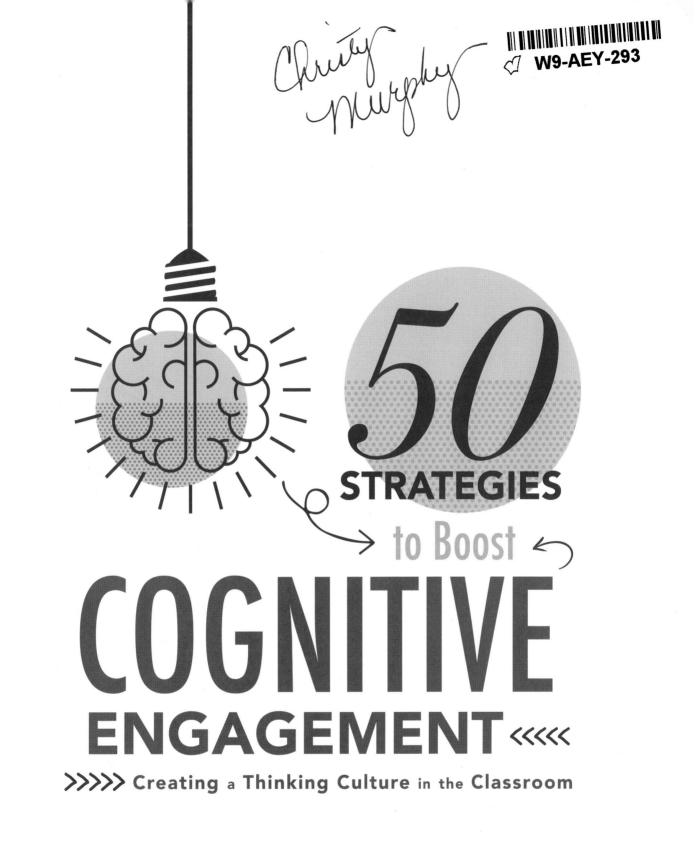

50
STRATEGIES
to Boost
COGNITIVE
ENGAGEMENT «««
>>>>> Creating a Thinking Culture in the Classroom

Rebecca Stobaugh

Solution Tree | Press *a division of* Solution Tree

555 North Morton Street
Bloomington, IN 47404
800.733.6786 (toll free) / 812.336.7700
FAX: 812.336.7790

email: info@SolutionTree.com
SolutionTree.com

Visit **go.SolutionTree.com/instruction** to download the free reproducibles in this book.

Printed in the United States of America

Library of Congress Cataloging-in-Publication Data

Names: Stobaugh, Rebecca, author.
Title: Fifty strategies to boost cognitive engagement : creating a thinking
    culture in the classroom / Rebecca Stobaugh.
Description: Bloomington, IN : Solution Tree Press, 2019. | Includes
    bibliographical references and index.
Identifiers: LCCN 2018045176 | ISBN 9781947604773 (perfect bound)
Subjects: LCSH: Critical thinking--Study and teaching. | Problem
    solving--Study and teaching. | Cognitive learning.
Classification: LCC LB1590.3 .S785 2019 | DDC 370.152--dc23 LC record available at
    https://lccn.loc.gov/2018045176

Solution Tree
Jeffrey C. Jones, CEO
Edmund M. Ackerman, President

Solution Tree Press
President and Publisher: Douglas M. Rife
Associate Publisher: Sarah Payne-Mills
Art Director: Rian Anderson
Managing Production Editor: Kendra Slayton
Senior Production Editor: Todd Brakke
Senior Editor: Amy Rubenstein
Copy Editor: Evie Madsen
Proofreader: Elisabeth Abrams
Cover Designer: Laura Cox
Editorial Assistant: Sarah Ludwig

This book is dedicated to my children. May they always challenge themselves to reach their full potential.

Acknowledgments

A special thanks to Rebecca Fields and Laura Beavers who suggested classroom examples and recommended several of the strategies I profiled, and to Marge Maxwell who provided insightful feedback.

Solution Tree Press would like to thank the following reviewers:

Terry Byfield
Business Teacher
Indian Hills Middle School
Prairie Village, Kansas

Melissa Cartwright
Seventh/Eighth-Grade Teacher
Helper Middle School
Helper, Utah

Teresa Dobler
Science Teacher
Washington Latin Public Charter School
Washington, DC

Tami Ewell
Language Arts Teacher
Copper Mountain Middle School
Herriman, Utah

Jodi Hebert
First Grade Teacher
D.C. Virgo Preparatory Academy
Wilmington, North Carolina

Sean Maloney
Fourth-Grade Teacher
Brooklyn Elementary School
Brooklyn, Connecticut

Visit **go.SolutionTree.com/instruction** to download the free reproducibles in this book.

Table of Contents

About the Author

Rebecca Stobaugh is an associate professor at Western Kentucky University, where she teaches assessment and unit-planning courses in the teacher education program. She also supervises first-year teachers and consults with school districts on critical thinking, instructional strategies, assessment, technology integration, and other topics. Previously, she served as a middle and high school teacher and a middle school principal.

Rebecca has authored several books, including *Assessing Critical Thinking in Middle and High Schools*, *Assessing Critical Thinking in Elementary Schools*, *Real-World Learning Framework for Elementary Schools*, *Real-World Learning Framework for Secondary Schools*, and *Critical Thinking in the Classroom*. Rebecca regularly serves on accreditation teams and writes grants to support K–12 professional development. She is the executive director and former president of Kentucky ASCD (Association for Supervision and Curriculum Development). Rebecca received the 2004 Social Studies Teacher of the Year Award from the Kentucky Council for the Social Studies.

She earned a bachelor's degree from Georgetown College, a master's degree from the University of Kentucky, and a doctorate in K–12 education leadership from the University of Louisville.

To book Rebecca Stobaugh for professional development, contact pd@SolutionTree.com.

About the Contributors

Lauren Tanner is a curriculum coordinator and former English and language arts high school teacher in Bowling Green, Kentucky. She has been teaching since 2011 and has served as the head of the English department, on multiple literacy committees, and as a testing coordinator. She has a master's degree in curriculum and instruction and is pursuing a Rank I in administration.

Alicia Wittmer is an elementary school teacher and was previously a reading interventionist. She fell in love with teaching and working with students while growing up in northern Kentucky. She has a master's degree in gifted education and talent development, as well as a gifted endorsement from Western Kentucky University.

Introduction

When students enter Mrs. Tanner's language arts classroom, they see their work posted on the wall. As class begins, they lead a discussion about their reading assignment from the night before. They pose questions to one another and share their thinking without fear of being wrong. Mrs. Tanner communicates the learning target for the day, but not the product. Students have a choice in how they demonstrate proficiency on the learning target. With classroom tasks framed around broad questions, students move around the room to the various furniture arrangements: workstations for individual reflection, group conversations, teacher-student conferences, and technology applications. Throughout the unit, students design authentic products like writing letters to the editor and hosting school poetry nights.

This model represents a new and necessary approach to instruction and learning. It is a model that shifts away from a culture of stand-and-deliver instruction to one that emphasizes a culture of thinking. With an increase in engagement and intentional thinking strategies, students can experience long-term understanding of the content. They learn and develop problem-solving and critical-thinking skills that will serve them well in their lives beyond school.

The purpose of this book is to offer you strategies that will help you transform your classroom from one of passive knowledge consumption to one of active engagement with activities that foster cognitive engagement and develop deep-level processing. It is about creating a thinking classroom culture.

But first, let's take a quick look at the changing demands of the professional workplace and the policy and assessment systems that make this book's content and strategies so valuable to both you and your students. Then, we'll establish the full scope of what you'll find in this book.

Changing Workplace Demands

Workforce needs are rapidly changing. In the 20th century, if a person could quickly produce facts and memorize information, he or she was considered intelligent. Through modern technology, anyone can retrieve information on almost anything within seconds. But how often is that information reliable or valid? How often does the user know how to interpret that information and make the most use of it?

The new, valued commodity for the 21st century is refined thinking skills. In *The Future of Jobs Report* (World Economic Forum, 2016), interviewers asked chief human resources and strategy officers from leading companies what employment skills they require. Table I.1 (page 2) highlights the changing needs industry experts expect as we transition from 2015 to 2020. Notice the increasing value of the bolded skills.

Table I.1: Top-Ten Skills for Employment

In 2015	In 2020
1. **Complex problem solving**	1. **Complex problem solving**
2. Coordinating with others	2. **Critical thinking**
3. People management	3. **Creativity**
4. **Critical thinking**	4. People management
5. Negotiation	5. Coordinating with others
6. Quality control	6. Emotional intelligence
7. Service orientation	7. **Judgment and decision making**
8. **Judgment and decision making**	8. Service orientation
9. Active listening	9. Negotiation
10. **Creativity**	10. **Cognitive flexibility**

Source: World Economic Forum, 2016.

Clearly, skills related to critical thinking are increasing in importance. Similarly, in a Hart Research Associates (2013) survey, 93 percent of employers agreed a job candidate's "demonstrated capacity to think critically, communicate clearly, and solve complex problems [was] more important than their undergraduate major" (p. 1). Job expectations are changing!

In the *Wall Street Journal*, reporter Kate Davidson (2016) writes, "Companies have automated or outsourced many routine tasks, and the jobs that remain often require workers to take on broader responsibilities that demand critical thinking, empathy or other abilities that computers can't easily simulate." In researching qualities of Google's top employees, surprisingly, *Washington Post* education reporter Valerie Strauss (2017) finds the company regards STEM (science, technology, engineering, and mathematics) expertise to be less important than six other key identifiers: (1) being a good coach, (2) communicating and listening effectively, (3) valuing different perspectives, (4) demonstrating compassion toward colleagues, (5) exhibiting strong critical-thinking and problem-solving skills, and (6) formulating connections between complicated concepts.

Despite all this, schools are not consistently preparing students for this world. The U.S. Chamber of Commerce Foundation (n.d.) states, "Somewhere along the road from education to employment, the system is not routinely equipping all students with all the skills they need to succeed" (p. 2). The skills the U.S. Chamber of Commerce Foundation (n.d.) cites as necessary align very closely with those that business leaders noted in table I.1.

- Teamwork and collaboration
- Problem solving and critical thinking
- Organization
- Interpersonal communication
- Leadership
- Work ethic and persistence
- Creativity
- Relationships and conflict resolution

These findings are not just common to the professional world. In *The Role of Education in Building Soft Skills*, researchers Alan D. Greenberg and Andrew H. Nilssen (2014) find that when teachers, administrators, parents, and students are asked about what qualities are most important, problem solving caps the list, with 65 percent finding it very important, followed by collaboration (56 percent), persistence (50 percent), creativity (37 percent), academic knowledge (33 percent), and leadership skills (35 percent).

The question that naturally evolves from this is, How do we move from knowing there is a need for cognitive engagement to ensuring our education system can deliver on it?

Policy and Assessment Systems Changes

These demands for student competencies are shaping national and international assessments. The Central Committee of the Communist Party states that education in China must begin to "emphasize sowing students' creativity and practical abilities over instilling an ability to achieve certain test scores and recite rote knowledge" (Zhao, 2006). The Organisation for Economic Co-operation and Development (OECD, n.d.), whose focus is to enhance economic progress and world trade, defines *global competence* as the ability to evaluate global and culture challenges from many viewpoints through a critical lens and comprehend how perceptions shape differences, so to effectively communicate with others from various backgrounds. The foundation of this global competence resonates on well-developed analytical and critical-thinking skills—interpreting the meaning of information, approaching problems logically, and evaluating the validity and reliability of information. To this end, the organization established the 2018 Programme for International Student Assessment (https://nces.ed.gov/surveys/pisa), a cognitive assessment program to measure understanding (along with analytical and critical thinking) while engaged in real-world problem solving on international issues.

Similarly, the Partnership for Assessment of Readiness for College and Careers (https://parcc-assessment.org) and Smarter Balanced Assessment Consortium (www.smartbalanced.org) are designing rigorous assessments to evaluate college and career readiness through critical-thinking tasks measuring analysis skills instead of rote memorization. Stanford professor emerita and president and CEO of the Learning Policy Institute Linda Darling-Hammond (2012) avows:

> Performance tasks ask students to research and analyze information, weigh evidence, and solve problems relevant to the real world, allowing students to demonstrate their knowledge and skills in an authentic way. The Smarter Balanced assessment system uses performance tasks to measure skills valued by higher education and the workplace—critical thinking, problem solving, and communication—that are not adequately assessed by most statewide assessments today. (p. 2)

The Every Student Succeeds Act (ESSA; 2015) also transfers the focus from remembering and recitation to higher-level thinking, as shown in one of the ESSA major areas directed toward access to learning opportunities focused on higher-order-thinking skills. Authors Channa M. Cook-Harvey, Linda Darling-Hammond, Livia Lam, Charmaine Mercer, and Martens Roc (2016) write:

> Rather than the rote-oriented education that disadvantaged students have regularly received, which prepares them for the factory jobs of the past, ESSA insists that states redesign education systems to reflect 21st-century learning. The new law establishes a set of expectations for states to design standards and assessments that

develop and measure high-order thinking skills for children and provides related resources for professional learning. (p. 1)

The evidence of the need for developing a thinking-based culture in all classrooms is clear. With all this in mind, let's examine how this book will help you build critical-thinking skills in your students and what it will take to make a thinking culture an everyday part of your classroom.

About This Book

This book will support educators as they seek to embed critical thinking into instruction by providing fifty easy-to-implement strategies that lead to high levels of student engagement that deepen learning. States, districts, and even individual schools all have valid ideas and systems in place they believe will serve student interests, but ultimately, it comes down to teachers.

As researchers Robert J. Marzano and Michael D. Toth (2014) write:

> If we hope to move students to these higher levels of skills and cognition, it's imperative that we equip teachers with the "how," those essential teaching strategies that will scaffold students to problem-solve and make decisions in real-world scenarios with less teacher direction. (p. 11)

Seventy-six percent of educators state they don't have sufficient knowledge and training to nurture creative problem solving (Adobe Systems, 2018). Similarly, in a large-scale study of teachers applying for National Board Certification, a key element differentiating those who earned and didn't earn certification was their ability to plan curriculum that transitions students from understanding to deeper learning outcomes (Smith, Baker, Hattie, & Bond, 2008). Possessing the ability to design tasks with high-cognitive-level outcomes is an advanced teaching skill.

This book will help you enhance your ability to design these high-cognitive tasks in the following ways.

- Chapter 1 fully defines *critical thinking* and *cognitive engagement*, details ways to involve students in deep-level processing strategies, and provides guidelines on establishing a thinking classroom culture.

- Chapter 2 focuses on Bloom's taxonomy revised (Anderson & Krathwohl, 2001), describing each level of its cognitive processes while also providing numerous classroom examples to highlight how you engage students at the levels most likely to engage their critical-thinking skills.

- Chapter 3 establishes the criteria for this book's strategies organization. It also clarifies the three supporting components of the strategies that produce the engagement necessary to allow critical thinking to happen.

- Chapters 4–7 contain the fifty strategies for critical thinking at the heart of this book. Chapter 4 provides strategies that emphasize the Understand level of Bloom's taxonomy revised (Anderson & Krathwohl, 2001); chapter 5 highlights strategies at the Analyze level; the strategies in chapter 6 align with the Evaluate level; and chapter 7 provides strategies that produce the highest and most demanding kinds of thinking, the Create level. These higher levels on Bloom's revised taxonomy (Anderson & Krathwohl, 2001) challenge students to think critically and problem solve, better preparing them for life outside of school.

- Chapter 8 wraps up this book by outlining several key aspects of a thinking classroom culture. The knowledge in this chapter is the cement that will hold all the strategy bricks together.

Each chapter ends with a series of Discussion Questions and a Take Action section that provides activities you can use to put this book's ideas and strategies to work.

When you consider the vital importance of thinking skills to students' future prospects, the need for all teachers to cultivate a classroom culture high in cognitive engagement is clear. If you're ready to make this essential transition, you need only turn the page.

CHAPTER 1

Understanding Cognitive Engagement and the Thinking-Based Classroom

Too often we give children answers to remember rather than problems to solve.
—Roger Lewin

Should education focus on ensuring acquisition of knowledge (that is, information, facts, and data) or building skills (creativity, communication, collaboration, and critical thinking)? Traditionally, the behavioral or transmission model emphasized that learning required reciting and reproducing information. This model focuses on transmission of knowledge through delivering content, not on the learner (Koenig, 2010). A thinking-based classroom looks remarkably different. It centers on building students' skills and their thinking processes (see table 1.1). It is a path to deeper learning, which is a high-leverage strategy to propel learning as students engage in complex tasks.

This all begs the question of what *thinking* is in the context of learning. To be sure, thinking covers a variety of categories and cognitive levels from information analysis to problem solving and effective collaboration skills. Bloom's taxonomy revised (Anderson & Krathwohl, 2001) is a key part of all this, and we'll cover those connections in detail in chapter 2 (page 11), but in this chapter, we start with a focus on two broad-based concepts that succinctly establish the core aspects of the thinking-based classroom—*critical thinking* and *cognitive engagement*.

Table 1.1: Transmission Model Versus Thinking Model

Transmission Model	Thinking Model
• Teacher-centered classrooms • One right way to answer a problem • Focus on grades • Testing culture • Students not allowed to talk • Speedy answers encouraged	• Learning-centered classrooms • Divergent ways to solve a problem • Focus on the learning process • Learning culture • Student discussions of diverse ideas and solutions • Authentic, intellectually demanding work

Source: Adapted from Ritchhart, 2015.

Critical Thinking

Critical thinking is a common descriptor in modern education, but it's not always one that teachers truly know how to define. *Critical thinking* is a reasoned approach to problems, decisions, questions, and issues. This kind of thinking is skillful and a precursor to all learning.

We can all identify times in our lives when we didn't think critically about a problem, decision, question, or issue. Maybe a few of these examples will resonate with you.

- Dated someone for superficial reasons (such as having nice hair, pretty eyes, or a cool car)

- Decided to go on vacation without considering possible consequences

- Took part in a class or professional development session without focusing on its content or mission

- Took a stance on an issue with little evidence or support

- Considered evidence from an unreliable source

By reflecting on times when you didn't engage your full cognitive self, you can start examining the attributes that do describe critical (or skillful) thinking. The following list describes the *Habits of Mind* related to critical thinking (Swartz, Costa, Beyer, Reagan, & Kallick, 2008):

- Persisting at a task that requires thinking
- Managing impulsivity in thinking and acting
- Thinking flexibly
- Striving for accuracy and precision
- Thinking interdependently
- Listening with understanding and empathy
- Communicating with clarity and precision
- Responding with wonderment and awe
- Creating, imagining, and innovating
- Taking responsible risks in thinking
- Finding humor
- Questioning and problem posing
- Applying past knowledge to novel situations
- Gathering data through all the senses
- Remaining open to continuous learning (p. 19)

Which areas of this list are your areas of strength?

Even if you are personally strong in several of these areas, or even if you feel you have strengths in all of them, that is only the start of the process. To truly establish a thinking-based classroom, you need to impart these qualities to each and every one of your students. Education author and consultant David A. Sousa (2011) states, "If something is worth teaching, it is worth teaching well" (p. 150).

Memorizing information does not tend to support transferring the learning to new situations, but when tasks require students to process information deeply and develop understandings, transference is more likely to occur. Being smart isn't memorizing a lot of facts. Sousa (2011) further emphasizes, "The cognitive research supports the notion that transfer occurs more easily if students have processed the initial learning in ways that promote deep, abstract understanding of the material, rather than emphasizing the rote application of superficial similarities" (p. 159).

True intelligence is the ability to solve problems, apply new learnings, and carefully evaluate. Author Rhoda Koenig (2010) comments, "Without this higher-level processing, we succeed at nothing more than adding to our students' 'bank' of inert knowledge" (p. 22). Research shows that students perceive cognitively challenging tasks as meaningful and intriguing (Marzano & Pickering, 2011). Professor John Hattie (2009) finds cognitive challenge to have an effect size of 0.57 on student learning.

Effect size, which is a numerical representation of an effort's impact on learning, derives from measuring the impact of implementing a change versus not doing so using an experiment group and a control group (Olejnik & Algina, 2000). An effect size of 0.57 is in the moderate to strong gain range, representing one to two years' worth of academic growth.

The point of emphasizing all of this is simple: as instruction becomes more complex and stimulating, students become more engaged in the learning process. The question becomes, How do you emphasize critical thinking in your own instructional practices? Education author Bonnie Potts (1994) identifies four key areas important for teaching critical thinking that remain resonant as a core rule set for establishing critical-thinking practices in your classroom.

1. Learning with others in a group setting

2. Posing open-ended questions that are ill-defined and challenge students to think creatively

3. Providing wait time for students to develop their thinking by asking questions, discussing with others, and refining their thinking before responding

4. Practicing critical-thinking skills in various contexts to ensure students apply the skill in new situations

The fifty strategies in this book all place an emphasis on one or more of these key areas, and when you join these aspects of critical thinking with components that foster engagement, your students will fully realize the benefits of a thinking-based classroom.

Cognitive Engagement

Closely related to critical thinking, *cognitive engagement* refers to the "psychological effort students put into learning and mastering content" (Fisher, Frey, Quaglia, Smith, & Lande, 2018, p. 135). When students are cognitively engaged, they might lose track of time and say things like, "Is class already over?" Some other attributes of cognitive engagement include persevering and learning from experiences, sharing learning with others, and enthusiastically engaging in the learning process (Fisher et al., 2018). I like to say, "The worker is the learner." I can recall going over review sheets or leading *Jeopardy!* review games; I was working really hard, but the students were not as engaged. As educators, our work must lie in designing rigorous tasks that lead students to grapple with content and engage in the heavy-lifting work called *learning*. When it comes to time spent in the classroom, your students should always be working harder than you are.

Given the importance of cognitive engagement to learning, how prevalent is it in schools? Authors John V. Antonetti and James R. Garver (2015) conducted a study based on 17,124 classroom visits. They conclude that a majority of the classrooms (87 percent) emphasize low-level thinking focused on knowledge and comprehension, 9 percent of classrooms require students to apply or analyze, and 4 percent of classrooms promote synthesis and evaluation. As part of this study, they define and measure a classroom's level of engagement based on three criteria: (1) *off-task classrooms* had a significant number of students not participating in classroom tasks, (2) *on-task* classrooms had students compliantly following the teacher's expectations in an orderly classroom, and (3) *engaged classrooms* were cognitively engaged (Antonetti & Garver, 2015). Table 1.2 summarizes these results. Are you surprised?

When measuring cognitive engagement, it is important to focus on student behaviors rather than teacher behaviors. This is where we see the relationship emerge between critical thinking and cognitive engagement. Notice how, when thinking levels shift from low to middle there is a 27 percent increase in engaged learning followed with a 13 percent increase when instruction moves from middle-to-high levels of thinking. Antonetti and Garver (2015) caution, "Attempts to improve student engagement without concurrent efforts to raise the thinking levels of student work can lead to learners enthusiastically participating in low-level tasks" (p. 30).

We find supporting evidence for this conclusion from a National Institute of Child Health and Human Development study, which examines fifth-grade

Table 1.2: Cross Tabulation Between Engagement Level and Thinking Level

Thinking Level	Number of Visits	Level of Engagement		
		Off Task	On Task	Engaged
Low	14,898	4 percent	94 percent	2 percent
Middle	1,541	Less than 1 percent	71 percent	29 percent
High	685	0 percent	58 percent	42 percent

Source: Antonetti & Garver, 2015, p. 81.

classroom observations (Pianta, Belsky, Houts, & Morrison, 2007). It finds 58 percent of students' time is spent on learning basic skills, with less than 13 percent on higher-level learning involving analysis and inference. Less than 5 percent of instructional time involves collaborative work, and less than 1 percent of students are highly engaged. It concludes students are either compliant or defiant, but few are truly engaged (Pianta et al., 2007).

To move students toward engagement with a strong critical-thinking component, Marzano and Toth (2014) analyzed more than two million classroom observations, finding the highest level of thinking tasks include hypothesis generation and testing and that these are apparent in less than 6 percent of instructional lessons. Marzano and Toth (2014) assert that for students to be successful on revised assessments and in college and careers, they must be able to analyze and synthesize. To do this, they posit that students need opportunities to take knowledge and apply it in authentic situations.

As you reflect on the data on the proliferation of classrooms with low cognitive engagement, ask yourself: "Do you see parallels to this data in your classroom or school district? What percentage of your instruction focuses on higher-level thinking?" If there is room to improve, that's OK. It's common for teachers to struggle with incorporating critical thinking. Fortunately, there are a few practical ideas that can support teachers in this transition.

Antonetti and Garver (2015) identify the following questions that highlight eight characteristics that ensure high-level cognitive engagement.

1. Does the activity, strategy, task, or idea allow for the student to personalize his or her response? Can they bring their life experiences into the activity and make it their own?

2. Are there clear and modeled expectations?

3. Is there a sense of audience above and beyond the teacher and the test? Does the activity have value to someone else?

4. Is there social interaction? Do students have an opportunity to talk about the learning and interact?

5. Is there a culture of emotional safety? Are mistakes valued because they are an opportunity to learn?

6. Do students have opportunities to choose within the activity?

7. Is it an authentic activity? This doesn't mean it always must connect directly to the student's world, but it should connect to reality.

8. Is the task new and novel? If kids are bored, is it hard to see engagement?

In their research, Antonetti and Garver (2015) determine that if three of the eight characteristics are present in a classroom, students demonstrate sustained cognitive engagement between 84 and 86 percent of the time. However, when two characteristics are present in classrooms, engagement levels drop to 16 percent of the time and further drop to less than 4 percent when only one characteristic is present.

Critical-thinking skills enable students to be successful in careers and in life, and classrooms offer tremendous power and opportunity to team critical thinking with student engagement. Such instruction can be challenging, while also being interesting and appealing to students. Given the research-backed importance of increasing levels of cognitive engagement, and to truly understand the fifty strategies in this book that accomplish this, it's important to examine the full scope of thinking as defined in Bloom's taxonomy revised (Anderson & Krathwohl, 2001). This is the purpose of the next chapter.

Discussion Questions

As you reflect on this chapter, consider the following five questions.

1. Review table 1.1 (page 5). Is your classroom instruction more focused on transmission or thinking? How can you further evolve your practices to make yours an increasingly thinking-based classroom?

2. How do you define critical thinking? What characteristics do you most value?

3. What evidence of critical thinking do you see in your classroom? How might you create more opportunities for it?

4. When you see your students demonstrating cognitive engagement, what does it look like? What evidence do you have that your students are engaged?

5. When you actively engage your students in learning, are they working at lower or higher levels of thinking? How can you shift more of this engagement toward higher levels?

Take Action

Use the following three activities to put this chapter's concepts to work in your own classroom.

1. Create a survey with the fifteen *Habits of Mind* (Swartz et al., 2008) related to critical thinking (see page 6). Ask your students to identify which habits they demonstrate on a routine basis, and then have them select a few habits they need to enhance. Using this information, determine some ways you can help them strengthen those habits.

2. Select an activity or assignment you use with your students and review it with the eight important characteristics of cognitive engagement listed in the Cognitive Engagement section (page 7). Evaluate whether the activity or assignment meets each characteristic. Identify ways to improve the assignment.

3. Work with a colleague and observe each other's classroom. Similar to Antonetti and Garver's (2015) research, chart the level of engagement in the classroom as off task, on task, or engaged, and the thinking level as low, middle, or high. Reflect on areas of strength and identify areas for improvement and how you can achieve that improvement.

CHAPTER 2

Applying a Taxonomy to the Thinking in Your Classroom

Children are not vessels to be filled, but lamps to be lit.
—Swami Chinmayananda Saraswati

There are many taxonomies for classifying levels of thinking; however, Benjamin S. Bloom's (1956) seminal work, *Taxonomy of Educational Objectives*, establishes a taxonomy or classification system. In *A Taxonomy for Learning, Teaching, and Assessing: A Revision of Bloom's Taxonomy of Educational Objectives*, editors Lorin W. Anderson and David R. Krathwohl (2001) suggest revisions that redefine the levels as Remember, Understand, Apply, Analyze, Evaluate, and Create. These revised levels are the focus of this chapter—a lens through which you can view the strategies in this book, and the filter through which the strategies are organized.

The first three levels—Remember, Understand, and Apply—often require convergent thinking with similar student answers to assignments. However, the Analyze, Evaluate, and Create levels typify the sort of divergent thinking that supports a variety of correct solutions or products. Needless to say, the strategies in this book focus much more heavily on aspects of critical thinking that focus on divergent solutions to challenging problems, although we do start at Understand-level strategies as a base for building these skills. Sousa (2011) sums up the thinking at each of these levels as follows.

- The Remember and Understand levels involve students acquiring and understanding information.

- The Apply and Analyze levels describe students transforming information through deduction and inference. (The Analyze-level strategies in chapter 5, page 39, all implicitly involve Apply-level thinking as part of the process.)

- The Evaluate and Create levels describe students generating new information.

The revised version of Bloom's taxonomy identifies cognitive processes under each level to clarify the level of thinking (Anderson & Krathwohl, 2001). It includes nineteen cognitive processes classified among the six levels (table 2.1, page 12).

To understand how to properly implement strategies for cognitive engagement at various critical-thinking levels, educators need to grasp the foundational knowledge of the depth of thinking required at each Bloom's level. I find that, without a rooted understanding of the level of thinking complexity, educators tend to misidentify Bloom's levels, often inaccurately believing their instruction is engaging students in higher levels of thinking.

Table 2.1: Bloom's Taxonomy Revised

Thinking Level	Cognitive Processes	
Remember	• Recognizing	• Recalling
Understand	• Interpreting • Exemplifying • Classifying • Summarizing	• Inferring • Comparing • Explaining
Apply	• Executing	• Implementing
Analyze	• Differentiating • Organizing	• Attributing
Evaluate	• Checking	• Critiquing
Create	• Generating • Planning	• Producing

Source: Anderson & Krathwohl, 2001.

To better interpret these Bloom's levels and cognitive processes, I describe each of them in the following sections, along with examples of student-focused tasks that align to each level's cognitive processes.

Thinking at the Remember Level

At the Remember level, learners must recover information they previously memorized. Although this is a low-level thinking process, memorizing information is important for higher-level thinking. For example, knowing the types of rocks can help students analyze problems with rock formations, a higher-level thinking skill.

There are two cognitive processes within the Remember level: (1) recognizing and (2) recalling.

Recognizing

Recognizing involves students selecting the correct memorized answer from a series of answer choices, like in a multiple-choice test. The following are examples of activities that use the recognizing cognitive process.

- Have students create a set of word cards and definitions based on textbook information using Quizlet (https://quizlet.com).

- Provide students with a list of terms and a list of definitions, and ask students to match them.

- Provide students with a series of shapes, and ask them to circle the shapes that are quadrilaterals, for example.

Recalling

Recalling requires students to provide a correct memorized answer from their memory, like for a fill-in-the-blank question. The following are examples of interactions that use the recalling sublevel.

- Ask students, "What feature is found at the top of a graph to tell the reader what topic is being displayed?"

- Say to students, "Through a process, plants use carbon dioxide to create oxygen and food. What is this process called?"

- Ask students, "What is the main function of each branch of the U.S. government?"

Thinking at the Understand Level

Where Remember-level thinking is critical for establishing foundational concepts, information that is not processed (or understood) at deeper levels is easy to forget. At the Understand level, students begin establishing new connections with the content.

There are seven cognitive processes associated with the Understand level: (1) interpreting, (2) exemplifying, (3) classifying, (4) summarizing, (5) inferring, (6) comparing, and (7) explaining.

Interpreting

When *interpreting*, students convert information from one form to another; this might mean changing text into paraphrases, pictures, graphics, or music. The following are examples of activities that use the interpreting cognitive process.

- Instruct students to use a novel's cover to explain what they think the book is about. (Convert pictures to text.)

- Instruct students to use a music-making program like GarageBand (www.apple.com/mac/garageband) to create a song describing one of the key terms for the unit. (Convert text to music.)

- Instruct students to examine a peer's or previous student's work on a mathematical problem and orally explain how that student solved it. (Convert graphics to paraphrased speech.)

- Have students listen to the story of a raindrop and its journey, and then instruct them to create a diagram to show the route the raindrop travels through the water cycle. (Convert text to pictures.)

- Instruct students to paraphrase a partner's answer after a Think-Pair-Share activity. (Convert speech to paraphrased speech.)

Exemplifying

With *exemplifying*, students must understand an existing concept and then find and suggest another example of that concept. These examples may include connections to other content areas or prior experiences. The following are examples of activities that use the exemplifying cognitive process.

- After having students learn about different types of graphs, instruct them to scan a report and locate similar examples of different types of graphs.

- After having students study the states of matter, instruct them to identify various chemical changes, such as making ice cubes, burning firewood, melting a snowman, or putting gelatin in a refrigerator.

- After providing students with several examples of similes from a text, instruct them to create their own original example of a simile.

- After having students learn about fact versus opinion, instruct them to locate an example of an author's opinion in a text.

Classifying

When *classifying*, students categorize information or items based on similar characteristics. For example, students group information under headings based on their common attributes. The following are examples of activities that use the classifying cognitive process.

- Instruct students to group mathematics equations into categories based on the basic number properties (such as associative property, distributive property, and so on).

- Instruct students to sort real-world pictures—such as a stop sign, a wheel, and so on—based on the subject's number of sides and angles.

- After explaining the difference between living and nonliving things, instruct students to read a story and sort objects in the story based on whether they are living or nonliving.

- Instruct students to sort new vocabulary into categories based on connotation.

Summarizing

When *summarizing*, students simplify information in a succinct statement. The summary could be about reading, watching a video clip, or observing a natural event. The following are examples of activities that use the summarizing cognitive process.

- Direct students to use sticky notes in the margin of a text to write down one sentence that summarizes each paragraph.

- After listening to a story, instruct students to write down three important plot points.

- After examining a word problem and modeling a valid answer to it, instruct students to describe the steps necessary to solve the problem.

- Have students identify the key points in a science video on force and motion.

Inferring

Inferring involves using evidence and reasons to make a conclusion. Inferences drawn with limited evidence can be inaccurate so it's important for teachers to model for students how to recognize and use valid and reliable evidence to support their conclusion. The following are examples of activities that use the inferring cognitive process.

- Instruct students to determine the next three numbers in a pattern. For example, "List the next three numbers in a pattern that begins: 345, 355, 365."

- Based on their use of microscope slides of different matter, instruct students to determine if an object is a solid or a liquid.

- Instruct students to use context clues to determine an author's opinion when it is not explicitly stated in the text.

- Instruct students to predict what will happen next in a text, based on clues from the reading.

- After having students watch a pot of boiling water for ten minutes, instruct them to describe what happens to the water level and what reasoning might explain the change.

Comparing

Comparing involves examining two different ideas or items to assess their similarities and differences. For example, students can use metaphors or analogies to make their comparisons. The following are examples of activities that use the comparing cognitive process.

- Instruct students to compare two solutions that slow or prevent wind from changing the shape of the land by providing two similarities and three differences between the solutions.

- Instruct students to examine the data on two graphs and determine how they are similar and different in terms of mean, median, and mode.

- Instruct students to identify similarities between two paragraphs with a similar theme.

- Instruct students to describe two similarities and two differences between two ecosystems.

Explaining

Explaining involves understanding cause-and-effect relationships. The following are examples of activities that use the explaining cognitive process.

- Instruct students to consider a mathematics problem that highlights the order of operations. Ask them to explain how changing the order changes the solution.

- Instruct students to assess a flowering plant from the school grounds that has wilted leaves and explain what might have caused the wilting.

- After having students read about the Boston Tea Party, instruct them to explain how they think England might react.

- Instruct students to explain how using dashes instead of commas might impact the readability of a text.

Thinking at the Apply Level

At the third level of Bloom's taxonomy revised (Anderson & Krathwohl, 2001), the Apply level involves executing certain procedures or steps to address a new problem. This usually involves teaching procedures to accomplish a task, such as teaching the steps to analyze a political cartoon, a procedure for analyzing a five-paragraph essay, or a method for finding the area of a triangle.

There are two cognitive processes in the Apply level: (1) executing and (2) implementing.

Executing

In *executing*, students must grapple with a new problem and identify a procedure to solve the problem. This might include solving for a variable in an algebraic equation, editing a paper for punctuation, and so on. At this lower-cognitive process within the Apply level, students should very quickly be able to identify a procedure and apply it to the new problem when there is one correct answer. The following are examples of activities that use the executing cognitive process.

- After demonstrating a method for adding three-digit numbers, instruct students to add two such numbers together; for example, 654 + 162.

- After presenting different objects in the room, instruct students to draw models of the waves that dropping the objects into the water would produce.

- After modeling an example, instruct students to write an original sentence demonstrating the same structure of the model sentence.

- After teaching the rules for semicolon usage, instruct students to add semicolons to a paragraph.

- After modeling the steps involved in free-throw shooting, instruct students to practice shooting free throws.

Implementing

Implementing tasks often involve more variables than executing tasks, and are therefore more challenging. This is because the procedure students must select to complete the task isn't immediately clear, and sometimes the problems might have more than one answer. The following are examples of activities that use the implementing cognitive process.

- Instruct students to answer the following problem: John had forty-five apples. While driving home, twelve rolled out of his truck. He stopped, and his neighbor doubled the apples he had. How many apples does John have now?

- Instruct students to create a grocery list of items they need to make spaghetti for their family. Students should use local grocery advertisements to help them stay within a given budget.

- Instruct students to use a six-step prewriting process to plan a letter to their principal about their thoughts on changes to the student cell phone policy.

- Instruct students to use the SOAPSTone (speaker, occasion, audience, purpose, subject, tone) process to identify each element in a two-paragraph newspaper editorial.

Thinking at the Analyze Level

At the Analyze level, learners use knowledge and understanding to complete higher-level tasks. If a student can search the internet for the correct answer or provide the teacher with an answer within a few minutes, the task is not at this level. This level is also the ground floor for the even higher-level thinking that goes on at the Evaluate and Create levels. "A key component of critical thinking is the process of analyzing and assessing thinking with a view to improving it. Hence, many consider the Analyze level as the beginning of deep-thinking processes" (Stobaugh, 2013, p. 28).

At the Analyze level, there are three cognitive processes: (1) differentiating, (2) organizing, and (3) attributing.

Differentiating

With this cognitive process, students must determine relevant and irrelevant source information. Differentiating is more complex than the Understand-level cognitive process of comparing since students must determine which information contributes to an overall structure. The following are examples of activities that use the differentiating cognitive process.

- Instruct students to determine which facts from a source you provide do not match characteristics of a given landform.

- Instruct students to highlight information from a relevant source that is not needed to solve a real-world problem.

- Instruct students to identify evidence in a related text supporting the claim that global warming is occurring.

- Instruct students to identify quotes from a story-based text that establish and support the theme.

Organizing

When *organizing*, students examine interactions and sequences of events to identify connections among relevant information. They must then design a new arrangement or structure for the information that depicts these relationships. To demonstrate their knowledge, students might construct charts, diagrams, outlines, flowcharts, or other graphic organizers to depict the interrelationships among the information. The following are examples of activities that use the organizing cognitive process.

- Instruct students to select a graph format that most appropriately organizes given data.

- After having students examine five real-world mathematical prompts, have them sort the prompts into two groups and explain how they are similar.

- Instruct students to categorize the twenty vocabulary words in three to five groups and explain what the words in each group have in common.

- Instruct students to create a graphic organizer or another visual depicting the claims and counterclaims for an argument.

Attributing

The cognitive process of *attributing* involves students identifying biases, assumptions, or points of view in information. Assessing the credibility of sources helps students analyze that information. The following are examples of activities that use the attributing cognitive process.

- Instruct students to read a primary source on a word-processing program and add a comment to the text when they see it express biases, assumptions, or points of view.

- Instruct students to examine the data related to students' perspectives on school lunches, and have them use the information available to determine what concerns this information reveals and if those perspectives are rooted in real or perceived issues.

- After reading the novel *The Awakening* (Chopin, 1993), instruct students to determine the author's perspective of gender roles. Students explain the perspective using at least five quotes from the text.

- Instruct students to determine the author's point of view in an article about gun violence. Students should cite textual evidence to support their conclusion.

- After reviewing the beginning steps of a peer's science experiment, instruct students to identify any biases or assumptions its creator made in his or her hypothesis.

Thinking at the Evaluate Level

To prepare students to survive and succeed in the modern world, evaluating information is a vital skill. As educator and leadership expert Douglas Reeves (2015) states, "Reluctance to criticize and evaluate is the ally of mediocrity" (p. 25).

At the Evaluate level, students examine information sources to assess quality and then make decisions based on specific criteria. When students engage in Evaluate-level tasks, they typically also deploy lower-level skills, particularly at the Analyze level. This makes evaluating a highly engaging cognitive process.

There are two cognitive processes at the Evaluate level: (1) checking and (2) critiquing.

Checking

Checking encompasses examining for fallacies or inconsistencies (Anderson & Krathwohl, 2001). In *Assessing Critical Thinking in Middle and High Schools*, I write, "Students possessing this cognitive ability pursue unsubstantiated claims, question ideas, and demand validation for arguments, interpretations, assumptions, beliefs, or theories" (Stobaugh, 2013, p. 33). To check a source, students might examine the author's qualifications, determine if it provides sufficient and valid evidence for its perspective, or assess if it uses reliable sources. The following are examples of activities that use the checking cognitive process.

- Instruct students to watch a peer group's ShowMe (www.showme.com) screencast recording that details the group's problem-solving steps as it attempts to solve a multistep, real-world mathematics problem. Students check their work and identify any errors.

- Instruct students to examine the inferences of a peer's analysis of an earthquake magnitude per region chart. Students determine if each inference is accurate based on the data and explain why.

- Instruct students to examine a peer's essay that provides evidence his or her fictional animal can survive in a particular habitat. Students determine whether the peer used sufficient and valid substantiation to support the survival of his or her new creation.

- Instruct students to read a political speech, and determine if its arguments are logical or fallacies.

- Instruct students to read "A Modest Proposal" by essayist Jonathan Swift (1996) and identify logical arguments and fallacies he makes in the text.

Critiquing

Critiquing involves using set criteria to evaluate various options. When critiquing, students identify reasons each option meets or does not meet the criteria, ultimately identifying the best choice. The following are examples of activities that use the critiquing cognitive process.

- Instruct students to use their knowledge about money and counting money to determine if Alexander, in *Alexander, Who Used to Be Rich Last Sunday* (Viorst, 1987), is making the best decisions. Students describe three choices Alexander makes during the story and use their mathematics skills to explain if those are good choices.

- Instruct students to work as a group to determine three traits important to high-quality paper towels. Groups test four brands of paper towels and note how each performs on each trait. Each group plans a short presentation sharing the brand it believes is the best based on its findings.

- Instruct students to examine a rubric for evaluating a persuasive letter they submit. In the self-evaluation column on the rubric, the students note their score for each rubric criterion. They highlight challenging key words in the rubric and state the reasons for their score.

- Instruct students to evaluate who would be the best author to bring to the school after a special presentation for examining the school budget. Students identify the kind of qualities the school should consider when deciding whom to select. After researching the authors, students also rate each on the identified qualities and prepare a digital presentation to persuasively convince the school's library media specialist that their author is the best choice.

- Instruct students to create a rubric to evaluate which new student-created plan for the school's website is the best. Students evaluate three such plans and record strengths and areas of improvement for each rubric indicator.

Thinking at the Create Level

The highest level of Bloom's taxonomy revised is the Create level and, not surprisingly, it is both the most nebulous and most complex (Anderson & Krathwohl, 2001). Sir Ken Robinson asserts that *creativity* is "a process of having original ideas that have value" (as cited in Azzam, 2009, p. 22). Developmental and cognitive psychologist Wendy L. Ostroff (2016) comments, "Creativity is imagination in action" (p. 76).

For our purposes, *creativity* involves having students organize information in a new way to design a product. At this level, students utilize the thinking processes of the Understand, Analyze, and Evaluate levels to design a new product that demonstrates understanding of content. On the importance of creativity to learning, best-selling author Robert Greene (2012) writes:

> First, it is through all of their hard work, the depth of their knowledge, and the development of their analytical skills that they reach this higher form of intelligence. Second, when they experience this intuition or insight, they invariably subject it to a high degree of reflection and reasoning. (p. 259)

The challenge for teachers is ensuring that the creative tasks they assign meet the necessary criteria. When students produce a poster or website, it does not necessarily mean the task is on the Create level. To be on the Create level, the task must ensure that students are engaged in brainstorming new ideas, identifying the best idea, planning a solution, and then designing a solution different from others.

Because Create-level content has multiple, demanding criteria, it's important that we explore this level of Bloom's taxonomy revised (Anderson & Krathwohl, 2001) a little deeper. Educational consultant Patti Drapeau (2014) establishes the following six criteria for students who think creatively:

- Express ideas other students don't think of.
- Like to choose their own way of demonstrating understanding.
- Ask questions that may seem off-task or silly.
- Enjoy open-ended assignments.
- Prefer to discuss ideas rather than facts.
- Prefer to try new ways of approaching a problem rather than accepted ways. (p. 6)

In schools, teachers can post problems or challenges with multiple solutions to inspire creative thinking. The structure of Create-level tasks might be different from a typical essay or multiple-choice assessment. In fact, it might be more performance oriented. As a performance assessment, teachers might establish work and assessment criteria that require students to exhibit knowledge and skills through some form of product, presentation, or demonstration showing they can transfer knowledge and skills into real-world contexts. Often such assessments have interdisciplinary connections (Hofman, Goodwin, & Kahl, 2015). There are many positive effects of Create-level performance assessments, including engaging in critical and creative thinking, personalizing learning with more meaningful tasks, engaging students in real-world tasks, and extending learning opportunities outside the classroom through collaboration (Hofman et al., 2015).

Reeves (2015) states there are four elements for supporting creative thought in schools: "(1) mistake-tolerant culture, (2) rigorous decision-making system,

(3) culture that nurtures creativity, and (4) leadership team that models and supports creativity" (p. 7). He asserts that creativity involves multiple first drafts to achieve a quality product. Reeves (2015) also identifies eight dimensions associated with creative thought.

1. **Research basis:** Students use research to support creative ideas.

2. **Multidisciplinary perspective:** Creative ideas consider different perspectives from multiple content areas.

3. **Source material:** Ideas build on previous thoughts.

4. **Clarity of guidelines:** Students receive consistent feedback through rubrics.

5. **Products:** Students create a product (blog, speech, and so on).

6. **Process:** There is documentation showing the evolution of students' thinking throughout the project.

7. **Collaboration:** The project involves some collaboration.

8. **Practice and error:** Students repeatedly practice, make errors, receive feedback, and make improvements.

Authentic tasks are a great way to plan a Create-level activity. Utilizing real-world problems is among the most influential instructional practices (Schroeder, Scott, Tolson, Huang, & Lee, 2007; Wenglinsky, 2004). When students are placed in real-world roles like journalists or investigators, they can engage in these higher-level processes. In these roles, students can engage in the complexities of solving authentic problems. See table 2.2, which compares realistic and real problems.

There are three Create-level cognitive processes: (1) generating, (2) planning, and (3) producing.

Generating

When students engage in the *generating* cognitive process, they explore various ideas or solutions to solve an ill-defined problem through hypothesizing and exploring various relevant options. Often, these new ideas begin as a possibility to explore (Johnson, 2010). To begin this process, students must thoroughly research to understand a topic so the ideas they generate have logical connections to that topic. Their own ideas should also be varied (signifying flexible thinking), unique, and detailed.

To improve the process for students, defer judgment on the quality of their ideas until the end of the brainstorming process; have them brainstorm many ideas related to the topic, because quality is related to the quantity of ideas they produce; have them list and recognize all ideas as they might inspire other ideas; and have them seek to add on or combine ideas to improve them (Treffinger et al., 2013). Verbs often connected with tasks that involve the generating cognitive process include *brainstorm*, *design*, *create*, *produce*, *construct*, and *improve*. Collaboration (such as having students brainstorm individually and then work in groups to select the best ideas) is also a critical enhancer to Create-level

Table 2.2: Realistic Versus Real Problems

Realistic Problems	Real Problems
Tasks or situations that are: • **Plausible**—Students recognize they could actually occur. • **Interesting**—Students expressed interest or have read, seen, or heard about them; they recognize them as pertinent to others. • **Engaging**—Students perceive them as worth their time and effort.	Tasks or situations that are: • **Pertinent**—Problems are actually present in the students' experience. • **Intensely involving**—Students feel personal concern about them; they have an impact or personal effect on the students' lives and experiences. • **Demanding**—Students perceive them as being important and necessary for investing time and effort. • **Immersed**—The task is part of the students' current personal experience (living it). • **Action essential**—A situation the students will actually do something about or take action on.

Source: Adapted from Treffinger, Schooner, & Selby, 2013, p. 76.

projects (Reeves, 2015). The following are examples of activities that use the generating cognitive process. Subsequent tasks for different cognitive levels within the Create level build off these examples.

- Instruct students to select a U.S. president who must run again in the next presidential election. They determine which previous president would be the best choice to serve in the modern era.

- Instruct students to generate several potential thesis statements in response to an argumentative prompt; for example, ask them, "Should students be able to grade their teachers?"

- Instruct students to brainstorm ways they could investigate if vibrating materials can make sound and if sound can make materials vibrate.

Planning

Planning is the second step in the Create process. After generating the ideas, students then need to evaluate their options and select the best idea to carry out the project. Using the Evaluate level of Bloom's taxonomy revised (Anderson & Krathwohl, 2001), students should sort, prioritize, categorize, and choose the best option (Treffinger et al., 2013). Typically, there is more than one way to solve the task, so students' final products should vary greatly. Revising existing ideas or throwing them out in favor of new ideas is also often part of the planning process. The following are examples of activities that use the planning cognitive process.

- After students select their presidential candidate from the past, instruct them to act as his campaign managers by proposing a plan for the candidate's political party on what they will do to ensure success in the next election.

- After students identify the best thesis statement for their project, instruct them to create an outline with the sources and evidence they will need to support their thesis statement.

- After students select the best way to investigate *vibration*, instruct them to plan their experiment by detailing what tasks they need to accomplish, what materials they need, and what their budget will be.

Producing

The final step in the Create-level process, *producing*, is to follow through with the plan and create the product. Creativity is a tricky thing to judge, but the following three criteria are very helpful: (1) novelty (an original outcome or process), (2) resolution (outcome addresses intended need), and (3) elaboration and synthesis (level of combining diverse components into a new, well-crafted product; Treffinger et al., 2013). Use a rubric like figure 2.1 (page 20) to assess students' level of creative-thinking dispositions. The following are examples of activities that use the producing cognitive process.

- Instruct students to pitch their campaign plan (their created product) to the class. Peers should use a rubric to select which presentation persuasively convinces the class that their candidate is the best choice.

- Instruct students to write an essay by developing their outline into full paragraphs that support the evidence they chose.

- Instruct students to perform an investigation and write up their conclusions from their experiment. Students share what they learned and how they might improve their investigation if revising.

Seeing the Big Picture

Notice that as students work at the higher levels of Bloom's taxonomy revised (Anderson & Krathwohl, 2001), the associated tasks typically require more of students and will take longer for them to complete. For example, if you ask students to name the main character in the story they could respond fairly quickly (Understand level); however, if you ask them to determine if the main character is a fraud by providing several examples of textual evidence (Evaluate level), this task requires more time for thinking. Most Create-level assignments should take several days or longer to complete. So, if you ask a question and hands immediately go up in your classroom to answer the question, your question was probably a low-level one.

Rating	Description
4 Expert: Unconsciously Competent	Thinks outside the box; has a variety of creative strategies to call on; enjoys generating creative solutions; examines alternative possibilities from many angles; has an active imagination; strives to find new, inventive ways to work on a task; expands the possibility of creative insight by researching a topic in great detail; is eager to seek advice and use the ideas of others to find solutions; frequently reflects and uses metacognition; offers detailed feedback about whether ideas are acceptable; uses a variety of media to present ideas and projects
3 Practitioner: Consciously Competent	Generates new ideas to solve problems; develops and uses several strategies to complete tasks; is inventive; does detailed research; generates options and possibilities from attained knowledge; finishes the task no matter the length of time; shows well-developed reflection and metacognition skills
2 Apprentice: Consciously Incompetent	Is beginning to volunteer one or two imaginative ideas; is increasingly developing strategies; needs encouragement to develop creative thinking; will stop persisting if answer is not gained after a short time; is developing metacognition with guidance
1 Novice: Unconsciously Incompetent	Says things such as, "I was never good at art," "I can't draw," "I'm not creative," and "I can't"; has no strategies to call on for new ideas; is afraid to be creative; will not seek alternative methods for solving new problems

Source: Boyes & Watts, 2009, p. 377.

Figure 2.1: Rubric for creating, imaging, and innovating.

Hopefully, these ideas spur your thinking on integrating critical thinking to engage learners in your classroom. Often, increasing the level of critical thinking does not require eliminating current assignments; rather, with some alterations, you can ratchet up your assignments to reach higher-thinking levels. As you grow to more accurately understand Bloom's taxonomy revised (Anderson & Krathwohl, 2001), you can better identify ways to enhance the level of critical thinking in your classroom.

Discussion Questions

As you reflect on this chapter, consider the following five questions.

1. Consider your current teaching practices. Approximately what percentage of classroom time do your students spend working at each level? What would you want to change about those percentages and why?

2. What are some activities you use that operate at lower-thinking levels? What steps could you take to raise them to higher-level-thinking tasks?

3. What is one activity in this chapter that you could use with your students? What changes could you make to tailor it to your students and instructional content?

4. What kinds of new projects could you introduce to your students that operate at the Create level and allow your students to demonstrate semesterlong or yearlong growth in their learning?

5. What traits will you look for in your students to know when they are working and thinking at higher levels?

Take Action

Use the following four activities to put this chapter's concepts to work in your own classroom.

1. Examine an assessment you use in your class to determine its thinking level.

2. Identify one classroom activity or assessment you use that operates at lower thinking levels and make adjustments to increase those levels.

3. Have students use an age-appropriate rubric to self-assess their level of critical thinking.

4. Have students use a debriefing matrix like the one in figure 2.2 to debrief about their project.

Identifying Positives	Seeking Clarification
Begin by listing the aspects of the activity or session that were positive or successful. Ask questions such as: • "What did we do that really worked well?" • "What were the best parts of this session or activity?" • "What happened exactly as planned or anticipated?"	Next, identify areas of uncertainty or aspects of the activity that were unclear. Ask questions such as: • "What wasn't clear to you about anything that happened?" • "What were you unsure or confused about, or what was puzzling or perplexing?" • "What do you wish you understood better or knew more regarding what we did (or did not do)?"
Seeking Improvements	**Seeking Novel Connections**
Consider anything that might not have been effective or successful by posing constructive questions, such as: • "How might we have improved or done this better or more effectively?" • "What do you wish we had handled differently and in what ways?" • "What might we have overlooked or forgotten?" • "What do you wish we had done more (or less)?"	Be alert for any discoveries or unexpected outcomes and their implications. Ask questions such as: • "What did we discover from this activity that we didn't know or hadn't tried before? Did any new possibilities come to mind?" • "What surprised us or happened that we didn't expect? What did we learn from that?" • "Are there any new ideas that we might want to try out in the future?"

Source: Treffinger et al., 2013, p. 212.

Figure 2.2: Creative thinking four-part debriefing structure.

CHAPTER 3

Developing Critical-Thinking Skills and Fostering Engagement

Hope is not a strategy.
—U.S. Air Force Special Ops pilot

Educators' understanding of effective instruction has shifted significantly, resulting in a move from teacher-directed to cognitively complex, student-directed instruction. As critical thinking is infused in student-directed tasks, students must actively apply their learning (individually and collaboratively). By establishing student-centered instructional strategies, you will challenge students "to successfully own their learning at the highest levels of complexity" (Marzano & Toth, 2014, p. 10).

This is not a quick process. For students to adjust to new expectations of rigor, they need opportunities to frequently engage in cognitively complex tasks. This means establishing a foundation with your students and building on it (see figure 3.1). With appropriate scaffolding, you can support students as they advance from basic applications of knowledge to complex tasks that demand Create-level content. Students will use this new knowledge to solve problems, make decisions, evaluate information, make inferences, critique the logic of arguments, and correct errors and misconceptions, all with less direction from you.

To assist teachers as they make significant shifts in their pedagogy to more student-centered, higher-order

tasks, instructional protocols and strategies can help teachers plan lessons to facilitate learning and direct students to take ownership of their learning. Marzano and Toth (2014) state:

> If we hope to move students to these higher levels of skills and cognition, it's imperative that we equip teachers with the "how," those essential teaching strategies that will scaffold students to problem-solve and make decisions in real-world scenarios with less teacher direction. (p. 11)

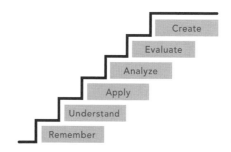

Figure 3.1: Scaffolding thinking levels from low to high.

The fifty strategies you are about to discover in chapters 4–7 take this bottom-up approach by establishing processes you can use at the Understand level and then progress to strategies for analyzing, evaluating, and creating. Table 3.1 is organized along these principles. Because the Remember and Apply levels are typically built into activities taking place on subsequent (higher) levels, there are no chapters on these two levels. Likewise, several of these strategies also invoke thinking at levels below them.

Remember, this book is about building a culture of learning that fosters cognitive engagement in everything students do. To that end, this chapter emphasizes the importance of providing students with ample opportunities to apply the strategies, and it establishes three metrics for the fifty strategies to demonstrate how they not only build critical thinking but also maintain engagement: (1) movement, (2) collaboration, and (3) media literacy.

Creating Opportunities for Engagement

Recall from chapter 1 that most classroom instruction (58 percent) operates at lower thinking levels, with only about 6 percent operating at the highest levels (Marzano & Toth, 2014). When it comes to helping students develop critical-thinking skills, this represents a massive loss of opportunity.

When students have multiple opportunities to build and refine their critical-thinking skills, they develop abilities to grapple with cognitively complex tasks. However, this doesn't happen if you don't hold students' attention as they take on work at increasingly higher cognitive levels. Writing for the Institute for Research and Reform in Education, Adena M. Klem and James P. Connell (2004) state, "Students who perceive the situation as challenging actively persist in the face of failure through the use of effort, strategic thinking, problem-solving, information-seeking, and experimentation" (p. 262).

The goal is high student participation *and* high cognition, thus cognitive engagement. Educators Ron Ritchhart, Mark Church, and Karin Morrison (2011) propose that students engage in authentic intellectual activity by "solving problems, making decisions, and developing new understanding using the methods and tools of the discipline" (p. 10). Achieving this requires teachers to act as facilitators, guiding students to solve complex, real-world problems and thereby having them assume ownership of their own learning.

The following sections establish the roles of movement, collaboration, and media literacy in maintaining engagement as students make their journey toward becoming high-level critical thinkers. Table 3.2 (page 26) lists how each of this book's strategies primarily align with these engagement criteria (although several strategies cross these lines). You will note that the majority of the strategies fall into the collaboration category, as this is the most common way to achieve engagement.

Engaging With Movement

Brain research reveals a strong connection between cognitive and motor processes (thinking and movement). Sousa (2011) states, "It seems that the more we study the cerebellum, the more we realize that movement is inescapably linked to learning and memory" (p. 353). Movement increases the amount of oxygen in the blood fueling the brain, which, in turn, helps the brain perform tasks (Sousa, 2011). In a study in which high school students were given tasks after walking ten minutes, the academically lower group of students obtained significant increases in the Remember- and Understand-level tasks from the Programme for International Student Assessment, while also demonstrating improvement in both the Apply and Analyze levels (Mualem et al., 2018). Not surprisingly, research also shows instructional tasks that use movement while teaching content deepen students' understanding and increase energy levels (Marzano & Pickering, 2011).

These connections make clear the importance of including kinesthetic approaches to your instructional practices. Not only do they improve learning but also are a terrific way to foster engagement and, when used to reinforce instruction, help students retain information (Paivio, 1991). In addition, kinesthetic tasks are particularly positive for students of low socioeconomic backgrounds (Helgeson, 2011), which is more reason to incorporate movement into classroom instruction whenever feasible. You will find this movement also positively affects classroom management.

Table 3.1: Summary of Strategies Classified by Bloom's Taxonomy Revised Levels

Understand	Analyze	Evaluate	Create
Strategy 1: Vocabulary-Building Movement	Strategy 7: Concept Attainment	Strategy 25: Four Corners (Remember to Evaluate)	Strategy 44: Affinity Diagram
Strategy 2: Inductive Learning	Strategy 8: Metaphor (Understand to Analyze)	Strategy 26: Rank Order	Strategy 45: Problem Solving
Strategy 3: Matrix	Strategy 9: Media Metaphor (Understand to Analyze)	Strategy 27: Questioning Protocols (Remember to Evaluate)	Strategy 46: Carousel Brainstorming
Strategy 4: Ten Most Important Words	Strategy 10: Quote It! Code It! (Understand to Analyze)	Strategy 28: Inferencing	Strategy 47: SCAMPER
Strategy 5: Build Background Knowledge	Strategy 11: Visual Thinking	Strategy 29: Jigsaw With Case Studies	Strategy 48: Hits and Spots
Strategy 6: Content Links	Strategy 12: Concept Maps (Understand to Analyze)	Strategy 30: Think-Pair-Share Continuum	Strategy 49: Six Thinking Hats (Evaluate to Create)
	Strategy 13: Mind Maps (Understand to Analyze)	Strategy 31: Decision Making	Strategy 50: Inferential Ladder (Understand to Create)
	Strategy 14: Hear, Think, and Wonder (Understand to Analyze)	Strategy 32: Peer Critiquing	
	Strategy 15: Anticipation Guide	Strategy 33: Evaluate Around the Circle Jigsaw	
	Strategy 16: Cubing	Strategy 34: Investigation	
	Strategy 17: Consensogram (Understand to Analyze)	Strategy 35: Evaluate an Author's Reasoning	
	Strategy 18: Fishbone Cause-and-Effect Analysis (Understand to Analyze)	Strategy 36: Media Analysis	
	Strategy 19: Directed Reading-Thinking Activity	Strategy 37: ReQuest (Understand to Evaluate)	
	Strategy 20: Overheard Quotes (Understand to Analyze)	Strategy 38: Find the Fiction	
	Strategy 21: Discrepant Event (Understand to Analyze)	Strategy 39: Quads	
	Strategy 22: Extent Barometer	Strategy 40: Claims, Evidence, Reasons	
	Strategy 23: SWOT Analysis	Strategy 41: Color-Coded Critical Feedback	
	Strategy 24: Gallery Walk (Understand to Analyze)	Strategy 42: Rank, Talk, Write	
		Strategy 43: Affirm and Challenge Quotes	

Table 3.2: Instructional Strategies for Engagement

Movement	Collaboration	Media Literacy
Strategy 1: Vocabulary-Building Movement	Strategy 4: Ten Most Important Words	Strategy 9: Media Metaphor
Strategy 2: Inductive Learning	Strategy 5: Build Background Knowledge	Strategy 10: Quote It! Code It!
Strategy 3: Matrix	Strategy 7: Concept Attainment	Strategy 11: Visual Thinking
Strategy 6: Content Links	Strategy 8: Metaphor	Strategy 14: Hear, Think, and Wonder
Strategy 20: Overheard Quotes	Strategy 12: Concept Maps	Strategy 26: Rank Order
Strategy 24: Gallery Walk	Strategy 13: Mind Maps	Strategy 36: Media Analysis
Strategy 25: Four Corners	Strategy 15: Anticipation Guide	
Strategy 30: Think-Pair-Share Continuum	Strategy 16: Cubing	
Strategy 39: Quads	Strategy 17: Consensogram	
Strategy 42: Rank, Talk, Write	Strategy 18: Fishbone Cause-and-Effect Analysis	
Strategy 43: Affirm and Challenge Quotes	Strategy 19: Directed Reading-Thinking Activity	
Strategy 44: Affinity Diagram	Strategy 21: Discrepant Event	
Strategy 46: Carousel Brainstorming	Strategy 22: Extent Barometer	
Strategy 48: Hits and Spots	Strategy 23: SWOT Analysis	
	Strategy 27: Questioning Protocols	
	Strategy 28: Inferencing	
	Strategy 29: Jigsaw With Case Studies	
	Strategy 31: Decision Making	
	Strategy 32: Peer Critiquing	
	Strategy 33: Evaluate Around the Circle Jigsaw	
	Strategy 34: Investigation	
	Strategy 35: Evaluate an Author's Reasoning	
	Strategy 37: ReQuest	
	Strategy 38: Find the Fiction	
	Strategy 40: Claims, Evidence, Reasons	
	Strategy 41: Color-Coded Critical Feedback	
	Strategy 45: Problem Solving	
	Strategy 47: SCAMPER	
	Strategy 49: Six Thinking Hats	
	Strategy 50: Inferential Ladder	

Engaging With Collaboration

Strategies that include student collaboration provide numerous benefits. You already know from the introduction of this book that employers identify problem-solving and collaborative skills as the two key soft skills to prepare students for work life (Greenberg & Nilssen, 2014). By collaborating, students learn to handle controversy and different perspectives while accomplishing a task, which fosters deep cognitive learning.

Another benefit of collaboration is the increased level of student engagement. In *The Role of Education in Building Soft Skills*, teacher Gareth Hancox (as cited in Greenberg & Nilssen, 2014) states:

> If you watch two learners working on something together, you see that their learning is deeper. They are the ones making the discoveries and asking questions, and consequently teachers are not prescribing all of the information to the children, and instead letting the children have ownership of their learning. (p. 12)

Collaboration increases active participation and student ownership of learning. Often via collaboration, the end result is a better outcome and improved student learning. But there is another reason that collaboration is a great format for engagement and learning—it prompts questions.

During the collaborative process, students often pose many questions to deepen their understanding of a task. Questioning shows students are actively engaged in learning, thus making learning visible (Ostroff, 2016). Unfortunately, questioning in classroom environments is something that research finds erodes over time.

In studies, preschool children ask seventy-six questions per hour to understand and gain information (Chouinard, Harris, & Maratsos, 2007); however, in kindergarten those are reduced to two to five questions in a similar time frame. Dismally, by fifth grade, students ask between zero and two questions per school day (Engel, 2011). Interestingly, an analysis shows top technology geniuses and inventors possess one common feature—asking great questions (Dyer, Gregersen, & Christensen, 2011).

When students ask a question, their intrinsic motivation shows in their internal desire for understanding.

Ostroff (2016) states, "Whoever asks the questions holds the power" (p. 100). Students need to know teachers value their questions, and when they know that, questioning can be an ignitor for critical thinking. (Strategy 11: Visual Thinking, on page 46, provides some question stems to spark student questioning.)

Engaging With Media Literacy

Media, which includes online videos, television, newspapers, magazines, movies, songs, cartoons, pictures, and posters, is pervasive in society. The capacity to view media, however, is not the same as understanding it. That requires a specific literacy skill set. For the purposes of this book, *media literacy* is the "ability to access, analyze, evaluate, and communicate messages in a variety of forms" (Chen, Wu, & Wang, 2011, p. 85).

Media literacy education increases higher-level-thinking skills in students rated as low and medium school achievers (Jeong, Cho, & Hwang, 2012; Webb & Martin, 2012). Further, using media to learn is tied to higher rates of student engagement and teacher creativity in instruction. It's also a daily, sometimes hourly, aspect of students' lives; it's a part of their culture. The National Council for the Social Studies (2016) states:

> At the core of learning is Literacy—the ability to access, analyze, evaluate and produce communication. Media literacy expands the traditional concept of literacy to include the forms of communication that dominate the lives of our students. If our students are to be literate, we must teach them the skills and habits of literacy for print and non-print mediated messages. (p. 183)

Given this, bringing media into the learning environment is not just a way to grab students' attention but also connect with them. But what is it that makes media so powerful?

Media has points of view and values. Students can learn how to use it (and how others use it) to influence people's behaviors, attitudes, and beliefs. Ithaca College professor Cyndy Scheibe and media literacy strategist Faith Rogow (2012) detail four main areas associated with media literacy: (1) understanding the media messages, (2) analyzing the message purpose, (3) making reasoned evaluation of media credibility and point of view, and (4) reflecting on how the media aligns to students' values and beliefs. Likely, you can already see how these skills translate into all the levels of Bloom's taxonomy revised (Anderson & Krathwohl, 2001). The fact that effectively using media to aid in students' learning is also a great way to hold their attention is icing on the cake.

In the following chapters you will see how movement, collaboration, and media literacy join with the fifty strategies for building students from the Understand level to the Create level, and developing a culture of true critical thought in your classroom.

Discussion Questions

As you reflect on this chapter, consider the following five questions.

1. What instructional strategies do you use to promote student movement?

2. What strategies do you find most effective for engaging students in critical thinking and collaboration?

3. How do you integrate media to engage students in critical thinking?

4. What are challenges with incorporating movement, collaboration, and media in classrooms?

5. What other strategies do you use to promote cognitive engagement in your classroom?

Take Action

Use the following three activities to put this chapter's concepts to work in your own classroom.

1. Review the instructional strategies for engagement in table 3.2 (page 26). Highlight the strategies you currently use in your classroom.

2. Analyze one of your units of study. Record a chart similar to the one in table 3.2 listing the strategies you use that utilize movement, collaboration, and media.

3. Select one lesson you use that needs more cognitive engagement. Identify one way you could integrate more movement, collaboration, and media into that lesson.

CHAPTER 4

Implementing Strategies for Understand-Level Thinking

The noblest pleasure is the joy of understanding.
—Leonardo da Vinci

In this chapter, you will find six instructional strategies that focus on learning at the Understand level of Bloom's taxonomy revised (Anderson & Krathwohl, 2001). Each of the following instructional strategies requires students to deploy cognitive skills at the Remember level (recognition and recall), along with a combination of Understand-level cognitive applications like interpreting, exemplifying, classifying, summarizing, inferring, comparing, or explaining content. Icons with each strategy indicate which steps (levels) of the taxonomy the activity touches, as well as its primary tool for engagement (movement, collaboration, or media literacy).

With each strategy, you will find a brief introduction that explains its concept and purpose, a classroom example, a series of steps for implementing the strategy, a list of variations you can choose to implement, and a section detailing additional classroom examples based on different content areas.

Strategy 1: Vocabulary-Building Movement

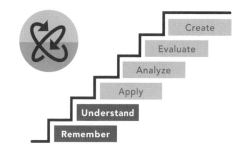

Vocabulary-Building Movement is a strategy to help students develop their vocabulary using movement. Education expert Eric Jensen (2019) writes extensively on the powerful connection between physical activity and students' long-term memory and attentional focus across all age groups. In particular, he builds on the work of Betty Hart and Todd R. Risley (2003) to reflect the necessity of vocabulary building for students from poverty who often enter the classroom behind their peers.

Research also suggests that using physical movement to represent concepts is effective with younger (preK–5) students. When concepts are abstract, iconic or representational gestures can depict objects or events to enhance understanding (Kendon, 1988). For example, students might put their arms directly in front of them to represent parallel lines. Metaphoric gestures, in contrast, make references to visual images but are more abstract. Students might symbolize the word *dictatorship* by putting one arm above their head with one finger up, noting "one" and meaning the leader is all powerful.

For students who have trouble explaining a concept, gesturing offers insight into the students' understanding (Church & Goldin-Meadow, 1986). Psychologist and child development expert Jean Piaget (1959) believes that gestures play an important role in students' learning, development, and communication. In agreement, learning scientist Wolff-Michael Roth (2001) says gestures are a key component of children's cognitive development. Using hand gestures as representations for abstract concepts enhances student learning (Collins, 2005). A vocabulary word is easier to remember if taught with a gesture.

CLASSROOM EXAMPLE

A second-grade class is learning ten vocabulary words from a story students are reading and analyzing. In pairs, students create gestures to match each vocabulary word and definition. When reviewing the vocabulary words, the students use their gestures while reciting the definitions.

Strategy Steps

Use the following three steps to help you implement the Vocabulary-Building Movement strategy.

1. Determine and then introduce the vocabulary words you want your students to learn.

2. Introduce students to a series of gesture-based vocabulary strategies. Here are several vocabulary-building movement strategy options you can use (Stobaugh & Love, 2015).

   • *Use hand gestures*—Have students create their own representational gestures, demonstrating the word in concrete ways. In addition, students could design gestures that depict words in a more abstract fashion. For example, students might decide a concrete gesture to demonstrate understanding of *precipitation* is to hold their hands up high and wiggle their fingers and then slowly lower their hands to emphasize that precipitation falls to the ground.

   • *Form a group statue*—To make it more interactive, assign students to groups and have them use their bodies to represent a word. For example, to illustrate the word *conservation*, two students could be in the center and the third student could wrap his or her arms around the others.

   • *Create a model*—As an individual or in groups, give students building resources (such as sticky notes, markers, and building blocks) and instruct them to create an abstract model to represent the word. For example, students might make a small tower in which the sticky notes represent the *judicial branch* (it handles the sticky issues), a building block depicts the *legislative branch* (it makes the laws, the building blocks of societal rules), and the craft stick represents the *executive branch* (it has one key figure, the president, leading it).

3. Allow students to choose one of the three ways (hand gesture, group statue, or model) to demonstrate their understanding of vocabulary terms.

Variations

You can use the following variations in association with this strategy.

• Have students create a video where they create dance moves related to the terms they are learning.

• You can vary students' use of the hand gesture strategy by having them act out their gestures and play a game of charades.

Additional Content-Area Examples

This section provides examples of some ways you can connect this strategy to your teaching in different content areas.

• A language arts teacher instructs students to develop hand motions to represent the meaning of Greek and Latin roots. For example, one group suggests a pulling motion to represent the word *tract*.

- In a unit on plant biology, a student group creates a gesture of spreading seeds (using hand gestures to gather seeds from a bag and shake them out onto soil) to depict *pollination*. The group shares aloud with the rest of the class how the gesture aligns with pollination.

- A mathematics teacher assigns students into groups of four, provides each group with building materials, and instructs them to create models related to the geometric formulas in their unit of study.

- In a unit on the civil rights movement in the United States, a social studies teacher forms groups of four students and instructs them to use the group-statue strategy to illustrate or symbolize a concept or term related to the movement. Students then provide three reasons for how their statue depicts that concept or term.

Strategy 2: Inductive Learning

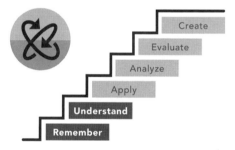

Broadly speaking, inductive teaching and learning are methodologies for engaging students in higher-order thinking. Inquiry-based learning, project-based learning, discovery learning, and so on are all forms of inductive learning (Prince & Felder, 2007). The *Inductive Learning* strategy focuses on students using inductive learning to group and classify information to build deeper understanding. You can use this strategy as a preassessment to gauge students' existing knowledge of a topic or as a review to assess their learning.

- -
CLASSROOM EXAMPLE

A teacher hands out twenty key terms involved in the production of a play. These words range from *script* to *center right*. He puts students in pairs and groups

the words based on common characteristics. Each student pair then creates a descriptive label for each grouping. As a class, students share their ideas and make connections between background knowledge and the groupings they created.

- -

Strategy Steps

Use the following four steps to help you implement the Inductive Learning strategy.

1. Create a list of terms, visuals, or data. When you are developing students' vocabulary, for secondary students, use fifteen to twenty-five terms. For younger students (grades preK–5), fewer terms are appropriate (around five to ten). The terms you select should be relevant to the ongoing learning in your class.

2. Determine a delivery method for allowing students to see and interact with the selected terms. For example, you could display the terms on a digital wall or provide students with written or printed materials.

3. Have students sort and group words based on common characteristics or shared features, either individually or as a group. Students should identify descriptive titles for the groups of words they categorize together.

4. Conduct a class discussion on how students determined their groupings and what categories they came up with.

Variations

You can use the following variations in association with this strategy.

- Have students brainstorm terms to use for this activity instead of using teacher-provided terms.

- Use this strategy as a preassessment to see if students understand the relationships between terms.

Additional Content-Area Examples

This section provides examples of some ways you can connect this strategy to your teaching in different content areas.

- A language arts teacher gives students twenty pivotal quotes from a novel they have read and asks them to sort and classify the quotes.

- A science teacher selects a list of various animals and instructs students to determine groups and classifications for them. Students consider and discuss each animal's behaviors, appearance, habitats, and so on.

- A mathematics teacher instructs students to group various shapes based on their attributes.

- In a unit on Native American culture, a social studies teacher instructs students to work in groups and gives each group a box of items representing a specific Native American tribe. Students work together to classify the artifacts.

- A visual arts teacher gives students various pieces of artwork and instructs them to use their existing knowledge to group the pieces according to how they look or appear to look. The teacher uses the students' results to lead a discussion on art history, color usage, brushstrokes and techniques, and movements in art.

Strategy 3: Matrix

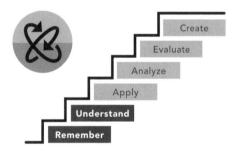

The *Matrix* strategy exposes students to a variety of perspectives while at the same time assesses students' understanding of a topic or lesson. The Matrix strategy involves having students examine two variables or ideas and observe how those ideas interact. Each axis represents a variable on a scale of 0 to 10, and students then consider their viewpoint before determining where they would appear on the matrix (see figure 4.1). The strategy provides time for students to deeply think about two ideas while physically moving to post their data points. When determining what criteria to apply, note that many informational texts pose arguments that consider two opposing ideas. The Matrix strategy is an excellent conversation starter for these kinds of texts.

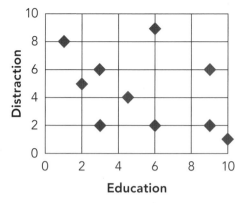

Figure 4.1: Matrix activity graph.

· ·

CLASSROOM EXAMPLE

A teacher gives each student an individual matrix while posting a large display on chart paper in the classroom. Students consider the educational benefits of using cell phones in class while also reflecting on the risk of distraction. Students decide how they rate each item. For example, one student loves using technology in class and rates a nine on that axis, but he is also a little concerned about the distraction and rates that a six. However, two others at his table rate slightly differently. Students place their rating on their matrix, then plot it on the classroom matrix (see figure 4.1). The teacher organizes students into small groups to reflect on the data and consider topics for a whole-class discussion.

· ·

Strategy Steps

Use the following seven steps to help you implement the Matrix strategy (Stobaugh & Love, 2015).

1. Select two variables to use in forming the matrix. The interaction of these variables should spur thought-provoking discussions and expose diverse viewpoints.

2. Have each student create a matrix on paper and mark his or her rating. For example, a student might apply a rating of 9 on a scale of 0 to 10 to a topic of high importance (preserving the environment) but apply a rating of 2 to a topic of minimal importance (financial support of environmental projects). The student would

then mark the intersection of those points on his or her matrix.

3. Instruct students to use the space below their matrix to justify their opinion in several sentences. Encourage students to use readings or other materials to support their answer.

4. Create a large matrix on chart paper, and post it on the wall. Have students use sticky notes (or dots) to mark their rating on the classroom matrix, creating a cluster graph.

5. Form students into two concentric circles—an inside and outside circle with students facing each other. Instruct students to examine the data and ask them the following questions.

   • "What do you notice in the data?"

   • "Do you observe any patterns, and what do they tell you?"

   • "What surprises you?"

   • "What can you infer, and what conclusions might you draw?"

   After each question, invite students to discuss their answers with the student in front of them.

6. After discussing, have the students on the outside circle move three spots to the right so they are with a new partner to discuss the next question.

7. Have students share their conclusions in a whole-group discussion.

Variations

You can use the following variations in association with this strategy.

• Near the end of a unit of study, put students in groups and have each group generate a topic and two variables to analyze based on their unit learning. The class should then select one or more of the group-generated ideas and complete the matrix activity.

• To gauge how opinions have changed from the beginning of the Matrix strategy to the end, have students use different color sticky notes (or dots) to indicate if their opinion changes at the end of the discussion. This provides a useful

visual for how many students changed their minds about the topic.

Additional Content-Area Examples

This section provides examples of some ways you can connect this strategy to your teaching in different content areas.

• A language arts teacher designs a matrix that analyzes the importance of the format relative to the impact of haiku writing.

• A science teacher designs a matrix that analyzes the importance of studying space with the costs involved.

• A mathematics teacher designs a matrix that analyzes the importance of the process to solving a mathematical problem to the importance of finding the correct answer.

• A social studies teacher designs a matrix that analyzes how much risk a business can take relative to the potential profit involved in taking that risk.

• A careers teacher asks students to chart how much effort they put into a resume on a scale from 10 to 1 (10 being maximum effort and 1 being minimal effort) and their grade on the assignment (from one to ten points).

Strategy 4: Ten Most Important Words

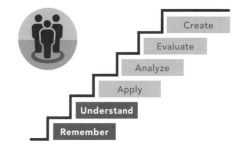

Vocabulary is very important to students, particularly those who come from poverty (Jensen, 2019); they will carry it throughout their lives. As with the Strategy 1: Vocabulary-Building Movement strategy, the vocabulary students know will enhance their learning experience and breadth of knowledge. The *Ten Most Important Words* strategy helps students identify key vocabulary terms and increase their understanding of them by making connections between those terms and the crucial knowledge that constitutes learning targets.

CLASSROOM EXAMPLE

After learning about environmental sustainability and the impact of people on the world around them, a teacher instructs students to read an article about the recycling process. Students identify ten key vocabulary terms in the article, and record their choices on individual sticky notes. The class compiles the vocabulary terms in one chart and discusses the patterns students observe.

Strategy Steps

Use the following five steps to help you implement the Ten Most Important Words strategy.

1. Provide each student with ten sticky notes.

2. Have students read or interact with a new source of information, like articles, websites, science data, and so on. The crucial factor is that the source contains plenty of relevant vocabulary-building words for students to choose from.

3. Instruct students to read or view the content you select and determine what they believe are the ten most important words mentioned. Students write each word they identify on a sticky note.

4. Using empty wall space or section of the floor, have a student announce a vocabulary word he or she selected and instruct him or her, along with any other students who identified the same term, to adhere their notes to the selected area. As each term is added to the mass, the sticky notes begin to form a giant bar graph depicting the number of times a student identified a key vocabulary word.

5. Conduct a whole-class discussion on any patterns students observe. As part of this discussion, identify words that are outliers, the reasons students gravitated to some words and not others, and any key words not well represented (or not at all) that students may

need to become more familiar with. Through discussion, the class makes connections to the learning and the vocabulary terms.

Variations

You can use the following variations in association with this strategy.

*   Use Padlet (https://padlet.com) or another digital wall technology to post words and move the digital posts around to group common answers.

*   After learning more about the terms, the groups could review their original selection of words and determine if they still believe those are the key words for the lesson.

Additional Content-Area Examples

This section provides examples of some ways you can connect this strategy to your teaching in different content areas.

*   A language arts teacher instructs students to read a section of a famous play, such as *The Tragedy of Romeo and Juliet* (Shakespeare, 1935), and identify ten common Shakespearean phrases.

*   A science teacher instructs students to read a data analysis summary for a science experiment and identify the ten most important words to understanding the results of the experiment.

*   A mathematics teacher instructs students to analyze a complex, real-world mathematical prompt and use the strategy to find the ten words most important to understand in the prompt.

*   Before creating a brochure about their community, a social studies teacher instructs students to read a professionally created brochure about New York City to help them identify key words found in this type of product that they could use about their own region.

*   A health teacher instructs students to read an article about the cardiovascular system and identify the ten most important words.

Strategy 5: Build Background Knowledge

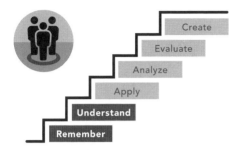

Build Background Knowledge represents a protocol you can use to pique students' interest in reading by having them make preliminary predictions, read a new text, explore an additional expert text, and then return to review their initial predictions (Expeditionary Learning, 2013). Through this strategy, students create a mind map and incrementally augment their understanding as they receive additional information. With each new source of information, students use a different color marker to show the progression of the learning with new ideas included on the mind map. You will find that Strategy 15: Anticipation Guide (chapter 5, page 53) and Strategy 29: Jigsaw With Case Studies (chapter 6, page 81) offer a natural evolution to higher thinking levels for this concept.

CLASSROOM EXAMPLE

To begin a unit on money, a teacher reads aloud "Smart," a poem by Shel Silverstein (n.d.), as students follow along. Individually, students think about what the poem means. The teacher briefly explains that money is important in our world and students will explore more information to learn about U.S. money. She assigns students to groups, and the groups use a black marker on chart paper to record their initial thoughts about the poem and any background information they observe using a mind map structure. The teacher then reads aloud an information sheet on the different types of U.S. coins. Students follow along and make notes about any new and relevant information. Groups then discuss what they have learned and add to their mind map using a red marker. Next, the teacher provides each group member a card with specific information about each different coin. Students highlight any new information on the card

and then share their new learning with the group. Using a purple marker, students add to their mind map. Finally, the teacher reads the poem again and groups use an orange marker to note any new conclusions. Each group is invited to share its thinking and conclusions based on its mind map.

Strategy Steps

Use the following twelve steps to help you implement the Build Background Knowledge strategy.

1. Select a topic and some associated texts that progressively bolster students' knowledge of that topic. These should consist of an original, mystery text to pique students' interest; a common text all students will read next that elaborates on the topic in more detail; and finally, some expert texts that different group members will read to understand the topic even better.

2. Create groups of four or five students. Provide each group with four different color markers (black, red, orange, and purple) and chart paper.

3. Distribute a short mystery source, which could also be a photograph, song, graph, map, poem, or video. Your main goal with this source is to ignite students' interest in the topic.

4. Instruct students to individually record their initial thoughts about the topic.

5. Provide background information as necessary to understand the mystery text. For example, in the Classroom Example for this strategy, the teacher sets the purpose of the lesson: learning about money.

6. In their groups, have students discuss their preliminary thoughts and any changes to their thinking based on the background information. Groups should then use their chart paper to create a mind map with visuals and text using their black marker.

7. To solidify understanding, provide a common text for all students to read. As students read, they should record an *N* or highlight any *new* information on a copy of the text.

8. Have groups discuss and add any new, important information they observe to their mind map using their red marker.

9. Distribute the expert text to each member of the group. Often, the best expert text will represent different perspectives on the core topic and challenge students' thinking from the previous texts. Students will again code *N* or highlight any *new* information on a copy of the expert text.

10. Group members should share what they learned from the expert text and then add any different, significant information to their mind map using their purple marker.

11. Review with students the original mystery text and instruct them to note any new thoughts or insights on the mind map using their orange marker.

12. Instruct groups to analyze how their thinking evolved based on the various colored notes at each part of the process. Invite groups to share their findings and conclusions.

Variations

You can use the following variations in association with this strategy.

- Along with readings, use multimedia texts (videos, pictures, music, and so on) to provide students with a variety of sources.

- Have students use a digital tool, such as a word processor or Padlet, to create their mind maps.

- Instruct students to walk around the classroom and review other groups' mind maps noting similarities and differences to their own maps.

Additional Content-Area Examples

This section provides examples of some ways you can connect this strategy to your teaching in different content areas.

- Prior to starting *A Raisin in the Sun* by Lorraine Hansberry (2004), a teacher instructs students to read the poem, "Harlem" by Langston Hughes (1990), the play's namesake. The teacher then shares that they will be reading a book about dreams and hopes for the future. In groups, students record their ideas about how the poem and the background knowledge are related. Students then examine the images in the cover of the book and add new understandings to their mind map. Finally, expert groups examine various pictures of the Great Depression. After group members share their learning, they examine the poem another time and finalize the group's mind map.

- A science teacher instructs students to observe two pictures related to the fable "The North Wind and the Sun" (Aesop, 2014). One features the sun bearing down on a man, and the other features a fierce wind blowing at a man. After sharing with the class that the lesson was on weather, the teacher asks students to record their thoughts about the weather on their group's mind map. Next the students read the fable and add on to their thinking about weather. Each expert group then watches one informational video on either solar energy or wind power and reports back to its home group by adding on to its mind map. Finally, groups examine the original pictures again, refine their mind map, and discuss their thoughts with the class.

- A mathematics teacher instructs students to listen as she reads *Inch by Inch* by Leo Lionni (1960) to begin a measurement unit. The teacher informs students that they will be learning about measuring in the next unit and places them in groups, instructing them to create a mind map about how the story uses measurement. Students then read a teacher-assigned expert article about conducting proper measurements. They continue to record their thoughts, and share with their classmates. Next, students form expert groups and measure shapes around the classroom. Students return to their home group and listen to the story one more time before finalizing their mind map and sharing their thoughts.

- Before beginning a unit on the civil rights movement, a social studies teacher instructs students to examine photos of sit-ins and protests and then work in groups to make initial inferences about the time period using a mind map. Next, students read Martin Luther King Jr.'s (1963) speech, "I Have a Dream," to determine key ideas of the civil rights movement and justify their previous inferences. Finally, expert groups examine various segments from the *Eyes on the Prize* (Vecchione & Else, 1990) and report back to their home group supplementing their mind map. Students review the initial sit-in and protest photos one more time while completing their mind map.

- An art teacher instructs students to examine four paintings. The teacher informs the class that they will be learning about translation, reflection, rotation, and symmetry and provides a simple example of each concept. After, groups discuss the paintings and lesson topic and record ideas on a mind map. In expert groups, students then view real-world pictures that show examples of translation, reflection, rotation, and symmetry and add their thoughts on these to the mind map. Home groups then re-examine the paintings and use their new learning to note evidence of the mathematical concepts in the art.

Strategy 6: Content Links

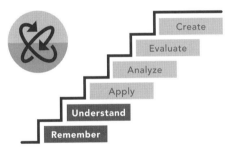

The *Content Links* strategy encourages students to compare key terms, symbols, or pictures and identify similarities or associations (Guillaume, Yopp, & Yopp, 2007).

CLASSROOM EXAMPLE

A teacher gives each student a postcard that represents one of the nine climate regions in the United States. Each student and one other peer compare their pictures to determine similarities and differences in the climate regions. Students record their hypotheses and the key defining climate features for each region on a note-taking guide. After discussing, students find other partners and continue the process by finding peers that have a postcard of the other climate regions.

Strategy Steps

Use the following steps to help you implement the Content Links strategy.

1. Create a list of key terms, symbols, or pictures from the lesson content.

2. Write each key term, symbol, or picture on separate note cards.

3. Distribute a note card to each student. Multiple students could have the same term, symbol, or picture. For example, and as in the Classroom Example for this section, you could make three sets of the climate notecards. If a student meets another student that has the same notecard he or she has already discussed, both students would just move on to find another partner.

4. Instruct students to walk around the room and find someone whose note card item is related to theirs in some way (while not being the same).

5. In pairs, have students discuss the relationship between their items.

6. Have students repeat the process; find another person and determine the relationship between the terms, symbols, or pictures on their cards. Then, signal them to stop but remain in their final pairings.

7. Have the final pairings take turns sharing the connections between their terms, symbols, or pictures with each other.

Variations

You can use the following variations in association with this strategy.

- Instead of providing students with established items, give students blank cards and have them choose a term or graphic related to their classroom learning.

- After step 7, have the final partner student pairs share their connections with the entire class.

- To establish associations, invite students to share with the class the most interesting, most difficult, and easiest terms, symbols, or pictures.

Additional Content-Area Examples

This section provides examples of some ways you can connect this strategy to your teaching in different content areas.

- A language arts teacher provides each student with the name of a character from the last five books they've read as a class. Students pair with peers who have different characters. Student pairs then try to find connections between their two characters.

- A science teacher provides a card that lists a system of the human body to each student. Students pair with peers who have different body parts. Student pairs then try to find connections between their body parts, such as how they connect to or support each other.

- A mathematics teacher provides students with cards that show mathematical symbols, terminology, and word problems. Students pair with peers who have different cards. Student pairs then try to determine ways they can use their cards together to solve problems.

- A social studies teacher provides students with note cards and instructs them to each record an important term in the unit. Students pair with peers who have chosen different terms. Each pairing discusses how the terms are related and tries to find connections to the broader unit.

- A business teacher provides students with cards that contain specific workplace etiquette tips. Students pair with peers who have a different tip. Each pairing discusses its tips and tries to establish connections to what these tips communicate about workplace etiquette.

Discussion Questions

As you reflect on this chapter, consider the following five questions.

1. Which strategies in this chapter already align with your existing instructional practices? What small changes could you make to improve these practices to enhance student thinking for understanding?

2. What are two strategies for building understanding that you could use in the next month?

3. What is your favorite movement-based strategy from this chapter? What makes it a great fit for your students?

4. What variation can you come up with to enhance a strategy in this chapter you intend to adopt?

5. What are some ways you can tailor a strategy in this chapter for your specific curriculum?

Take Action

Use the following three activities to put this chapter's concepts to work in your own classroom.

1. Pick one strategy that you want to use with your students and create a plan for how you could utilize it in your classroom.

2. After using a strategy you've adopted with your students, ask them whether they enjoyed the strategy and how you can improve it for the next time.

3. Observe another teacher who uses critical-thinking strategies that develop understanding. Write down your reflections and ideas about what you notice and how you could adopt them into your own teaching.

CHAPTER 5

Implementing Strategies for Analyze-Level Thinking

No problem can withstand the assault of sustained thinking.
—Voltaire

In this chapter, you will find eighteen instructional strategies that focus on learning at the Analyze level of Bloom's taxonomy revised (Anderson & Krathwohl, 2001). Each of the following instructional strategies requires Analyze-level cognitive applications like differentiating, organizing, or attributing content. Some of the following strategies also tap cognitive applications at the Remember, Understand, or Apply levels. Icons with each strategy indicate which steps (levels) of the taxonomy the activity touches, as well as its primary tool for engagement (movement, collaboration, or media literacy).

Within each strategy, you will find a brief introduction that explains its concept and purpose, a classroom example, a series of steps for implementing the strategy, a list of variations you can choose to implement, and a section detailing additional examples based on different content areas.

Strategy 7: Concept Attainment

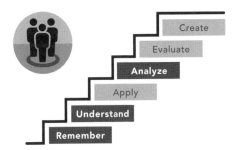

The *Concept Attainment* strategy has students use a structured-inquiry process to determine the attributes of a group or category. As students compare and contrast examples with the attributes of the concept with examples without those attributes (or with different attributes), they distinguish examples of a given group from the examples of the other. Figure 5.1 (page 40) shows an example of this based on this strategy's Classroom Example.

As students learn to sort out relevant information through classifying, they can make connections and deeply understand a concept. Additionally, using more complex clues that require students to distill information and identify similarities and differences can also require analytical-thinking skills (Silver, Strong, & Perini, 2007). Students often like this strategy because

	Idea A	Idea B
Clue one	_Beauty and the Beast_	_Cast Away_
Clue two	_Titanic_	_Jaws_
Clue three	_Twilight_	_The Martian_
Common theme	_Love conquers all_	_Man versus nature_

Source: Cameron, Landau, & Cameron, 1997; Godfrey, Mooradian, Morgan, & Hardwicke, 2008; Hanks, Rapke, Starkey, Zemeckis, & Zemeckis, 2000; Hoberman, Lieberman, & Condon, 2017; Kinberg et al., 2015; Zanuck, Brown, & Spielberg, 1975.

Figure 5.1: Movie-themes clues.

it feels like a game to identify the key idea. The strategy is also very effective at hooking students' attention at the beginning of a lesson or unit while requiring complex cognitive processing.

CLASSROOM EXAMPLE

A teacher presents students with an initial set of clues: a picture from _Beauty and the Beast_ (Idea A; Hoberman, Lieberman, & Condon, 2017) and one from _Cast Away_ (Idea B; Hanks et al., 2000). Students work in groups to determine the attributes of both. She then provides a second set of clues with additional examples: _Titanic_ (Idea A; Cameron et al., 1997) and _Jaws_ (Idea B; Zanuck, Brown, & Spielberg, 1975). Students then attempt to determine the common attributes between the two A ideas and two B ideas. Finally, she gives students the final clues: _Twilight_ (Idea A; Godfrey, Mooradian, Morgan, & Hardwicke, 2008) and _The Martian_ (Idea B; Kinberg et al., 2015). Students finalize their thinking about these components and the teacher asks, "Do you have a guess?"

The students decide that the Idea A movies all had the theme, _love conquers all_, whereas the Idea B movies had the theme, _man versus nature_. See figure 5.1.

Strategy Steps

Use the following nine steps to help you implement the Concept Attainment strategy.

1. Identify the core concept you want students to understand or analyze. For example, at the Understand level, students could identify basic qualities between living and nonliving things.

To push students' thinking to deeply analyzing a concept, pick something more abstract, like the term _cooperation_.

2. Identify the key attributes that represent the concept you chose.

3. Develop positive (_yes_) and negative (_no_) examples that exhibit these attributes. For example, you can present these in the form of text, objects, pictures, or video clips.

4. Model an example using this concept so students understand the process.

5. Organize students into groups and present a _yes_ and a _no_ example (the first two clues). Give groups approximately three to five minutes (depending on the topic's complexity) to think about the differences between the clues and jot down tentative hypotheses about their ideas of the concept.

6. Present the second set of clues and give students an additional three to five minutes (again, depending on the topic's complexity) to refine their hypotheses.

7. Finally, introduce the third clue set. Provide groups another one to five minutes to further adjust their hypotheses.

8. Have groups share what they think are the common attributes of the positive examples and their educated guess on the mystery concept.

9. Lead a closing discussion revealing the core concept and how it relates to all the clues. Acknowledge the groups whose hypotheses were related or correctly guessed the topic. Explain how the core concept will be that day's instructional focus.

Variations

You can use the following variations in association with this strategy.

- For younger students (preK–3), you can use just one or two sets of examples to reduce the complexity of this strategy.

- Once groups figure out the categories, have them propose their own, new set of clues back to you so they can test if their hypotheses are correct. For example, as in the classroom example for this strategy, students might suggest another book or movie for the themes *man versus nature* and *love conquers all*. As students share their examples, the teacher would clarify any misunderstandings and provide additional examples as necessary.

- After introducing each set of examples, have the groups share the attributes of the *yes* and *no* examples so you can record them on the board or classroom display.

- Consider presenting all confirming examples first, and then follow with a series of contradictory nonexamples. For example, in figure 5.2, the first-column criteria are examples of conserving water, while the second column lists examples of wasting water.

- To add movement to this exercise, have each student move around the room to find a clue about the topic. Provide students with four to six clues, with some students having the same clue. Each student then makes an inference about what he or she believes is the lesson topic. Each student then finds someone with a different clue, and the two share their inferences. Each student pairing then revises his or her inference about the lesson topic. Finally, each pair merges with another pair to share their conclusions and further refine their ideas about the lesson focus. These groups then share their ideas with the whole class.

Additional Content-Area Examples

This section provides examples of some ways you can connect this strategy to your teaching in different content areas.

- A language arts teacher presents students with examples of nouns and then nonexamples or other types of words. Students use the Concept Attainment strategy to identify which fit into each category to determine how all the examples are related.

- A biology teacher instructs students to examine characteristics of cells. The teacher presents clues in the first column that represent characteristics of an animal cell, while the second column examples highlight characteristics of a plant cell. Through the presentation of clues, the students must compare the clues and draw conclusions to figure out the pattern of these characteristics.

- A mathematics teacher presents students with examples of regular geometric shapes and nonexamples of irregular polygons. Students must properly determine which fall into each category and why.

- A social studies teacher instructs students to examine three sets of quotes. The first quote in each set references *democracy*, and the second references *monarchy*. Students must brainstorm the common attributes among the quotes in each group and determine which falls into each category.

- To begin a unit on music history, a music teacher has students listen to Renaissance music followed by an example of music from the Romantic era. Students must analyze the differences between the first and second songs. The teacher then plays two more segments from each period to help students deepen their analysis.

	Examples	Nonexamples
Clue one	*Turning off the faucet while you are brushing your teeth*	*Showering for more than five minutes*
Clue two	*Fixing leaky pipes*	*Running a load of laundry with two shirts*
Clue three	*Using a bucket of water to wash the car*	*Running water continuously when washing dishes*
Common theme	*Conserving water*	*Wasting water*

Figure 5.2: Water-conservation clues.

Strategy 8: Metaphor

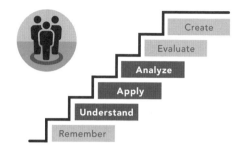

A *metaphor* is a comparison between unlike things with some similarities. The *Metaphor* strategy uses this concept to deepen understanding and stimulate creativity as students make comparisons between two things that don't initially seem alike but have something in common (Carpenter, Sweet, & Blythe, 2012). Often students can connect new information to previous learning to build personal connections with the content, thus personalizing the lesson. Having students use a graphic organizer, like the one in figure 5.3, can help them organize their thinking.

At the Understand level of Bloom's taxonomy, students can make metaphors of critical vocabulary terms (such as, evaporation is similar to Christmas decorations going away after the holiday). At the Analyze level, students craft metaphors that represent a larger body of information with multiple similarities. Students could create a metaphor that represents a character in a book, showcasing several similarities. For example, a student could select Boo Radley from *To Kill a Mockingbird* (Lee, 1989) and compare him to a zombie.

CLASSROOM EXAMPLE

After studying the U.S. Constitution, a teacher instructs students to create a metaphor of the key ideas embedded in the document by making at least four comparisons. In groups, students list key ideas represented in the U.S. Constitution and then brainstorm potential metaphors. One group decides to compare the U.S. Constitution to a manual stapler. The group records several similarities in a graphic organizer and then explains these comparisons. Figure 5.3 represents the group's work.

The U.S. Constitution is like a manual stapler.	
Similarity	**Description**
Limitations	*The stapler is limited in its power. A manual stapler needs a person to operate it just like the U.S. Constitution is built on the idea of popular sovereignty—power from the people. In addition, there are limits to the powers of the government just as the stapler has a limited function (to staple). The stapler can't hole punch or tape things together.*
Republicanism	*Often in classes, one student or the teacher staples papers for everyone else to speed up the process. Similarly, in the United States, citizens vote on representatives who serve in government to represent the citizens.*
Separation of powers	*A manual stapler has several parts working together to function. For example, the metal base of the stapler creates the structure of the tool. This base is like the judicial branch, as justices interpret laws grounded on the base—the U.S. Constitution. Inside the stapler, there is a spring that pushes the staples forward. This spring represents the executive branch, as the president is expected to enforce laws across the country. There is also the human operator who presses down on the stapler. The human operator represents the U.S. Congress, which is made up of 535 state representatives who make the laws.*
Checks and balances	*For the stapler to work correctly all parts must be functioning. The human operator must press down with enough power to eject the staple but not too hard as to crush the stapler. The spring inside the stapler needs enough tension to push the next staple forward. Similarly, the U.S. Constitution establishes some checks and balances to make sure all the branches are operating effectively. For example, the Supreme Court justices can declare a law unconstitutional, and the president can veto a law made by Congress.*

Figure 5.3: Metaphor graphic organizer.

*Visit **go.SolutionTree.com/instruction** for a free reproducible version of this figure.*

Strategy Steps

Use the following five steps to help you implement the Metaphor strategy.

1. Determine the topic for the metaphor or a list of concepts that students could choose for the comparison. Typically, the larger the body of information students must consider, the higher the thinking level.

2. Divide the class into equal-sized groups of two or three students.

3. Instruct groups to brainstorm potential ideas for the metaphor and select the best concept. Alternatively, you could provide options for students to use in the comparison (such as the stapler in the Classroom Example for this strategy). Encourage students to be creative and select unusual ideas that challenge their thinking.

4. Have groups record the similarities and descriptions on a graphic organizer (see figure 5.3).

5. Have groups share their thinking by creating new groups composed of a representative from each of the initial groups. Members of each initial work group can number off, and then all the students with the same number can form a new group to share their initial group's metaphor.

Variations

You can use the following variations in association with this strategy.

- If you teach younger students (preK–2), you can have them draw a picture of their metaphor and illustrate the similarities.

- For each group (or for the whole class), prepare a bag with four or five items that are metaphorical representations of the content students have learned. For example, you could use the following random objects in a bag for students to select among to make their metaphor: tape, hammer, banana, feather, and light bulb. Have students analyze the items to try to draw conclusions or connections between each object and the content.

Additional Content-Area Examples

This section provides examples of some ways you can connect this strategy to your teaching in different content areas.

- After reading a book, a language arts teacher instructs students to walk around the room and view various objects (such as a vase of flowers, onions, a brick, file folders, or a soft drink). After viewing the objects, the teacher has students go to the object they think represents the text's main idea and develop a list of similarities between the object and the main idea.

- A science teacher instructs students to create a metaphor to represent an assigned element from the periodic table.

- A mathematics teacher instructs students to use order of operations and identify similarities between the mathematical process and another step-by-step process they follow in their daily lives.

- A social studies teacher instructs students to select a commercial to represent a famous historical leader and explain the similarities.

- A physical education teacher instructs students to create a metaphor for badminton. For example, students could compare badminton to a particular food and explain why they made that comparison.

Strategy 9: Media Metaphor

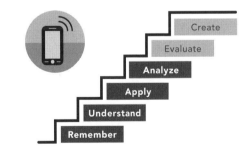

In the previous strategy, you learned the benefits of using metaphors to make unfamiliar concepts more meaningful by connecting them to what students already know. You can have students take this a step further and connect to their interests by using *Media Metaphor* to integrate media into the strategy. For example, students could compare a main character in a book to a favorite scene from a movie or a commercial or to highlight the differences between Thomas Jefferson and Alexander Hamilton. You can see an example of this in figure 5.4.

Other ideas for using metaphors with media include students finding media with similarities to concepts like recycling, the distributive property, and commas. Choosing media that represents abstract concepts challenges students to deeply understand a topic and then consider various options to determine which best represents the topic—or to use their critical-thinking skills (Tsirkunova, 2013).

CLASSROOM EXAMPLE

After reading William Shakespeare's (1935) *The Tragedy of Romeo and Juliet* in their English language arts class, students engage in a class discussion of Juliet's relationship with Romeo. The teacher prompts students to enter into groups of three and

find a song, commercial, or movie clip that represents the relationship. The students connect lyrics in the song or words in the commercial or movie clip to evidence from the text to support their decisions. Figure 5.4 shows an example of their work.

Strategy Steps

Use the following three steps to help you implement the Media Metaphor strategy.

1. Select a topic as the basis for the strategy.

2. Identify a song, commercial, movie clip, or social media post that loosely connects with the topic your students identified, or allow students to choose the media comparison as in the classroom example for this strategy.

3. Have groups share relevant connections with the class.

Song Lyrics	Connection
"'Cause all of me/ Loves all of you . . . You're my end and my beginning —John Legend, "All of Me"	The song "All of Me" perfectly captures the love between Romeo and Juliet. Juliet describes her love as "boundless" and "infinite": "My love as deep; the more I give to thee,/ The more I have, for both are infinite" (2.2). A similar love is portrayed in John Legend's song in which the speaker describes the act of giving everything he has to his love. Similarly, this love is boundless.
"Can I have your daughter for the rest of my life? . . . Tough luck, my friend, but the answer is no!" —MAGIC!, "Rude"	The song "Rude" by MAGIC! is a great representation of the forbidden love between Romeo and Juliet. In act 1, scene 5, Juliet states that her "only love [has] sprung from [her] only hate," and that Romeo is her "loathed enemy." This is similar to the song "Rude" because the speaker asks the father for his blessing and he will not allow their marriage. In both situations the couples are not allowed to be together, but they love each other despite not having their parents' permission.
"What if we rewrite the stars? . . . You'd be the one I was meant to find" —Zac Efron, "Rewrite the Stars"	The song "Rewrite the Stars" is similar to the fated love of Romeo and Juliet. In the beginning of the play, the Chorus describes the pair as "star-crossed lovers," implying that their love is meant to be. Both speakers, the one in Efron's song and the Chorus, believe strongly in the influence that fate can have on life and love.

Figure 5.4: Music metaphor.

Variations

You can use the following variations in association with this strategy.

- Use this strategy at the beginning of the school year as a way to get to know students. Have students use themselves as part of the metaphor; for example, have students select a song that tells something important about themselves. This task encourages students to describe themselves while critically thinking.

- Have students add dance moves to go along with certain parts of the song to represent the mood of a character from a novel or a famous historical figure.

- To organize their thinking, have students use a graphic organizer like the one in figure 5.4.

Additional Content-Area Examples

This section provides examples of some ways you can connect this strategy to your teaching in different content areas.

- A language arts teacher explains to students that songs often have the parts of a plot diagram. The teacher instructs students to find a song and explain (by citing the lyrics) how all the elements of the plot diagram are represented in the song. To extend the learning, the teacher has groups create a soundtrack that represents the most important plot points of the whole text.

- After explaining there are many different ecosystems around the world, a science teacher instructs students to find a song and explain how that song represents a specific ecosystem.

- After studying the associative and distributive properties, a mathematics teacher instructs students to find media that relate to these properties.

- Explaining that geography shapes the way people live, a social studies teacher instructs students to find two movie clips that demonstrate understanding of this concept.

- After learning about budgeting, an economic teacher instructs students to identify a song that they can connect to wise budgeting practices.

Strategy 10: Quote It! Code It!

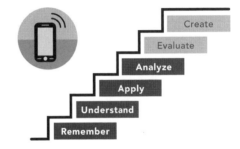

Similar to the Strategy 9: Media Metaphor, the *Quote It! Code It!* strategy has students use quotes from a teacher-selected song to connect with a concept (its code) and then describe the meaning or interpretation (demonstrate critical thinking). This strategy is unique in that it challenges students to find multiple concepts in one media source while classifying information. For example, students could find examples of figurative language or causes and effects. A graphic organizer like the example in figure 5.5 is ideal for this purpose.

Focus: Analyzing geography themes
Name of Song: "Rocky Top"
Lyrics by: Felice and Boudleaux Bryant (1967)

Quote It!	Code It!	Meaning or Interpretation
"ol' Rocky Top"	Place	This phrase represents <u>place</u> because the mountain is a physical characteristic of a location.
"moonshine still"	Place	The moonshine still represents <u>place</u>, a cultural characteristic of this area in Appalachia.
"once two strangers climbed ol' Rocky Top"	Human-environmental interaction	People climbing the mountain connect to the theme <u>human-environmental interaction</u> because people change the environment as they create trails.

Figure 5.5: Quote It! Code It! graphic organizer example.

*Visit **go.SolutionTree.com/instruction** for a free reproducible version of this figure.*

. . . .

CLASSROOM EXAMPLE

A teacher instructs students to identify the geography themes in the lyrics to the song "Rocky Top" (Bryant & Bryant, 1967). Using a graphic organizer (see figure 5.5, page 45) to explain their thinking, students analyze the song lyrics to identify (code) and explain its geography-related themes.

. . . .

Strategy Steps

Use the following five steps to help you implement the Quote It! Code It! strategy.

1. Select a song students can analyze from a certain focus.

2. Inform students of the purpose of listening to the song.

3. Provide students with a blank Quote It! Code It! graphic organizer (like the example in figure 5.5, page 45). Explain the directions for using the organizer. In the first column, students quote lyrics from the song. Students classify information and note the category in the second column. Finally, students explain the connection between the quote and the classified information.

4. Play the song, and provide students with a printed transcription of the media source as a reference (or provide them with access to a resource to replay the media in their groups).

5. In pairs or in a group discussion, have students share their thinking.

Variations

You can use the following variations in association with this strategy.

- Have students record their thinking on chart paper or digitally and share their work with the class.

- Record on notecards phrases within the media and some code categories. Give each group an envelope with the phrases and code category, and instruct students to match the phrases to the code. Have students explain their reasoning.

Additional Content-Area Examples

This section provides examples of some ways you can connect this strategy to your teaching in different content areas.

- A language arts teacher instructs students to listen to a movie clip and identify dialogue in the clip that connects with key characters in a novel or text they have read.

- A science teacher plays the song "Rocket Man" (John & Taupin, 1972) and instructs students to identify the key consequences of space travel.

- A mathematics teacher instructs students to listen to a song and select words or phrases that connect three geometric shapes. Students should justify their reasoning.

- A social studies teacher instructs students to listen to the song "Roller Skate" (Crow & Trott, 2017) and complete the Quote It! Code It! strategy by identifying how technology has changed culture.

- An art teacher instructs students to select several social media posts and connect each with a different art period. Students must justify the connections they selected.

Strategy 11: Visual Thinking

Visual Thinking centers on image discussions by using art to teach visual literacy, thinking, and communication as students listen and express themselves (Yenawine, 2013). When repeated, this critical-thinking strategy can help students internalize the process and utilize it to analyze other images. In doing so, it equips students to make new, complex, and detailed connections and understandings that support deeper learning. Because it provokes student thinking on multiple levels, it produces a high level of engagement and questioning.

This makes it a great way for you to hook students' interest when beginning a lesson or attempting to make connections in new learning.

. . . .

CLASSROOM EXAMPLE

A political science class is learning about government from the colonial era. The teacher presents students with a political cartoon and asks them to answer established prompts while examining the art. Students use evidence in the art to make connections related to what they are learning about colonial-era government and the purpose of the artwork.

. . . .

Strategy Steps

Use the following four steps to help you implement the Visual Thinking strategy.

1. Have students examine a work of art, map, cartoon, time line, or image that is related to their learning.

2. Discuss students' observations by posing questions such as, "What's going on in this picture?" "What do you see that makes you say that?" and "What more can you find?" The first question should be open-ended to promote discussion but encourage understanding. Subsequent questions can examine students' reasoning and evidence. Students identify parts of the image related to their observations.

3. Listen to and consider the alternate perspectives each student contributes, and then put students in small groups to further discuss. Encourage as many interpretations as possible. Provide students with the following question stems to help them probe deeper.

   - What can you conclude? What evidence supports that conclusion?

   - What is your opinion of _____?

   - What is the most interesting part?

   - What is the purpose of _____?

   - Compare two parts of the _____.

   - What is the problem?

4. Have students share their answers during a whole-group discussion. Their goal is to point to as many interpretations as possible.

Variations

You can use the following variations in association with this strategy.

- Adapt this strategy to solve real-world mathematics problems or to analyze quotes or a passage (Yenawine, 2013).

- For younger students (K–5), when posing questions in step two, you can be more specific, such as, "What do you see in this picture?" Students can then support their ideas with evidence from the art.

- After completing the strategy process, assign students a related writing task, such as an essay comparing the various perspectives of a map profiling American westward expansion.

Additional Content-Area Examples

This section provides examples of some ways you can connect this strategy to your teaching in different content areas.

- A language arts teacher gives students a series of quotations from a novel they are about to read, along with images the teacher selected. Students choose a quotation and match it with an image. In doing so, they are making predictions about the context of the quotations and about the text they will be reading.

- A science teacher instructs students to examine a time line of major scientific discoveries related to a topic they are studying. The teacher asks students, "What was the turning point for the people involved in making the discoveries?" The teacher then asks students, "What was most important about it?" The teacher has students compare two of the discoveries and their impact on society.

- A mathematics teacher instructs students to analyze a time line containing world population numbers over a three-hundred-year time span. Based on their mathematical analysis of the data, students discuss what they observe, what they find most interesting, any problems they identify, and what evidence might support a possible solution to those problems.

- A social studies teacher instructs students to examine the painting, *The Landing of William Penn* (Ferris, 1920). The teacher has students answer questions regarding what's going on in the painting, like What makes it interesting? What might be the purpose of the painting? and Does the painting accurately represent history?

- A humanities teacher instructs students to view visual artwork and music from the same historical period. The teacher prompts students to discuss key elements of that particular historical period. Students then create a picture they believe represents the period based on their conclusions.

Strategy 12: Concept Maps

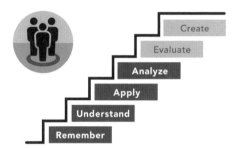

Concept Maps help students organize information they have learned, such as through readings. Usually these maps take on a tree-like structure, as in figure

5.6. Research suggests that Concept Maps have positive benefits for knowledge retention (Nesbit & Adesope, 2006) and metacognitive accuracy (Redford, Thiede, Wiley, & Griffin, 2012). Through this strategy, students learn to identify important information. Often, teachers develop graphic organizers to support students' understanding, but if students can select which type of Concept Map best represents the information and then develop it on their own, they can stretch their thinking even further. With more complex readings, students can create diagrams depicting interactions between concepts and ideas. Various Concept Maps can depict different methods of organizing information, including hierarchical or cause and effect. Using a web-based Concept Map, such as those found at Lucidchart (www.lucidchart.com) or MindMeister (www.mindmeister.com), you can challenge students to create as many connections as possible.

. . . .

CLASSROOM EXAMPLE

A teacher provides elementary students arranged in groups of four or five with informational texts about interesting animals, such as the aye-aye. Each group creates a Concept Map, like the one in figure 5.6, on chart paper describing the animal and then shares it with the class. Using the individual Concept Maps, the class creates a larger Concept Map together, linking all their thoughts and ideas.

. . . .

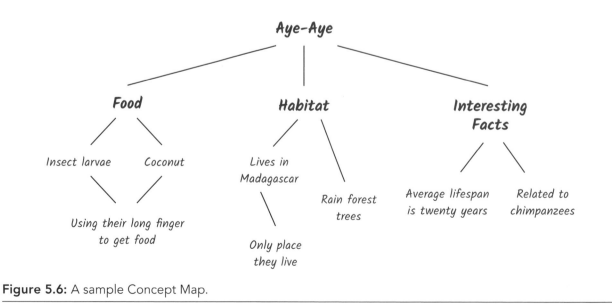

Figure 5.6: A sample Concept Map.

Strategy Steps

Use the following five steps to help you implement the Concept Maps strategy.

1. Select a drawing medium like paper, whiteboards, or digital tools for students to use. There are several digital tools to support students' creations including Smart Art and other drawing tools from Microsoft (https://microsoft.com/en-us), Bubbl.us (https://bubbl.us), and Lucidchart (https://lucidchart.com). A benefit of using digital tools is that they are easy for students to edit and share.

2. Instruct students to determine the central idea for the subject or topic. Give them about five minutes to brainstorm and refine their main concept.

3. Once students establish a main concept, have them select associated concepts. These associated concepts should support the central idea. Depending on the age of the students and complexity of the concept, students should identify ten to twenty-five associated concepts that support the central idea. Students may need to conduct research on the concept to collect information.

4. Students should then organize their associated topics. For example, they could select a hierarchical format with general ideas leading to more specific ones at the bottom. They could use shapes and lines to group similar associated concepts. They could depict connections and relationships with larger text sizes, different colors, or shapes.

5. Provide about five minutes for students to refine their Concept Map. Students should examine the links to see if they accurately represent the content or idea.

Variations

You can use the following variations in association with this strategy.

- Allow younger students (preK–2) to use images instead of text to represent core and associated ideas on their Concept Maps.

- To increase collaboration, have students trade their Concept Maps with one or more peers for feedback and allow them about five minutes to refine their work based on the feedback they receive. Or, have students produce their Concept Maps as a group project and have each group present their work as part of a class discussion.

Additional Content-Area Examples

This section provides examples of some ways you can connect this strategy to your teaching in different content areas.

- A language arts teacher provides students with an informational text on current eating habits in the United States. Students create a Concept Map identifying the main idea with supporting details.

- Following a study on changes in matter, a science teacher has students create Concept Maps in pairs to show the different types of changes in matter, and the knowledge connected with changes in matter.

- A mathematics teacher asks students to create a Concept Map to preassess their understanding before beginning a unit on shapes.

- In a unit on the Revolutionary War, a social studies teacher instructs students to create a Concept Map depicting the changing beliefs of the colonists that led to a declaration of independence and war against Great Britain.

- At the beginning of a music history unit for a preassessment, a music teacher plays a selection of a famous musical piece such as *The Nutcracker Suite*'s "Dance of the Sugar Plum Fairy" (Tchaikovsky, n.d.). In groups, students create a Concept Map by brainstorming descriptions of the type of music (such as instruments, tempo, and dynamics) and interpretations (such as the composer's intentions, a possible story line, and inferences on where this piece falls within musical history).

Strategy 13: Mind Maps

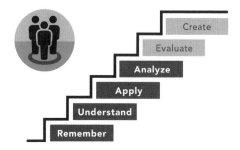

Like Concept Maps, *Mind Maps* display a visual representation of concepts. Unlike Concept Maps that could include several concepts, Mind Maps start with one, key idea in the center and radiate outward with specific examples or ideas (see figure 5.7). Students can use words, symbols, or images to describe each idea and then further elaborate on these with additional branches. Mind Maps are useful as a visual formative assessment of students' understanding because they challenge students to make connections between various pieces of information. This helps students learn concepts better than through traditional linear formats and note taking (Farrand, Hussain, & Hennessy, 2002).

CLASSROOM EXAMPLE

In science class, students begin analyzing differences among animals. To solidify the learning, students write *classification* in the middle of their chart paper. After reviewing the fifteen other terms, each on cards the teacher provides, the group discusses how to place them on the Mind Map (such as a reptile, invertebrate, and so on) to accurately depict the relationship between the words and the term, *classification*. See figure 5.7.

Strategy Steps

Use the following five steps to help you implement the Mind Maps strategy.

1. Select a central idea that represents what students will explore and place that idea in the center of a page or large chart paper.

2. Instruct students to work within groups to brainstorm and design branches from the main idea with words, phrases, or pictures. Each branch may then have subsequent divisions that further define the concept.

3. Students can add color and change text sizes to highlight points, emphasize connections between information, and clarify relationships between terms. For example, they could use blue arrows to represent positive connections between terms and red arrows to indicate negative relationships.

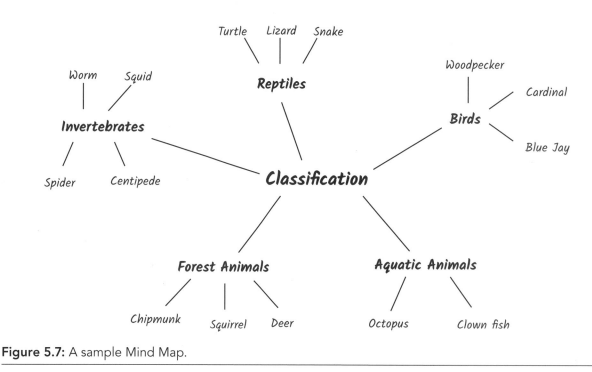

Figure 5.7: A sample Mind Map.

4. Students should then present and explain their arrangement to other groups.

5. Conduct a final discussion with questions. Ask questions like, "How did listening to the explanations of others help you to more deeply understand the topics?" and "What terms do you think should be added or deleted from the stack? Why?"

Variations

You can use the following variations in association with this strategy.

- To help younger students (preK–2) to show relationships among terms and ideas, create a set of index cards with the central idea and branching elements. Display the cards on a flat surface (such as chart paper, a floor, a large desk, or using magnets and a magnetic board). In small groups of two to four, have students arrange all the branching ideas using the arrow cards to show subsequent clarifications of an idea. Have students justify how their Mind Map accurately depicts the information to the class.

- Instead of using index cards, print the words and cut them into strips, or create a digital wall using tools like Padlet (https://padlet.com), Lino (https://linoit.com), or Coggle (https://coggle.it).

- Have students add pictures to their Mind Maps and use color and text size to better clarify relationships between terms. For example, red arrows could represent positive connections between terms, and black arrows could indicate negative relationships.

- Have students examine other groups' Mind Maps and use sticky notes to record questions for the other groups to consider.

Additional Content-Area Examples

This section provides examples of some ways you can connect this strategy to your teaching in different content areas.

- After learning about the different types of text structures, a language arts teacher provides students with different related texts and instructs them to design a Mind Map on text structure with branches detailing their understandings.

- A science teacher instructs students to analyze different celestial bodies (stars, planets, moon, comets, and so on) and prepares fifteen cards with associated terms. To solidify the learning, students write the word *classification* in the middle of their chart paper. After receiving the cards from the teacher, students review the fifteen terms on cards provided and discuss in groups how to place them on the Mind Map to accurately depict the relationship between the words and the core term.

- A mathematics teacher provides students with various proofs and theories. She directs students to design a Mind Map to categorize them and determine relationships between them to show their understanding.

- A social studies teacher provides students with cards listing the fifteen key economics terms they learned for a unit and instructs them to organize the cards into a Mind Map to show their understanding.

- A career and technical education teacher instructs students to design a Mind Map depicting the elements necessary to be ready for college or career.

Strategy 14: Hear, Think, and Wonder

Hear, Think, and Wonder is a strategy that encourages students to deeply analyze song lyrics (Connell, 2014). After listening to the song and recording their initial thoughts, students are given a purpose for reviewing the song and, when they listen the second time, they are focused on scrutinizing the lyrics for that goal. By analyzing music and lyrics together, students can learn about themes, character traits, symbolism, inference, and so on. By using songs that connect with your curriculum's content, you can help students make connections to your teaching, develop their learning in ways that they might not with just the core content alone, and connect to many students' personal interest in music. To help them with this strategy, have students use a graphic organizer like the one in figure 5.8.

· ·

CLASSROOM EXAMPLE

Students listen to "Bohemian Rhapsody" (Mercury, 1975) while reading their own copy of the lyrics. The students complete the first row of the Hear, Think, and Wonder graphic organizer by recording what they hear, think about, and wonder. In pairs or groups, the students complete the second row of the organizer by noting what they read in the lyrics, then think about, and finally understand. (See figure 5.8.) They share their notes to begin their whole-group discussion of the song.

· ·

Strategy Steps

Use the following four steps to help you implement the Hear, Think, and Wonder strategy.

1. Choose a song related to a current lesson and instruct students to listen to the entire song and complete the first row in the Hear, Think and Wonder graphic organizer (see figure 5.8). Tell students to record words and phrases they hear, what those words and phrases make them think about, and what they make them wonder.

2. Have students work in pairs and share what they record.

3. Have students listen to the song again for a specific purpose, such as its theme, concept, and so on.

4. Students should read the music lyrics and think about how the song connects to the lesson's learning target. They should use the *I read* column to record specific lyrics from the song that connect to the learning target. In the *And I think* column, students should explain how these lyrics relate to the learning target. Finally, in the *So, now I understand* column, students should draw conclusions about the main point or theme of the song and how it connects to the learning target.

Variations

You can use the following variations in association with this strategy.

- Instead of music, use a video clip. For example, you could have students analyze a segment of a media interview with an author, legislator, or world leader. Students could also analyze a scene from a movie to identify themes in literature or a historical event.

- Instead of music, use images with this strategy. Instead of having a *hear* column in the graphic organizer, replace it with *observe*. After analyzing

Learning target: I can analyze how and why the speaker in the song develops.		
I hear . . .	**And that makes me think . . .**	**Now I wonder . . .**
Anyway the wind blows, doesn't really matter to me, to me	*The speaker is carefree and says that nothing matters, but he is out of touch with reality.*	*Why does he believe nothing matters? Why can't he escape reality?*
I read . . .	**And I think. . .**	**So, now I understand . . .**
Mama, life had just begun But now I've gone and thrown it all away	*The speaker has done something terrible (committed murder), and his decision will cost him his life.*	*The speaker is feeling sorry for himself because he has committed murder. He believes that this terrible decision has ruined his life and now he has nothing to live for.*

Figure 5.8: Hear, Think, and Wonder graphic organizer example.

*Visit **go.SolutionTree.com/instruction** for a free reproducible version of this figure.*

the image, have students read more about the topic and record information in the second row about how the picture and readings are related.

Additional Content-Area Examples

This section provides examples of some ways you can connect this strategy to your teaching in different content areas.

- In connection to a unit on William Shakespeare's (1935) *The Tragedy of Romeo and Juliet*, a language arts teacher provides students with the lyrics to "Love Story" (Swift, 2008) and then plays the song for them. The students complete the first row of the Hear, Think, and Wonder graphic organizer, recording what they hear, think about, and wonder. In pairs or groups, students complete the second row of the organizer noting what they read in the lyrics, then think about, and finally understand. They share their notes as a class to begin their whole-group discussion of the song and draw connections to *The Tragedy of Romeo and Juliet* (Shakespeare, 1935).

- In a unit on static electricity, the teacher has students listen to the "Electric Boogie" (Livingston, 1983) and use a Hear, Think, and Wonder graphic organizer to compare its lyrics to the real process and traits of static electricity.

- In a unit on solving for variables in an equation, the teacher has students listen to the "Cupid Shuffle" (Bernard, 2007) and use a Hear, Think, and Wonder graphic organizer to identify how its lyrics connect with this mathematical process.

- In a unit on the Great Depression, the teacher has students listen to the song "Electric Avenue" (Grant, 1982) and use a Hear, Think, and Wonder graphic organizer to identify how its lyrics reflect specific aspects of this period in U.S. history.

- In a unit on the music of the American South in the early 1900s or 1920s, the teacher has students listen to the "Homeless Blues" (Grainger, 1927) and use a Hear, Think, and Wonder graphic organizer to identify how

historical factors of the time resonate within the song's lyrics.

Strategy 15: Anticipation Guide

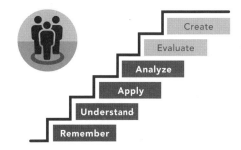

You can use the *Anticipation Guide* strategy to build students' curiosity in a reading topic while also activating their prior knowledge. Tapping students' prior knowledge is a proven way to help students acquire new learning (Marzano, 2004). Using this strategy prior to reading, students mark statements as true or false and then, after the reading, they review the answers and make changes as needed. Whether they change an answer or not, students also record textual evidence that defends their marks. Use an Anticipation Guide (see figure 5.9, page 54) to facilitate this process. Because students indicate the statements prior to reading, it stimulates students to lean on prior knowledge, inciting their interest and providing a purpose for reading.

. . . .

CLASSROOM EXAMPLE

A teacher provides students with an Anticipation Guide related to their readings on amendments to the U.S. Constitution. (See figure 5.9.) Students read the three teacher-provided statements about constitutional amendments, and mark them as true or false in the *Before* column. After reading the amendments, students then re-examine the statements and note in the *After* column whether they now believe the statements are true or false. In addition, students record textual evidence in the final column. Small groups discuss their markings and evidence, allowing students time to add additional proof or revise their thinking. In a whole-group discussion, students raise their red card (false) or green card (true) to indicate their stance on each statement and then share evidence.

. . . .

True or False		Statement	Evidence
Before	After		
F	T	1. The most important amendment is listed first.	*While all the amendments are important in different ways, the First Amendment preserves protection for religion, speech, press, assembly, and petition, which are bedrocks of individual freedom.*
T	T	2. The majority of amendments grant individuals rights.	*Amendments one through nine outline basic freedoms for people. Amendments thirteen through fifteen abolish slavery, establish due process, and expand voting rights. These fifteen amendments, over half, extend citizen rights. The Twenty-Fourth Amendment prohibits poll taxes, and the Nineteenth and Twenty-Sixth Amendments give women and eighteen-year-olds the right to vote.*
T	F	3. There are many amendments that could be deleted because they are not relevant today.	*Although the U.S. Constitution is over two hundred years old, really only three amendments seem out of date. The Third Amendment addresses quartering of soldiers, which has not been an issue since the United States began, and the Eighteenth and Twenty-First Amendments established prohibition and then repealed that stipulation, respectively. The other amendments represent key markers in history of important changes, as well as clarification of processes.*

Figure 5.9: Anticipation Guide example.

*Visit **go.SolutionTree.com/instruction** for a free reproducible version of this figure.*

Strategy Steps

Use the following eight steps to help you implement the Anticipation Guide strategy.

1. Choose a reading for students and set up an Anticipation Guide with several statements based on the information in that reading. At least one statement should be true, and at least one should be false. To be higher level, statements should not be facts from the reading, but inferences drawn from the text or statements that represent misconceptions. Regardless, each statement should sound plausible to ensure higher-level thinking. Statements that do not necessarily have a correct answer and fit these criteria will encourage discussion and debate.

2. Before reading, individually or in small groups discuss the statements with your students and instruct them to mark each one as true or false.

3. Have students read the assigned text.

4. After reading, have students review each statement again and identify if the statements are true or false using the After column. In the final column, students should record evidence from the text that supports what they marked.

5. Allow students about five to ten minutes to discuss in small groups their markings and evidence.

6. Provide each student with a red card and a green card. Read the first statement and then have students raise their red card if they believe the statement is false, and their green card if they believe it is true *before* reading. Have them put their cards down. Then, ask students to show which colored card represents their thinking *after* reading.

7. Conduct a whole-class discussion on the reading, allowing students to share their textual evidence and reasons for why they changed or didn't change their markings.

8. Repeat step six and step seven using the other statements.

Variations

You can use the following variations in association with this strategy.

- Have students do this strategy individually or in groups; note, however, that group discussions can expose other perspectives and reasoning.

- Instead of using the red and green cards, have students go to one side of the room or the other to represent true or false. After students debate and share their evidence for their answers, those persuaded to change their mind can move to the other side.

- In the Evidence column of the Anticipation Guide, have students list specific quotes from the text to support their thinking.

- Have grades preK–2 students stand up to indicate statements they believe are true and sit if statements are false. After reading aloud the text, the class can discuss evidence from the text that affirms or denies each statement and decide if the statement is really true or false.

- When asking students to determine their initial evaluation of each statement (step two), you can also conduct a classroom poll so students or groups can share their markings and preliminary reasons prior to reading.

Additional Content-Area Examples

This section provides examples of some ways you can connect this strategy to your teaching in different content areas.

- A language arts teacher uses the book *Fireflies* (Brinckloe, 1986) to present a statement: how a person's actions cause a positive or negative effect on the environment. The teacher instructs students to mark the statement as true or false, read the book, and then review and revise their initial thinking based on what they read.

- In a unit on energy and physics, a science teacher offers students an initial statement: kinetic and potential energy are generated from rolling a ball down a hill. The teacher then instructs students to record on an Anticipation Guide if they believe the statement is true or false. Students then research the topic and review and revise their thinking based on what they learn.

- A mathematics teacher instructs students to quickly read a word problem. On their Anticipation Guide, the teacher asks students to mark as true or false the following statement: to solve this word problem, you need to first calculate the volume. Students then carefully examine the problem and work out the answer, revising their initial answer as necessary.

- In a unit on government, a social studies teacher poses a statement to students that reflects debatable aspects of the branches of government, such as that Congress is the most powerful, and instructs them to use an Anticipation Guide to record their initial thinking on the topic. Students then research the branches of government and review and revise their thinking.

- In a study on composers in the Baroque period, a music teacher gives students statements in an Anticipation Guide that reflect contested issues about their music. For example, Johann Sebastian Bach was one of the most influential composers of the Baroque period. Students record their initial thoughts and then research the topic and review and revise their thinking.

Strategy 16: Cubing

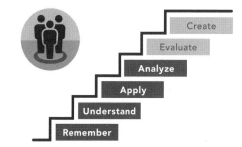

Cubing is a strategy that challenges students to examine a topic from different perspectives by using a labeled cube or die to assign students a topic from a specific, but randomly derived approach. There are a variety of ways to obtain such a cube. For the Teachers (n.d.) recommends buying a foam cube from a teacher supply store, or making your own out of paper (see www.fortheteachers.org for a printable design) or simply using an ordinary die and assigning specific actions to the numbered dots on it.

Regardless of how you obtain or make your cube, use the following labels or assignments for each of the six faces: (1) describe, (2) compare and contrast, (3) associate, (4) analyze, (5) apply, and (6) argue for or against. Sides one through three reinforce learning at the Understand level of Bloom's taxonomy, whereas sides four through six push thinking to the Analyze level. You can adapt these labels as necessary to fit the context of the task. (See the content-area examples.)

. . . .

CLASSROOM EXAMPLE

The class is learning about recycling leading up to Earth Day. The teacher uses the recycling theme as a topic. The teacher divides the class into groups and instructs students to write about the topic using the *describe* side of the cube. One group member rolls the cube to determine the next prompt, and he or she repeats this process two more times. To reflect, the teacher hosts a whole-group discussion that includes questions about the most difficult, least difficult, and most enjoyable prompt.

. . . .

Strategy Steps

Use the following seven steps to help you implement the Cubing strategy.

1. If this is your first time using this strategy with your students, explain the six types of thinking the cube faces represent. The following lists some of the traits you can use to explain the labels.

   - *Describe*—Provide attributes, details, or characteristics.

   - *Compare and contrast*—Identify similarities and differences.

   - *Associate*—Make connections with another object or idea.

   - *Analyze*—Identify different perspectives.

   - *Apply*—Explain how to use it.

   - *Argue for or against*—Identify advantages and disadvantages.

2. Prepare enough cubes for students to use individually or share. Record the six key words in step one on each side.

3. Assign students to groups of three or four and pass out the cubes. Tell students to turn their cube to the first or *Describe* side.

4. Announce the topic and provide around five minutes for students to write a description of the topic.

5. After the allotted time, instruct students to take turns sharing their writing with their group. By listening to others, students build their own understanding.

6. Have students roll the cube to determine the next prompt in each group. If the group rolls the cube and gets a prompt they have already completed, the group should reroll the die. Repeat this process as you prefer.

7. To conclude the writing and discussions, as a whole class, have groups discuss questions like the following.

   - Which prompt was the least difficult?

   - Which prompt was the most difficult?

   - Which prompt was the most enjoyable?

   - Which prompt was most beneficial for learning new information?

   - Describe how your knowledge of the topic has progressed (Nessel & Graham, 2007).

Variations

You can use the following variations in association with this strategy.

- When defining labels for a mathematics class, have students use the following guidelines, which I adapted from a presentation by educator Sholom Fried (2010).

   - *Describe* how you would solve the problem.

   - *Analyze* how this problem develops your mathematical thinking and problem-solving skills.

   - *Compare or contrast* this problem to a different problem. (You should specify the different problem.)

   - *Demonstrate* how someone could apply this problem or a problem like it to their work or life.

- *Change* an aspect of the problem (such as a number, element, or sign) and explain how this change affects it.

  - *Create* a challenge word problem, or *Diagram* or *Illustrate* the solution to the problem and explain the visual.

- Instead of writing, have students share their thinking with the group and take notes on what they hear from other students.

- To differentiate based on students' readiness to learn, use cubes with different prompts at various thinking levels.

Additional Content-Area Examples

This section provides examples of some ways you can connect this strategy to your teaching in different content areas.

- A language arts teacher labels a cube with the following six headings specific to analyzing poetry: (1) describe, (2) pretend, (3) critique, (4) compare, (5) question, and (6) connect. After reading a poem, students roll the cube to determine if they will: (1) describe it, (2) pretend they wrote it, (3) critique it, (4) compare it to another poem, (5) create questions about it, or (6) connect it to their lives. Students roll the cube three times and complete three of the tasks.

- A science teacher outlines for students a natural phenomenon (a tornado, an earthquake, a blizzard, and so on) and has them use the cube method to: (1) describe it, (2) compare and contrast it with another natural phenomenon, (3) associate it with another science concept, (4) analyze why we do or do not have this natural phenomenon where we live, (5) determine the best way to protect yourself, or (6) pose a thoughtful question about one phenomenon to group members.

- A mathematics teacher gives students a specific algebraic problem and has them roll a cube three times to determine how to approach it. Use the mathematics-based option from the Variations section for this strategy.

- After studying the Roman Republic, a social studies teacher has students in small groups

roll the cube and discuss the prompt using the default cube labels.

- A visual arts teacher shows students a famous piece of artwork to examine, including its notable features and historical context. Using the standard cube prompts outlined for this strategy, groups record their ideas about the artwork and discuss them.

Strategy 17: Consensogram

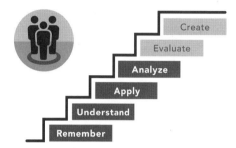

When utilizing *Consensogram*, the teacher poses a survey-style question to students, who then collectively record and display the combined data as a bar graph (see figure 5.10, page 58). The questions should offer students a range of answers, such as a rating scale from zero to ten in one-degree increments or a series of ratings like *none, minor, moderate,* and *extremely high* or *not important, somewhat important, important,* and *very important.* This bar graph becomes the basis for group discussion, allowing students to share viewpoints and consider other perspectives. In addition, students not only get an opportunity to physically move to post their ratings, they also draw on higher-level thinking skills when analyzing the data and drawing conclusions. The Teacher Toolkit (https://bit.ly/1BHbKha) has some additional downloadable Consensogram templates to use.

. . . .

CLASSROOM EXAMPLE

A teacher gives students a recording sheet with a question about the economy with scale ratings: *absolutely, mostly, somewhat,* and *not at all* (see figure 5.10, page 58). The question asks about the extent the new Walmart in town positively impacts the local economy. After students complete their sheet, the teacher invites them to use sticky notes and record their ratings, creating a class bar graph. Students then get into groups to discuss the data and draw conclusions.

. . . .

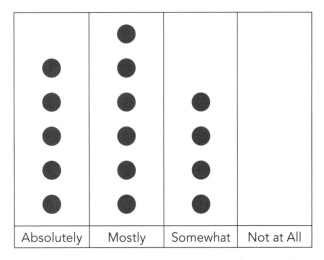

| Absolutely | Mostly | Somewhat | Not at All |

Figure 5.10: A Consensogram strategy bar graph.

Strategy Steps

Use the following four steps to help you implement the Consensogram strategy (Stobaugh & Love, 2015).

1. Prepare and distribute a task sheet and ask students to note the questions they need to answer and the ratings scale they will use. Students should individually complete a task sheet and record their rating for each question. Below each question, each student should justify his or her rating.

2. On a large piece of chart paper, establish a rating scale or other rating indicator, like zero to ten increments, and use sticky notes or colored dots to record all students' ratings on the chart paper, creating a bar graph that clearly depicts data for the class.

3. Pair students and instruct them to examine the data. Students should stand facing their partners around the perimeter of the room. Post the following questions for pairs to discuss: What do you notice in the data? What patterns are noticeable? What surprises you? What conclusions might you draw?

4. Conduct a whole-group discussion sharing reactions to the data.

Variations

You can use the following variations in association with this strategy.

- Have students use different-colored sticky notes or dots to represent groups in the class. For example, it might be interesting to see how male students and female students respond differently to prompts. In addition, different class periods could use different color sticky notes to examine the varying opinions among the class periods.

- You could use the Consensogram strategy as a preassessment with students marking whether they were *not confident*, *confident*, or *very confident* on each of the unit learning targets. After teaching the learning target, have students use another color to mark the same chart and compare the changes. You can use the data to adjust your instructional focus and provide differentiated instruction based on the data.

- If it is contextually appropriate to do so, have students use evidence from other sources to support their ratings.

Additional Content-Area Examples

This section provides examples of some ways you can connect this strategy to your teaching in different content areas.

- A language arts teacher instructs students to use a Consensogram to self-assess how hard they worked on a recently completed writing piece.

- A science teacher instructs students to answer Consensogram questions related to the degree engineering impacts society.

- A mathematics teacher instructs students to determine the best next step in solving a problem. Students choose between the following options: *adding*, *combining like terms*, *eliminating irrelevant information*, or *subtracting*.

- A social studies teacher instructs students to analyze the importance of the Boston Tea Party as a catalyst of the American Revolution. Students choose their answers: *most significant cause*, *one of the causes*, or *minor cause*. Students collaborate in groups to come to a consensus.

- A physical education teacher polls students on to what degree dance shapes American culture based on the specific criteria: *greatly*, *a little*, or *not at all*. Students then discuss as a class why they chose their answer.

Strategy 18: Fishbone Cause-and-Effect Analysis

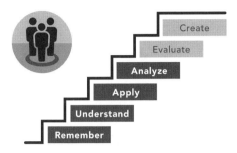

There are many cause-and-effect relationships, particularly those that center around problem and resolution. Helping students find the source of a problem can be an effective tool as they understand content and solve problems in their own lives. Whether students hope to enter the world of business, medicine, education, or some other, the ability to problem solve is an essential 21st century skill (Watanabe-Crockett, 2016a). With *Fishbone Cause-and-Effect Analysis*, students develop their problem-solving skills using a fishbone diagram. The mouth of the fish represents the problem or issue and the backbone branches off, representing multiple causes for the issue or problem (see figure 5.11, page 60).

CLASSROOM EXAMPLE

Students examine a mathematics problem and accompanying student work to identify mistakes and draw conclusions about the cause of any mistakes they find. They summarize their mistakes in a graphic organizer like the one in figure 5.11.

Strategy Steps

Use the following five steps to help you implement the Fishbone Cause-and-Effect Analysis strategy.

1. Identify materials that challenge students to determine the causes of a problem or issue. This might be by using a video, readings, scenario, or past student work that needs correction.

2. Make sure students understand the problem or issue and instruct them to examine the information available to them.

3. In groups or as individuals (if they are looking for mistakes in their own work), instruct students to identify several key causes for the problem. Each cause can have antecedent causes branching out of the fishbone diagram. Students use a blank version of figure 5.11, sticky notes, or chart paper to record the causes.

4. Ask students to explain each step in their diagrams to their classmates.

5. As a whole class, compare the differences and similarities among the causes or mistakes that each student or group presents.

Variations

You can use the following variations in association with this strategy.

- For some problems, you can have students rate the importance of each cause to the final problem or issue.

- Have students brainstorm additional problems or issues not listed in the source reading or material that could be a cause of the problem.

Additional Content-Area Examples

This section provides examples of some ways you can connect this strategy to your teaching in different content areas.

- A language arts teacher instructs students to identify a problem in "The Gift of the Magi" (Henry, 2005). In groups, students use a fishbone graphic organizer to brainstorm the sequence of causes leading to the problem.

- A science teacher organizes students into groups and instructs them to select a biological anomaly in people or animals. Students use a fishbone graphic organizer to determine its causes.

- A mathematics teacher instructs students to examine a scenario where they have run out of money for their back-to-school shopping. Students must use a fishbone graphic organizer to examine the financial decisions they made and identify the mistakes that caused the overspending.

- After reviewing the video *India's Geography Problem* (Wendover Productions, 2017), a social studies teacher organizes students into groups and instructs them to use a fishbone graphic organizer to identify what they believe are the

Adair bakes four dozen oatmeal raisin cookies, two dozen sugar cookies, and five dozen chocolate chip cookies. Adair likes to share with his friends and gives away two dozen oatmeal raisin cookies, 1.5 dozen sugar cookies, and 2.5 dozen chocolate chip cookies. How many total cookies does he have now?

1. Find number of cookies: *Oatmeal: 4 × 12 = 48; Sugar: 2 × 12 = 24; Chocolate chip: 5 × 12 = 60*

2. Find how many he gave away: *Oatmeal: 2 × 12 = 24; Sugar: 12 + 5 = 17; Chocolate chip: 12 × 2 = 24*

3. *Oatmeal: 48 + 24 = 72; Sugar: 24 + 17 = 41; Chocolate chip: 60 + 29 = 89*

4. Total: *72 + 41 + 89 = 192*

Fishbone Diagram

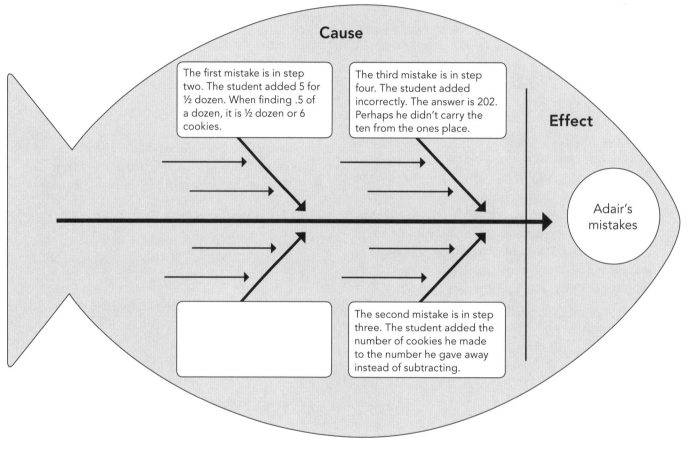

Cause

The first mistake is in step two. The student added 5 for ½ dozen. When finding .5 of a dozen, it is ½ dozen or 6 cookies.

The third mistake is in step four. The student added incorrectly. The answer is 202. Perhaps he didn't carry the ten from the ones place.

Effect

Adair's mistakes

The second mistake is in step three. The student added the number of cookies he made to the number he gave away instead of subtracting.

Source: Adapted from van de Vall, 2013.

Figure 5.11: Fishbone diagram example.

Visit **go.SolutionTree.com/instruction** *for a free reproducible version of this figure.*

five key challenges for India based on its geography. Students then conduct research to find more information about each challenge.

- After studying Johnny Cash and Elvis Presley in a unit about the history of rock and roll, a humanities teacher instructs students to use a fishbone graphic organizer to analyze issues both artists faced, particularly why one artist continued to make music for nearly sixty years while the other artist's career ended in tragedy.

Strategy 19: Directed Reading-Thinking Activity

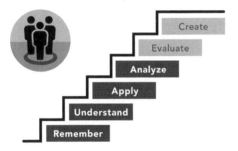

The *Directed Reading-Thinking Activity* strategy is an active-reading strategy where students make predictions and then seek to find evidence in the reading to corroborate or repudiate their hypotheses (Stauffer, 1975; TeacherVision, n.d.). Using this strategy, the teacher designates stopping points in the text for students to ask questions that help the teacher assess their comprehension. Prior to reading the next section of text, students should hypothesize what will happen, encouraging them to predict and then evaluate their predictions. This strategy helps establish a purpose for reading, stimulates inquisitiveness, strengthens comprehension, and encourages active immersion in the text.

CLASSROOM EXAMPLE

Before reading William Shakespeare's (1935) *The Tragedy of Romeo and Juliet*, students scan the text and images to make predictions. The teacher asks questions to spark interest: "What have you heard about this classic story?" "Should your parents be able to determine who you love?" and "Do you believe this story will have a happy ending and why?"

Students engage in a whole-class discussion before reading. Students then read an excerpt of act 1 and make guesses about what changes in the plot and characters are forthcoming. They supply evidence to support their theories based on their reading so far and prior knowledge. After reading the rest of act 1, students review and evaluate their predictions while making new predictions for the next section. Students repeat this process with each excerpt of the play. At the end, the teacher poses summary questions to check for understanding.

Strategy Steps

Use the following nine steps to help you implement the Directed Reading-Thinking Activity strategy.

1. Select a text and identify three or four stopping points that provide rich opportunities for students to make predictions. Plan a few thoughtful questions to ask students before they read.

2. Begin by allowing students to scan the title and examine any text features, such as headings, diagrams, and so on.

3. Ask students a few questions related to the reading to spark their interest.

4. Have students make predictions about what will happen and share those predictions as part of a whole-class discussion.

5. Instruct students to silently read until arriving at the next stopping point.

6. Have students review their predictions. Discuss if their initial thoughts were correct. Use the following questions to guide the discussion.

   - What do you think about your predictions now?
   - What did you find in the text to prove your predictions?
   - What did you read in the text that made you change your predictions?

7. Instruct students to predict what they will learn about or discover in the next few sections

or have them refine their existing predictions based on new evidence.

8. Repeat steps five through seven as needed to complete the reading.

9. Close with a few summary questions. These could include the following.

    • What is the main point the author is making in this story or article? What supports your answer?

    • Do you agree with the author's ideas or the character's actions? Explain why or why not.

    • What would you tell someone about this story or article if the person did not have time to read it?

    • Is this like something else you have read? Explain.

Variations

You can use the following variation in association with this strategy.

• For elementary grades, read the story aloud instead of having students read independently.

• In step four, assign students the following roles in their small groups: (1) summarizer, (2) questioner, (3) clarifier, and (4) predictor. After reading a block of text, one student would summarize it. Then, the next student would pose questions to the group. The clarifier then addresses misunderstandings. Finally, the predictor makes an educated guess on what would happen next. Have students change roles after they read the next block of text.

Additional Content-Area Examples

This section provides examples of some ways you can connect this strategy to your teaching in different content areas.

• While having students read sections of a novel, a language arts teacher instructs them to stop and make predictions about events to come. Following the reading, students write a short summary of the plot.

• While having students read about Benjamin Franklin's discovery of electricity, a science teacher instructs them to stop reading during key moments in Franklin's experiments to predict the outcome.

• Before starting calculations, a mathematics teacher instructs students to make predictions about results at each phase of the calculation.

• After having students read about the westward expansion in the United States, a social studies teacher instructs students to stop and predict major moments during this time period, such as what motivated people to move west, the difficulties of traversing the continent, and expansion's effects on slavery.

• A music teacher instructs students to listen to a song in ABA (or ternary) form, but only through the B section. At the end of the B section, students stop and predict what might happen next. The teacher asks, "Will the composer return to the A section, or will the composer create a new section resulting in rondo form, rather than ABA form?" Students discuss how each form would have changed the piece after listening to the final section.

Strategy 20: Overheard Quotes

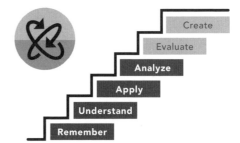

Overheard Quotes is a strategy to engage students in listening to various ideas and drawing meaningful conclusions about the information (Guillaume et al., 2007). This strategy is an effective way to hook students' interest while focusing them on a topic because, as students move around the room and hear quotes from peers, they are collecting clues to try to figure out the topic. In my experience, students enjoy being able to circulate and talk with classmates as well as the challenge to decipher the topic.

CLASSROOM EXAMPLE

A teacher selects music lyrics from multiple songs based on the theme *good versus evil*. The teacher writes these lyrics from various artists on different cards and distributes the cards to students. Students walk around the room, sharing various lyrics with each other. They then work in small groups to discuss the common themes, conclusions, and questions they found in the lyrics. In a whole-class discussion, students share their groups' ideas and questions. The teacher then reveals that the focus of the lesson is to explore several pieces of literature with the literary theme of good versus evil.

Strategy Steps

Use the following seven steps to help you implement the Overheard Quotes strategy.

1. Generate a list of quotes about a topic. Gather enough to give each student a different quote. Each quote should express a different idea or viewpoint, but each should align with an overarching theme.

2. Print the individual quotes or write them on index cards, and distribute the cards face down to students (one per student).

3. Direct students to read their quote and write down their initial thoughts about the quotation.

4. Have students circulate among their peers, sharing their quotes. Students should only share the quotes; they should not discuss them.

5. After they exchange quotes with five peers, have students discuss the following questions in small groups.

   • What common ideas are in the quotes?

   • What conclusions can you draw?

   • What questions do you have now?

6. Conduct a whole-class discussion about the ideas and conclusions the groups came up with.

7. Connect the quotes to the overarching theme or topic you want students to learn.

Variations

You can use the following variations in association with this strategy.

• Instead of providing students with quotes to share, post quotes on the walls and instruct students to meander around the room and read them.

• Instead of using quotes, provide students with physical items to examine, such as pictures, historical items from a time period, or props for a play.

• In stations around the room, offer a mixture of audio and video segments for students to listen to or view. After absorbing the clues, instruct students to draw conclusions about the topic.

Additional Content-Area Examples

This section provides examples of some ways you can connect this strategy to your teaching in different content areas.

• A language arts teacher organizes quotes that all have similar grammar mistakes. The teacher then instructs students to share their quotes with each other, work in small groups to determine similar characteristics among the mistakes they identify, and share their conclusions with the class.

• A science teacher gives each student a quote card that represents a different viewpoint on global warming. The teacher instructs students to share their quotes with each other, work in small groups to determine similar characteristics among their quotes, and share their conclusions with the class.

• A mathematics teacher gives students cards with common statistics that people often misinterpret. The teacher instructs students to share their statistics with each other, work in small groups to determine similar characteristics among their statistics, and share their conclusions with the class.

• A social studies teacher distributes to students a series of notecards with quotes from movies about compromise. The teacher instructs students to share their quotes with each other, work in small groups to find commonalities among their quotes, and share their conclusions with the class.

- A career and vocation education teacher provides students with quote cards with bad advice on how to get a job. The teacher instructs students to share their advice cards with each other, work in small groups to find commonalities among the advice and what it means, and share their conclusions with the class.

Strategy 21: Discrepant Event

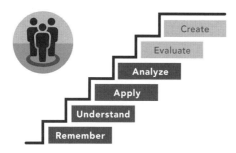

Engagement is crucial for students to think critically about a topic (Jensen, 2019). To that end, a *Discrepant Event* is an event that is unexpected, puzzling, or surprising. It is an event that immediately engages students and causes them to think as they seek to understand the mystery. For example, a science teacher might cause an explosion, or a social studies teacher might read a relationship break-up note resembling the arguments in the U.S. Declaration of Independence. These events quickly seize students' attention and engage them in critical thinking as they seek to find an explanation through inquiry-based learning. Teachers can use various tools to create Discrepant Events, like a demonstration, video clip, engaging reading, or science experiment.

CLASSROOM EXAMPLE

A teacher asks students if gummy worms are alive. The class agrees that they are not alive; however, students then examine gummy worms spontaneously wiggling in a cup. In groups, students make conjectures as to why the worms appear to be moving. They then discuss possibilities, with some students believing that a chemical reaction is happening in the cup causing the worms to move. From there, groups try to determine the potential chemicals causing the reaction. Each group shares its hypothesis, and

then the teacher reveals the secret: the teacher had soaked the worms in baking soda and then added vinegar, which created a reaction that forms gas bubbles that rise to the surface, making the worms move.

Strategy Steps

Use the following six steps to help you implement the Discrepant Event strategy.

1. Brainstorm or research materials that align to the content to spark inquiry-based learning among your students. Decide on your Discrepant Event.

2. Focus your students' attention on what they are about to observe, but do not reveal too much. You want them to feel surprise or shock.

3. Conduct your Discrepant Event so that students can experience it.

4. In small groups, have students discuss possible reasons for the event as they attempt to understand the Discrepant Event and develop questions about it.

5. Have each group select a spokesperson to share the group's thinking.

6. If no groups can decipher the cause of the Discrepant Event, reveal what really happened. Only reveal the cause *after* all groups have had a chance to present. Congratulate any group that succeeds in identifying the cause.

Variations

You can use the following variations in association with this strategy.

- Instead of having students present their best guess, have them develop *yes* or *no* questions to ask you to help them to try to understand the event. For example, in the gummy worm demonstration in the Classroom Example, groups might ask the teacher if there was a chemical reaction happening. The teacher would confirm this and encourage other groups to ask additional questions to help them formulate their hypothesis.

- You can use Discrepant Events to address student misconceptions—like the idea that more (longer) writing isn't always better than less (shorter) writing. You might show students two pieces of writing, one short (that received top marks) and one long (that received a low grade). Focus the ensuing discussion on the specific traits of the shorter work that make it superior.

Additional Content-Area Examples

This section provides examples of some ways you can connect this strategy to your teaching in different content areas.

- A language arts teacher reads two different letters about prom night written from a teenager's point of view. One letter divulges many details about the teenager's exciting night with her "dreamy" date. The other letter references the nice time she had with her friends and emphasizes her good behavior. The teacher asks students to determine the purpose of both letters. The teacher hopes that students will conclude the letters were written for two different audiences—one, a friend and the other, a grandmother. This activity engages students in a lesson about the importance of knowing your audience.

- A science teacher places a balloon on a wall in the classroom. The balloon sticks to the wall and floats, even though it is not filled with helium. Students discuss the possible reasons for the floating balloon. The teacher hopes students will correctly identify that the teacher rubbed the balloon to create static electricity, allowing it to "stick" to the wall.

- A mathematics teacher displays examples of student work that show multiplying numbers with positive and negative exponents with the same base. Students examine the problems to determine a mathematical process for them.

- As students enter class, a social studies teacher selects a few of them for a group. The teacher allows these students to choose what the class will do and tells them they can move around the room whenever they choose; however, they also are responsible for enforcing the classroom rules. The teacher requires the other students to do a worksheet, and allows this to continue for the first few minutes of class. Then, the teacher has students form small groups to discuss their

feelings about what happened. At the end, the teacher tells students that the selected students represented the Roman plebeians and the others represented the patrician social class.

- A drama teacher shows students a media clip of a comedian. Working in groups, students try to figure out the comedian's tricks for making people laugh.

Strategy 22: Extent Barometer

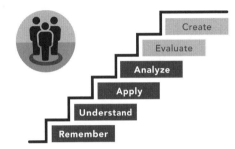

Another way to have students improve their analysis and thinking skills is to have them use a graphic organizer like the one in figure 5.12 (page 66) to examine a situation or topic from several perspectives. This helps them understand an issue more deeply and aligns with the Analyze level. By using the attributing cognitive process at this level, students identify biases, assumptions, and points of view in information. The *Extent Barometer* strategy challenges students to identify the pros and cons of an issue and then rate their level of agreement with the perspective or idea.

. . . .

CLASSROOM EXAMPLE

After engaging students in learning about NASA and the planets, the teacher asks them to consider a specific perspective about the topic: "The U.S. government should fund a space mission to Mars." Students work in groups to brainstorm three different perspectives about it. One group decides to examine the points of view of NASA, taxpayers, and U.S. Congress members.

On a graphic organizer, students record the pros and cons of each perspective (see figure 5.12). After groups develop several pros and cons for each perspective, they generate questions they would ask to spark discussion from each point of view. Each group poses its questions to the other groups, seeking answers from the perspective assigned to

Question or Statement: The U.S. government should fund a space mission to Mars.				
Perspective	Pros	Cons	Questions	Extent Barometer
NASA	Believes in potential to discover new ideas and inventions; achieve an American dream to further explore outer space	Concerned about potential to contaminate Mars with Earth microbes; might use up scarce financial resources, limiting other explorations (such as to the moon)	If we don't go, might the Chinese overtake the United States in space missions?	
Taxpayers	Are curious about the potential for life on Mars	Fear trip would be expensive and money could be better spent to solve key social issues and clean up the environment	What is the best way for our country to continue space travel with reasonable budgets?	
U.S. Congress members	Believe exploration will build U.S. prominence globally	Think exploration would be costly and potentially not worth the reward	Will either political party support this initiative?	

Figure 5.12: Pros and cons graphic organizer.

*Visit **go.SolutionTree.com/instruction** for a free reproducible version of this figure.*

those groups. At the end of the debate, students consider all the evidence and arguments they heard and rate the extent to which they agree or disagree with them on a scale from one to five on a barometer-themed graphic organizer. For example, one student colored in all the barometer boxes for the NASA perspective because she felt the evidence was clear that the space mission should be funded; whereas she only colored in one barometer box for the tax-payers because she felt the argument for their stance was weaker.

Strategy Steps

Use the following five steps to help you implement the Extent Barometer strategy.

1. Identify the topic you want students to analyze. It's critical to select something that allows students to see the topic from multiple perspectives.

2. Assign students to groups and instruct them to identify several different perspectives on the topic and record them in a pros and cons graphic organizer like the one in figure 5.12.

3. As a group, have students identify the pros and cons of the issue along with any questions they have about this perspective.

4. Host a classroom debate and assign each group a perspective. Each group should be prepared to ask the other groups questions and defend its point of view.

5. After reflecting on all the ideas presented, students complete the Extent Barometer strategy by coloring in the barometer to indicate their agreement. For example, coloring in all five segments on the barometer shows strong agreement with that perspective; whereas, coloring in one box indicates little agreement with the perspective.

Variations

You can use the following variations in association with this strategy.

- After the debate, have students write a persuasive essay about the topic or develop a multimedia presentation to give to the class.

- Instead of using a pros and cons graphic organizer, have students use a data-based graphic organizer like the one in figure 5.13. This version allows students to record data that support each perspective and then chart their agreement with each perspective.

Additional Content-Area Examples

This section provides examples of some ways you can connect this strategy to your teaching in different content areas.

- A language arts teacher asks students to consider whether social networking sites are good for society. Students work in groups to consider different ways people use (or don't use) social media and how they would approach this question.

- A science teacher asks students to consider whether people should use a vegan diet. Students work in groups to consider the perspectives of medical professionals, dieticians, meat lovers, and vegetarians, and how they would approach this question.

- A mathematics teacher displays several student work samples showing different ways to solve a problem. Students identify the pros and cons for each method for each student work sample.

- A social studies teacher asks students if it should be the responsibility of the U.S. government to provide internet service for every citizen. Students work in groups to consider the perspectives of people who have trouble accessing or affording internet service, people who have

Question or Statement:		
Perspective	Data	Extent Barometer

Figure 5.13: Data-based graphic organizer.

Visit go.SolutionTree.com/instruction for a free reproducible version of this figure.

easy access to it, internet service providers, and elected government officials, and how they would approach this question.

- An art teacher asks students how people from different periods in history would view a painting. Students work in groups to identify the historical eras and evaluate how people from those eras might react to the painting in question.

Strategy 23: SWOT Analysis

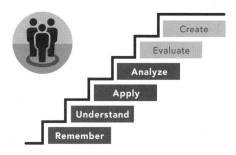

Businesses often use *SWOT* (*strengths, weaknesses, opportunities,* and *threats*) *Analysis* to examine a situation, plan a project, or explore the competition ("SWOT Analysis," n.d.). However, you can adapt this strategy for your classroom when you want students to analyze a problem or situation by defining objectives, considering all relevant factors that might affect achieving those objectives, and determining if objectives are attainable ("SWOT Analysis," n.d.). In doing so, students learn to analyze a situation or problem from multiple angles. All you need is for students to fill out a simple graphic organizer, like the one in figure 5.14.

CLASSROOM EXAMPLE

Student grades were lower for the quarter than normal, so the teacher asks students to think about the class and their progress and to prepare a SWOT Analysis to achieve the objective of improving their outcomes in the future. Students individually reflect on the quarter and complete a SWOT graphic organizer (see figure 5.14). Students then share their analysis with a partner with a focus on the opportunities for improvement. The teacher invites students to share some of the opportunities they listed as a way to improve class results going forward. Based on student feedback, both the teacher and the students make adjustments to increase student success.

Strategy Steps

Use the following five steps to help you implement the SWOT Analysis strategy.

1. Identify a problem or situation your students can use the SWOT Analysis strategy to examine. The item you identify should offer students a clear objective.

2. Organize students in groups and instruct them to analyze the problem or situation through the four lenses: strengths, weaknesses, opportunities, and threats.

3. Each group should use its graphic organizer (see figure 5.14) to establish strengths, weaknesses, opportunities, and threats.

Objective: *Increase overall grades for the entire class.*	
Strengths	**Weaknesses**
Group work, interesting content	*Speed of class, need more review before tests*
Opportunities	**Threats**
Provide practice quizzes to gauge progress.	*Bad grades come from not understanding content.*
Conclusion: *We think it is possible to improve graded outcomes by providing more content reviews before tests and offering us practice quizzes so we can assess our progress.*	

Figure 5.14: SWOT Analysis example.

Visit **go.SolutionTree.com/instruction** *for a free reproducible version of this figure.*

4. When complete, students leave their graphic organizer in a station and rotate between stations to view the other groups' reflections and conclusions. Students place a check mark on insightful ideas and conclusions, jot any questions they have on sticky notes, and leave them on each group's graphic organizer.

5. After viewing others' charts, student groups should refine their own SWOT Analysis by adding new ideas, answering questions left by other groups, and restating their conclusions.

Variations

You can use the following variations in association with this strategy.

- When groups are working on refining their charts, have them prioritize the most important ideas in each section.

- If a traditional letter-size sheet of paper for the graphic organizer is insufficient for a group activity, create organizers on larger sheets of chart paper.

Additional Content-Area Examples

This section provides examples of some ways you can connect this strategy to your teaching in different content areas.

- A language arts teacher instructs students to use SWOT Analysis to explore the character Jay Gatsby from *The Great Gatsby* (Fitzgerald, 2018). Their objective is to determine if he is a hero or fundamentally flawed.

- A science teacher instructs student groups to propose a solution to reduce the impact of a weather-related hazard. Groups present their solution and use SWOT Analysis to examine the solutions from other groups to provide feedback on their design.

- A mathematics teacher instructs student groups to collect data for a statistics project. Each group presents its findings while the other groups use SWOT Analysis to evaluate and provide feedback to the group for final revisions.

- A social studies teacher instructs students to pick a country involved in World War I and use SWOT Analysis to determine their objective for entering the war and whether their objective was a realistic goal to achieve.

- A music teacher instructs students to identify a musician or band from the rock and roll era and use SWOT Analysis to determine if the individual's or band's music impacted their contemporaries.

Strategy 24: Gallery Walk

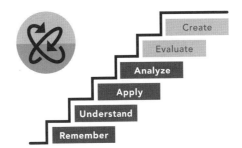

Gallery Walk is an instructional strategy where students in small groups rotate around the classroom to various stations and respond to thoughtful questions, documents, images, texts, or situations. You can use this strategy as a preassessment activity, and to brainstorm new ideas, introduce new content, or review prior learning. The benefit of the Gallery Walk strategy is students can engage in movement around the classroom as well as take part in focused discussions with peers to highlight different perspectives and allow them to reflect on their ideas. By utilizing small groups, more students engage, which encourages more timid students to participate. Although you can use Gallery Walk for lower-level thinking activities like summarizing information, at the Analyze level, students can organize complex information and draw accurate conclusions.

- -

CLASSROOM EXAMPLE

An elementary classroom is discussing different Native American tribes and traditions. The teacher breaks the class into small groups and has the groups rotate around separate stations. Each station has several images and an artifact of a different tribe and its traditions, along with chart paper for students to record on. Groups rotate to each station, recording on the chart paper their ideas, questions they have about the images, and connections to previously recorded comments.

- -

Strategy Steps

Use the following five steps to help you implement the Gallery Walk strategy (Stobaugh & Love, 2015).

1. Identify major topics or concepts for students to consider, record them on chart paper (for students to also use), and post the chart paper at each station. Anything that enhances students' exploration and understanding is fair game, so use descriptions of key topics, images like political cartoons or paintings, or quotes or recordings from a novel or primary source. These could also include several higher-level questions based on reading a text or synthesizing information displayed around the room. For example, "Based on the reading, has equality been achieved in our nation?"

2. Create small groups of around four students. Give each group a different-color marker to use when noting its responses at each station (to make clear each groups' input). Groups should identify an initial recorder while rotating the role to a new person at each new station.

3. After each group designates its recorder, signal when you want groups to move to the first station. If you're using brainstorming prompts, it might only take one or two minutes for students to record their thoughts, but if you have students answering higher-level questions, it might take additional time for them to process and reflect. In this case, three or four minutes might be more appropriate. Groups should record their ideas and questions on the chart paper.

4. Have groups rotate to another station after a designated time period. You can determine any rotation pattern you want, just be sure to explain it to your students. When students read comments from other groups and have a question, they can place a question mark on the chart to discuss the item later as a class. Students should add new ideas and not repeat ideas previous groups have already posted. Students should continue until they have visited all the stations.

5. Initiate a whole-group discussion or reflection summarizing students' learning, addressing the questions posted, and highlighting good ideas posted.

Variations

You can use the following variations in association with this strategy.

*   After a reading, have students respond to the following three prompts on chart paper at each station: (1) comments or personal reactions, (2) questions, and (3) predictions.

*   You could also post mathematics problems, political cartoons, or images on your classroom's walls at different stations. Instead of using chart paper, have students record their thoughts in their notes.

*   After all groups complete the rotation, have them do another, faster rotation to each station to allow them to review the items other groups recorded on the chart paper.

*   To wrap up the Gallery Walk, have students synthesize their learning in a graphic organizer, summary paragraph, or in groups by circling several key information points on each chart (Simon, n.d.).

Additional Content-Area Examples

This section provides examples of some ways you can connect this strategy to your teaching in different content areas.

*   A language arts teacher instructs students to review various quotes on a recent Victorian-era reading. Students scan the quotes on chart paper at various stations around the room, select a quote, and record why it is their favorite (or not) by marking on the chart paper how it reflects the period (Guillaume et al., 2007). Groups rotate and add questions or additional comments about each quote.

*   A science teacher instructs students to review key ideas in their unit on types of resources by answering open-ended questions at each station such as, How can we conserve natural resources in our community?

*   A mathematics teacher places different mathematical problems on chart paper around the room and has groups rotate to check solutions to the problems, while also showing other ways to arrive at the solutions.

- A social studies teacher instructs student groups to examine a political cartoon on chart paper and identify one key piece of the cartoon critical for understanding it. Students then note on the chart paper what they identify. Groups rotate around the room, viewing other cartoons, and identifying additional important information in each cartoon.

- A humanities teacher instructs students to rotate between stations that include artwork, samples of music, and videos of dances. Groups record in their notebook how each shows the rebirth of culture explorations.

Discussion Questions

As you reflect on this chapter, consider the following five questions.

1. Which strategies in this chapter already align with your existing instructional practices? What small changes could you make to improve these practices to enhance student thinking for analysis?

2. What are four strategies for building analysis skills that you could use in the next month?

3. What is your favorite strategy from this chapter that is based on media literacy? What makes it a great fit for your students?

4. What variations can you come up with to enhance a strategy in this chapter you intend to adopt?

5. What are some ways you can tailor a strategy from this chapter for your specific curriculum?

Take Action

Use the following three activities to put this chapter's concepts to work in your own classroom.

1. Pick just one strategy that you want to use with your students and create a plan for it specific to the content you teach.

2. After using a strategy you've adopted with your students, ask them whether they enjoyed the strategy and how you can improve it for next time.

3. Observe another teacher who uses critical-thinking strategies that develop analysis skills. Write down your reflections and ideas about what you noticed and how you could adopt them into your own teaching.

CHAPTER 6

Implementing Strategies for Evaluate-Level Thinking

It is the mark of an educated mind to be able to entertain a thought without accepting it.
—Aristotle

In this chapter, you will find nineteen instructional strategies that focus on learning at the Evaluate level of Bloom's taxonomy revised (Anderson & Krathwohl, 2001). Each of the following instructional strategies requires Evaluate-level cognitive applications like checking or critiquing content. Some strategies also tap cognitive applications at the Remember, Understand, Apply, or Analyze levels. Icons with each strategy indicate which steps (levels) of the taxonomy the activity touches as well as its primary tool for engagement (movement, collaboration, or media literacy).

Within each strategy, you will find a brief introduction that explains its concept and purpose, a classroom example, a series of steps for implementing the strategy, a list of variations you can choose to implement, and a section detailing additional classroom examples based on different content areas.

Strategy 25: Four Corners

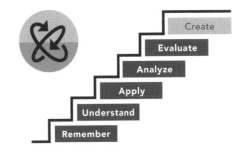

The *Four Corners* strategy engages students in moving while deeply thinking about class topics and then collaborating on them. Using this strategy, you pose a question to students and have them move to a corner of the room to indicate their answer. Students then discuss the topic in small groups and report their conclusions to the whole group.

There are many positive aspects to this strategy. Each student makes a decision and then, based on his or her choice, converses with others with similar thinking. Engaging students with this strategy encourages them to listen to various perspectives and use critical-thinking skills as they reflect on their own thinking and critique the thinking of others.

Because this strategy allows students to collaborate and express their knowledge of a topic, you can use it to formatively assess students while promoting rich conversations in small groups. Use this strategy to pre-assess students' prior knowledge of a topic, prepare for a debate, or stimulate thinking and conversation after they read a text, and provide time for students to process their learning. At the conclusion of the strategy, you can provide feedback on the quality of evidence or support provided by each small group as well as address any misconceptions.

CLASSROOM EXAMPLE

After learning about the water cycle, a class discusses each stage of the cycle and its role in the environment. The teacher prompts the students to think about which stage of the water cycle is the most important. The teacher labels points around the room for each cycle stage, and students move to the point that matches their opinion. As they do this, they form groups and present their argument to the full class based on evidence.

Strategy Steps

Use the following five steps to help you implement the Four Corners strategy.

1. Select a thoughtful question that does not have a correct answer but is controversial, leads to discussion, and offers several answer choices.

2. Prepare students for group conversations by having them record their initial ideas about the question on a graphic organizer or note-card. Giving students three to four minutes to solidify their thinking helps prepare them to thoughtfully contribute in the next step.

3. Instruct students to move to the corner that aligns with their ideas. Students will then subdivide into clusters of two or three (to increase student engagement) to explain their choices. Groups should build their argument or case with evidence to try to persuade the other groups. If only one person is in a corner, then celebrate his or her courage and consider engaging that student directly to discuss his

or her thinking while other small groups are discussing their cases.

4. Have groups either select a spokesperson or randomly call on a student from each group to share the group's thinking. Afterward, allow groups about five minutes to pose questions to each other and debate answers.

5. After the discussion, if a group has persuaded students to change their viewpoint, instruct those students to switch corners and have further discussions with their new groups and explain their change in thinking.

Variations

You can use the following variations in association with this strategy.

*   You can use more or fewer corners than four. For example, after posing a question related to a binary issue, you could designate one side of the room for those who agree and the other side for students who disagree.

*   Use this strategy as both a prereading and postreading activity to gauge how students' thinking evolves after assimilating new information. For example, identify the key takeaways from an article students haven't read and ask them to choose a corner based on their existing knowledge and assumptions. After they read the article, repeat the activity and discuss how their thinking evolves.

*   Choose several key topics from a lesson and assign each to an area. Place chart paper that you've labeled with each topic, and have students move to the topic that was most challenging. Students can list on the chart paper questions they still have on that topic or pose those questions to the other groups. After each group has shared, students can move to the next most challenging topic for them, which will show you which areas may need more instruction.

Additional Content-Area Examples

This section provides examples of some ways you can connect this strategy to your teaching in different content areas.

- After students read a story, a language arts teacher instructs them to choose a character to be their friend. Each corner of the room corresponds with one of the key characters in the book, and students should support their answer with textual evidence.

- A science teacher instructs students to review the data in a report on climate science and determine if the data support the claim that climate change is largely human made. Each corner of the room represents a rating scale indicator: *strongly agree, agree, disagree*, and *strongly disagree.*

- To preassess their understanding of a new topic, a mathematics teacher instructs students to examine (anonymously) a previous student's student work from a multistep, real-world problem. The teacher designates each corner as part of a rating scale: *all correct, one mistake, two to three mistakes*, and *four or more mistakes.*

- A social studies teacher selects the ten amendments to the U.S. Bill of Rights and asks students to choose which one they could delete without having a significant impact on individual or collective freedoms. To prepare for the activity, students identify positive and negative aspects of deleting each amendment and then rank them in order of importance. The teacher designates ten spots around the perimeter of the classroom to represent each of the amendments.

- A mathematics teacher instructs students to examine the contributing factors that led to the Beatles' rise to fame: media coverage, talent, historical context, and personality. For each of the four corners, the teacher provides groups with a large sheet of paper with each factor labeled. Students write their thinking on the paper. Students then share their thinking with the class and try to persuade others to join them through a brief discussion or debate (TeachRock, n.d.).

Strategy 26: Rank Order

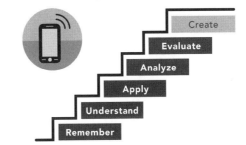

Building on the ideas of Strategy 9: Media Metaphor (page 43), the *Rank Order* strategy challenges students to analyze several pieces of music in relation to an established concept and then demonstrate understanding of both by ranking them and discussing their reasoning behind their rankings. Whereas the Media Metaphor strategy compared two items to find similarities, this strategy provides additional challenges as students must scrutinize comparisons among several songs and a concept and evaluate which song most effectively represents the topic.

· ·
CLASSROOM EXAMPLE

Students listen to "Taxman" (Harrison, 1966), "Take the Money and Run" (Miller, 1976), and "She Works Hard for the Money" (Summer & Omartian, 1983) to determine which song best represents the concept of sales tax. After individually ranking the songs, in small groups, students discuss using textual evidence from the song lyrics to support their opinion. The teacher conducts a class poll and instructs groups to share their reasons to support or contradict the poll results.
· ·

Strategy Steps

Use the following six steps to help you implement the Rank Order strategy.

1. Have students select three songs that represent a literary character, concept, time period in history, and so on.

2. Play the songs and provide students with the lyrics for each of them.

3. Instruct students to individually rank the songs based on which best aligns to the topic.

4. In small groups, have students share their ranking and discuss reasons for the rankings, citing textual evidence from the song lyrics. As a group, come to a consensus on the rankings.

5. Conduct a class vote. Groups should indicate their top ranking. With the vote, students should numerically show on their fingers their ranking choice. Record on the board how many groups voted for each music choice.

6. Conduct a whole-group discussion sharing reasons for the selection.

Variations

You can use the following variations in association with this strategy.

- Have students draw and create a visual summary of each song and then decide which song best represents the topic.

- Instead of using music, have students rank the order of other media, objects, or pictures.

Additional Content-Area Examples

This section provides examples of some ways you can connect this strategy to your teaching in different content areas.

- After reading *The Great Gatsby* (Fitzgerald, 2018), a language arts teacher instructs students to consider which song most reminds them of Jay Gatsby: "Firework" (Perry, Eriksen, Hermansen, Wilhelm, & Dean, 2010), "I'm Only Me When I'm With You" (Swift, 2006), or "Stronger (What Doesn't Kill You)" (Elofsson, Gamson, Kurstin, & Tamposi, 2012). Students listen to the songs, examine the lyrics, rank the songs in order, and vote for their top choice.

- After learning about magnets, a science teacher instructs students to listen to and decide which song best relates to *magnetic attraction*: "Can't Help Falling in Love" (Peretti, Creatore, & Weiss, 1961), "We Are Never Ever Getting Back Together" (Swift, Martin, & Shellback, 2012), or "Stuck Like Glue" (Nettles, Bush, Griffin, & Carter, 2010).

- After studying the calculation of surface area for different geometric shapes, a mathematics teacher instructs students to select which song best relates to this topic: "Wide Open Spaces" (Gibson, 1998) or another song of their choosing.

- A social studies teacher instructs students to use their understanding of the British and colonial relationships by ranking which nursery rhyme best connects to this topic: "Baby Bumblebee," "I'm a Little Teapot," or "The Eensy Weensy Spider."

- A family and consumer science teacher instructs student groups to brainstorm songs that align with an authoritarian parenting style. After justifying why each song a group selected relates to this topic, it decides that "Run the World (Girls)" (Knowles & Nash, 2011) was most closely connected to the topic.

Strategy 27: Questioning Protocols

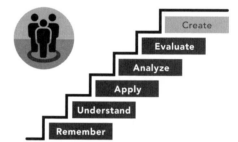

Questioning Protocols can engage students in a variety of equally useful methods crucial to the thinking-classroom concept, because when students ask questions, they engage in high-level thinking (Jensen, 2019; Watanabe-Crockett, 2019). Yet, just 58 percent of students say they feel comfortable asking questions (Fisher et al., 2018). Fortunately, for those who struggle, there are methods for encouraging them to ask questions including giving them adequate time to develop and refine their questions, providing protocols to guide their questioning, and fostering a supportive and positive environment. Also, Questioning Protocols can help students as they construct questions. To help students formulate questions, you can distribute question stems, such as What evidence supports _____? or What is another perspective on _____?

Where the questions come from matters. Educators can replace teacher-led questions and their accompanying silent pauses with student-developed, thought-provoking questions to ignite engaging discussions that center on quality thinking. Authors and codevelopers of Questioning and Understanding to Improve Learning and Thinking (QUILT) Jackie Acree Walsh and Beth Dankert Sattes (2017) assert:

> In true discussion, the teacher gives over to students the responsibilities of (1) generating and posing questions of importance; (2) inviting all to participate actively, to put their voices into the mix; (3) questioning to get behind one another's thinking—to request evidence or an explanation for reasoning; (4) giving and receiving formative feedback; (5) engaging continually in individual reflection to self-assess and monitor their thinking and understanding; and (6) protecting the fragile culture in which such an open exchange of ideas can occur. (p. 177)

Although it is tempting for teachers to provide feedback during discussions, teachers should consider other ways to contribute to the discussion, including encouraging another student to ask a question; inviting the student to elaborate on his or her point; or paraphrasing what the student stated (Dillon, 1988).

It is helpful to provide students with interpretive materials like statements, pictures, passages, and media clips as a catalyst for student questioning.

- **Statements:**
  - *Read the statement and create questions*—"A good story ends with a happy ending."
  - *Examine the statement and generate questions*—"You must follow the scientific method."
  - *Evaluate the statement and design questions*—"All people are equal."
  - *Read the following statement and think of questions you have*—"All U.S. citizens have freedom."

- **Pictures:**
  - *Scrutinize the four pictures of animals in our world*—Develop questions a scientist might ask. (Note that all the pictures would depict how animals use camouflage.)

- *Analyze the political cartoon*—Develop questions that would help you understand its meaning.
  - *Examine the cartoon strip*—Think about how the cartoon relates to the book. Create questions that explore this connection.

- **Passages:**
  - *Read the editorial*—Formulate questions that can be used in the discussion about point of view.
  - *Read a short passage or page from a story*—After reading, create questions that could help the illustrator add detail to the story.

- **Media clips:**
  - *Watch a clip related to workplace behaviors*—Locate a relevant video clip (such as a scene from the television show *The Office*) and create questions about appropriate workplace behaviors.
  - *Watch a clip related to experimentations*—Locate a relevant video clip (such as an episode on amazing science experiments from the YouTube channel, Home Science; https://bit.ly/1yEcAYr) and develop questions about one of the experiments.
  - *Connect to the humanities*—Examine a visual work of art, listen to a musical selection, or watch a video of a type of dance from the same historical time period. Develop questions about each in relation to the time period.

There are a variety of protocols you can use to establish Questioning Protocols that promote student questioning, including the following. (Note that each strategy begins with selecting subject material for students to question.)

- **Think-Pair-Square-Share:** In this strategy, students individually form questions, share them with a partner, merge with another pair to select a single question to share with the class, and finish with a whole-group discussion on the final question from each group (Stobaugh, 2016).

- **10 by 10:** This strategy stretches students to generate a larger quantity of questions as a means to practice and improve their questioning skills (Stobaugh, 2016). Students work individually or in small groups to generate ten questions about a subject. They then select what they regard as their best question for whole-group discussion.

- **Priority Questions:** This Questioning Protocol has students as a whole group post as many questions as they can think of. As they do so, they record each one, and then use group discussion to prioritize the quality of each question. During the brainstorming process, the teacher should refrain from giving examples of questions or evaluating any questions students pose. This promotes a safe environment and prevents any negative comments from hijacking the process and stopping the flow of questions. As part of a whole-group discussion and prioritization process, highlight the differences between closed questions (those answered with a word or two) and open questions (those that require elaboration), and encourage students to identify which questions fall into each category. The group should select the three most important questions (the Priority Questions) for further discussion.

- **DIG (detail, inference, and global):** This strategy gives students a structure for generating questions. After examining a statement, passage, picture, or media, students develop questions that address details, inferences, and global connections. Detail questions can be answered from information directly in a text. (According to the text, what happened next?) Inference questions require the reader to make conclusions regarding the text (Based on the information given, what inferences can you make?). Global questions ask the reader to make connections to current events or personal experiences (How does this text apply to your life?). Each student finds a partner. One student shares a question, and the other responds. The other student in the pair then poses his or her question. After discussing the two questions, the pair dissolves and each finds another partner to repeat this process (Give One, Get One, Move On).

You can use each of these protocols with the following strategy steps to encourage students to refine their questions prior to discussion.

Strategy Steps

Use the following four steps to help you implement a Questioning Protocol.

1. Have students examine a teacher-selected media clip, visual, quote, statement, or passage. The item you select should spark students' thinking.

2. Select a Questioning Protocol and explain it to students. If this is their first time using this protocol, make sure you model the process for them.

3. Provide time for students to formulate questions according to the protocol you select.

4. Based on the Questioning Protocol you select, establish a process for reporting or recording the questions students or groups came up with and conduct a discussion to evaluate and provide feedback on the results.

Variations

You can use the following variations in association with this strategy.

- *Question Continuum* is a more advanced Questioning Protocol that supports students as they refine the quality of their questions by considering the level of cognitive demand and the ability to spark student discussion. It involves using a display board or Padlet (https://padlet.com) to post a Question Continuum that has high and low interest levels and high and low complexity to gauge the degree to which a question inspires new ideas or sparks discussion. Optimal questions will have both high interest and high complexity. You can learn more about this variation in *Sparking Student Questioning* (Stobaugh, 2016).

- When using the Priority Questions protocol, you can have students divide into groups to determine the three priority questions. When students have completed the protocol, conduct a whole-class discussion.

Additional Content-Area Examples

This section provides examples of some ways you can connect this strategy to your teaching in different content areas.

- After reading four movie quotes about conflict, a language arts teacher instructs students to develop questions using Think-Pair-Square-Share. In pairs, students share their questions and discuss their answers. They then select the best two questions and merge with another pair and share the questions and confer. The teacher selects a few students to voice the best question out of each group of four to debate in a whole-class discussion.

- A science teacher shows students a picture with the outline of the United States during night-time, with lights more concentrated in certain geographical areas. With a partner, students use the 10 by 10 protocol to generate ten questions about the map in less than ten minutes.

- A mathematics teacher instructs students to use a Question Continuum to examine census data depicting income distributions for various ethnic groups. Working in pairs, students write two questions they have about the data with at least one being high in interest or complexity. The teacher selects a few of the student questions for a group discussion.

- During a unit on a historical conflict, a social studies teacher presents the statement, "Violence is necessary sometimes." In groups, students use the Priority Questions protocol to consider the statement and create as many questions as possible. Each group reviews its questions and selects the three most important questions to discuss as a class.

- A technology teacher instructs students to examine a video clip explaining how to create a video. In pairs, students use the DIG protocol to develop detail, inference, and global questions as the teacher rotates around the room, posing and answering questions.

Strategy 28: Inferencing

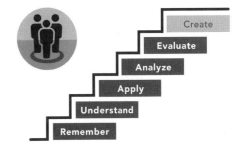

Marzano (2010) writes that *inference* is a foundational process relative to higher-order thinking. *Inferencing* means using logic based on evidence and reasoning to arrive at a conclusion. It's something that students do all the time without even thinking about it. For example, students make assumptions about what happens next in a story based on past experience with similar stories. Students can use supporting facts, examples, past experience, and logic and reasoning to defend their inferences. While *Inferencing* can be an Understand-level task, with more complex texts and illustrations, the task can reach the Evaluate level as students judge the credibility of information. Use a graphic organizer like the one in figure 6.1 (page 80) to help students ramp up their thinking.

• •
CLASSROOM EXAMPLE

A class compiles data about student preference for school lunches. Students use a graphic organizer (see figure 6.1) to record the facts and then draw inferences based on what they see and how they think the lunch menu should change based on these.
• •

Strategy Steps

Use the following three steps to help you implement the Inferencing strategy.

1. Choose a text, photograph, illustration, bar graph, media clip, or other interpretive materials for students to evaluate.

2. Organize students into groups and instruct them to create a Facts and Inferences Chart similar to the graphic organizer in figure 6.1. Using this organizer, students can list explicit information and draw inferences.

Facts (Explicit information)	Inferences (Implicit or implied information)	Opinions (What we think)
• Ten people in our class like pizza best. • Five people like sandwiches best. • Four people like tacos best. • Two prefer to bring their lunch.	1. Most people prefer to eat school lunches, with pizza being the most popular choice. 2. Not very many students bring their lunch. 3. Fewer people in our class like tacos compared to pizza and sandwiches.	While students like the pizza, they also choose that option because it always comes with grapes and cookies which are students' favorites.

Figure 6.1: Inferencing graphic organizer.

Visit **go.SolutionTree.com/instruction** *for a free reproducible version of this figure.*

3. Have each group rank its inferences according to how credible they are. Groups should list their top three credible inferences on chart paper and share them as part of a whole-class discussion.

Variations

You can use the following variations in association with this strategy.

- As a challenge, have students add an *Opinions* column and fill it with their own reflections about what their inference tells them.

- Use one of the strategies in Strategy 27: Questioning Protocols (page 76) to have students develop questions about the topic or subject based on the inferences they drew.

Additional Content-Area Examples

This section provides examples of some ways you can connect this strategy to your teaching in different content areas.

- A language arts teacher instructs students to read a short story in chunks. After each chunk, students answer a series of questions like, Why do you think the character made a particular decision? and What do you believe he will do next? Students answer these questions based on textual evidence and record their inferences on the chart.

- A science teacher provides a diagram to students that depicts the next ten days of weather in their hometown. In a graphic organizer, students record the facts and then draw inferences based what they already know about their local weather and how it affects daily decisions.

- In a unit on statistics, a mathematics teacher instructs students to survey the class about their favorite sport. Students record the facts and draw inferences using the data they collect.

- In a unit on the American Civil War, a social studies teacher instructs students to examine statistics about differences between the North and South prior to the start of the war, including population, farm acreage, value of the farm land, railway mileage, manufacturing establishments, and capital stock of banks. Students identify facts and develop inferences about the differences between the regions. In the opinions column, students record ways they would have used this information to successfully lead either the North or South.

- A humanities teacher instructs students to survey the class about either their favorite genre of music or favorite dance style. Students record the data and use them to draw inferences about their peers' interests in the arts.

Strategy 29: Jigsaw With Case Studies

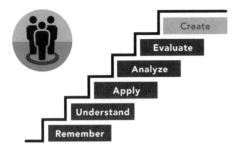

Jigsaw is a cooperative learning strategy that supports high levels of student engagement in that it segments a broader lesson into smaller pieces and directs students to break into groups and collaborate on just one piece. Students then share their new learning with other groups until every group understands each piece of the complete puzzle. *Jigsaw With Case Studies* is a slight modification of this traditional Jigsaw strategy because it challenges students to explore different points of view, such as those over disputed controversial issues (Brislin, 1999). Students read background information and analyze the issue through the lens of one perspective. They then pitch their ideas from their own perspective. To conclude, students examine the validity of the arguments, interpretations, and assumptions.

. . . .

CLASSROOM EXAMPLE

An elementary class is completing a unit of study on the author Kevin Henkes. The teacher divides the class into six groups, with each group assigned a different Henkes book. Each group reads the book it selected and records notes on the common writing and illustration trends in the book. One person from each group then meets with students from other groups to share the group's conclusions. The class then synthesizes the learning to identify common characteristics of each of Henkes's publications.

. . . .

Strategy Steps

Use the following six steps to help you implement the Jigsaw With Case Studies strategy.

1. Select a topic that students can examine through various perspectives.

2. Identify readings or other content you can use to foster a unique perspective so that each group will have a focused aspect of the broader topic to digest.

3. Establish the broader topic and case study to students. You could, for example, show a video clip, read a poem, or display a timeline that explains the background for the topic.

4. Create equal-size groups and assign each group a different perspective. Tell each group it is to become a knowledge expert about their perspective. Provide whatever additional information or resources students require to become experts, and then allow them ten minutes for group discussion. (You can extend this to allow groups more time to create persuasive presentation materials.)

5. Create new groups so each original group's expert and perspective are represented in each new group. Give students about twenty minutes to establish the merits of their perspective with their new group members. Group members should pose questions to the speaker to clarify his or her position, expose assumptions, or obtain validation for arguments, interpretations, assumptions, beliefs, or theories.

6. Conduct a class discussion on what students learned about each perspective along with the merits of each argument.

Variations

You can use the following variations in association with this strategy.

*   Instead of a whole-group discussion, after students complete their mixed experts group discussions, have them return to their original expert groups to share any new thinking.

*   As an assessment to complete after this activity, have students write an essay based on a perspective different from the one you assigned them.

Additional Content-Area Examples

This section provides examples of some ways you can connect this strategy to your teaching in different content areas.

- At the end of a poetry unit, a language arts teacher assigns students to small groups of three or four. Each group receives a different poem. After analyzing the poems, students break into new groups to share their analyses with different groups.

- For a science unit, the teacher gives students a hypothetical scenario where a city wants to build a bridge. The teacher assigns each group specific shapes that could be used or past designs of existing bridges. Groups must establish the merits of their assigned designs and then defend those merits to other groups.

- A mathematics teacher divides students into expert groups and instructs each to examine a different methodology for solving a real-world mathematics problem. In the expert groups, students determine if the methodology is correct and discuss if the processes are the most efficient way to arrive at the solution. In new groups, each person shares his or her work and then decides which student work example is the best.

- A social studies teacher assigns students to expert groups and tasks them with learning about and understanding a major ethnic group who immigrated in large numbers to the United States (such as from Mexico, Ireland, or Japan). Each group researches and develops a persuasive pitch on why its group had the strongest impact on American culture.

- A music class is vying to have its own composition selected as a new piece to be played at a gala event for a new community music hall. The teacher assigns groups to compose a melodic theme. The teacher then mixes the groups and has them defend why their composition best represents their community.

Strategy 30: Think-Pair-Share Continuum

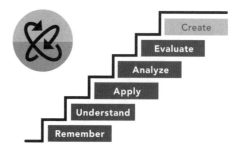

The *Think-Pair-Share Continuum* strategy provides students with an opportunity to think about their personal opinion on an issue while utilizing evidence to support their stance. Students then physically stand on a continuum and share their perspective. This provides opportunities for students to move around while also creating a visual representation of what each student believes.

CLASSROOM EXAMPLE

After reading an article about the challenges of cell phones in schools, a teacher invites students to take a stance on whether elementary students should have cell phones at school. The teacher explains that across the front of the classroom there is a continuum starting with *strongly agree, somewhat agree, somewhat disagree,* and then *strongly disagree* at the furthest corner. After recording their opinions, reasons, and supportive evidence on their own paper, students move to the spot on the continuum that aligns with their beliefs. In small groups, with others standing near them, students discuss their reasoning while recording any new ideas others mention. In the whole-group discussion, a representative from each area shares the group's reasons for its beliefs.

Strategy Steps

Use the following seven steps to help you implement the Think-Pair-Share Continuum strategy (Stobaugh & Love, 2015).

1. Identify a controversial or contested topic using historical documents, literary writing, current news, other informational texts, or a provocative statement.

2. Introduce the topic and explain to students the continuum across the room. Each side of the continuum will represent the polar opposite standpoints (*strongly agree* and *strongly disagree*) with regard to the topic.

3. To get students thinking, ask them to identify where they stand on the continuum. Have students record their stance on their paper and provide several reasons or evidence to support their viewpoint. (This is the *think* component of the strategy.)

4. Have students move and stand near the place on the continuum that represents their thinking.

5. Instruct students to find two or three other students near their location on the continuum and have them share their reasoning with each other for why they chose that area. Students should take notes on any new ideas or evidence. (This is the *pair* component of the strategy.)

6. Conduct a whole-group discussion by providing time for a representative from each area to persuasively pitch his or her stance, citing any evidence the group collects. (This is the *share* component of the strategy.)

7. Allow students to move to a different spot on the continuum if the evidence their peers presented persuades them to change their own position.

Variations

You can use the following variations in association with this strategy.

- To challenge students to formulate an argument regardless of their beliefs, have students draw a card that assigns their stance on the issue. Students should then join with others with a similarly assigned stance and develop an argument to support the position.

- Use this strategy as part of a pre- or postassessment. For example, you could ask

students how much they know about the instructional topic for the day, with one end of the continuum representing *I know a lot about this* and the other side representing *This is new to me.*

Additional Content-Area Examples

This section provides examples of some ways you can connect this strategy to your teaching in different content areas.

- A language arts teacher tells students that the French novelist Gustave Flaubert once stated, "The art of writing is the art of discovering what you believe" (BrainyQuote, n.d.). The teacher asks students to move to the area on the continuum based on the degree to which they agree or disagree with Flaubert's statement.

- A science teacher asks students if they think society should allow human cloning. Students move to the area on the continuum according to what they believe.

- A mathematics teacher asks students to examine student work from a real-world problem on probability that students worked on the previous day. The teacher asks students to move to an area along the continuum based on whether they believe the past students used an effective strategy. Students must support their position with evidence.

- A social studies teacher has students watch a video on the impact of social media on society. The teacher asks students to move to an area on a continuum based on whether they believe social media has a net positive or negative impact. Students must support their position with evidence.

- A vocational studies teacher asks students, "Should all students go to college?" The teacher instructs students to move to an area on a continuum based on what they believe. Students must support their position with reasoned opinions.

Strategy 31: Decision Making

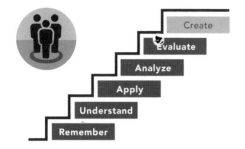

Decision Making is a strategy that challenges students to think at high cognitive levels while engaging in real-world thinking processes as they evaluate and select the best choice based on a question, situation, or dilemma the teacher identifies. The graphic organizer in figure 6.2 provides an example of how students can show their thinking. By engaging in this strategy, students learn a thoughtful way to approach making decisions in real life (Silver, Strong, & Perini, 2007). It encourages divergent thinking as students brainstorm possible options as well as convergent thinking in selecting the best choice. It also allows students to learn in ways they enjoy—working with classmates and taking a stand on a topic.

. . . .

CLASSROOM EXAMPLE

At the beginning of the school year, a teacher challenges groups to develop a class motto. After viewing a few examples of a motto, in a class discussion, students suggest key elements of an effective motto: motivating, short and simple, and memorable. In groups, students brainstorm potential options on chart paper. Each group selects its best motto and pitches it to the class. Using a graphic organizer

(see figure 6.2), students evaluate how each motto addresses the three criteria. At the conclusion of all the group presentations, students review their notes and record a ranking of which is the best motto.

. . . .

Strategy Steps

Use the following six steps to help you implement the Decision-Making strategy.

1. Brainstorm an open-ended question, real-world situation, or dilemma and have students come up with and justify multiple acceptable answers.

2. Instruct students to evaluate a teacher-identified item to determine what about it is the *most important, most influential, most essential, most changed,* or *most affected.* When possible, use real-world situations and connect with your students' interests to increase their motivation to complete the task. For example, Of the three proposed traits, which ones are most important in a great leader?

3. As a whole class (or in groups), instruct students to develop the criteria necessary to evaluate the solution. This might require them to do research to determine the appropriate criteria to use. For the example in step two, students could find that it is best to evaluate a leader based on his or her humanitarian efforts, lasting impact, innovation, or any other number of aspects.

4. Have students brainstorm and research three to six possible subjects, concepts, strategies, and so on that fit their selected criteria. With the

Motto	Motivating	Short and Simple	Memorable	Rank
1	*It encourages us to work hard and not to give up.*	*It is twelve words—fairly short and simple.*	*It is a memorable quote, but not as "cool" as other mottos.*	*2*
2	*All the words are positive and sum up what we want to be.*	*It is an acronym with four words.*	*Using "#SWAG" will be easy to remember.*	*1*
3	*It says the actions we should take, but seems more for younger grades.*	*It is twenty words long—too long to remember.*	*It seems more like a list of class rules.*	*3*

Figure 6.2: Decision-making graphic organizer.

*Visit **go.SolutionTree.com/instruction** for a free reproducible version of this figure.*

leader example, students would generate a list of leaders who had significantly impacted the world according to the criteria.

5. Have students evaluate each choice using a graphic organizer like the one in figure 6.2 to determine how each one fits with the selected criteria. Students then rank each choice accordingly.

6. Determine how you prefer to assess students' work. For example, you can have them turn in a graphic organizer or have them use it to prepare for a class debate. Students could also use their graphic organizer to write an individual persuasive essay or offer a presentation arguing for their top ranking.

Variations

You can use the following variations in association with this strategy.

- Have students assume the role of an individual or group from the past (or in some other way related to the topic) and then use a Decision-Making graphic organizer to assess if they would make the same decisions as that person or group. For example, ask students, "What choice would you make if you were Queen Isabella and King Ferdinand on whether to support Columbus's trip?" The students would then develop criteria and brainstorm choices.

- To differentiate and support some students based on age or ability, you can provide the criterion or alternatives, and simply have them do the evaluation and rankings in the graphic organizer.

- Often in real life, one criterion is more important than others when making a decision. For more advanced groups, have students weigh certain criteria more heavily than others. For example, if the student council is considering what would be the best fund-raiser, students could devise criteria, such as the potential for making the most money, the importance of creativity, and how much time to devote. However,

they would weigh generating money as the most important criterion when evaluating rankings.

Additional Content-Area Examples

This section provides examples of some ways you can connect this strategy to your teaching in different content areas.

- A language arts teacher poses a scenario to students—they are working for a book company and must select a book first published more than fifty years ago. The book must not be widely known, but must be appealing to the modern young adult market. The teacher instructs students to examine the literature options and the criteria for evaluating the books. Students then prepare a persuasive presentation to convince the president of the company to select their book.

- A teacher in a science class poses the question, What animal would be the best class pet? The students then determine the criteria and a list of three to six animals to evaluate. Students then use the Decision-Making graphic organizer to evaluate which animal would be best.

- A mathematics teacher poses a scenario to students—they are an executive for a professional basketball team and must review statistics for six player prospects and select the one player they would attempt to sign. The teacher instructs students to determine the players and criteria and then evaluate and rank them.

- A social studies teacher asks students to evaluate which leader in World War I made the most impact on the world. The teacher instructs students to determine which leaders to evaluate and the criteria for evaluation.

- A humanities teacher asks students which composer, visual artist, or dancer made the most impact in the world. The teacher instructs students to determine the criteria for evaluation as well as three to six historic contributors to the arts to evaluate.

Strategy 32: Peer Critiquing

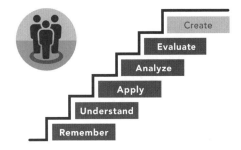

Peer Critiquing refers to the process of students sharing their work with other students for constructive feedback, which they can subsequently use to revise and perfect their work. This process lies at the heart of the Evaluate level. Peer feedback not only provides an opportunity for students to learn from the successes and mistakes of others but also is a way to achieve deep learning, as students evaluate whether a peer achieved the assignment's goals (Lynch, McNamara, & Seery, 2012). You can also use the peer-review process to provide formative feedback on student work to improve its quality prior to providing students with your own summative grade on their work.

Although peer feedback is often used with writing in language arts classrooms, you can use it with lots of other areas, including projects like presentations, podcasts, and website creation for analyzing mathematical processes, science conclusions, and interpreting political cartoons. Peer Critiquing promotes the student collaboration and higher-level thinking vital for student learning.

. . . .

CLASSROOM EXAMPLE

A science teacher prompts students to design a gravity-propelled race car to be the fastest car down a track. As a whole class, students determine the main three criteria that each small group must consider when constructing their car. To begin, students use an online simulation program to create their cars. The small groups then present their creations to the class and receive feedback from their peers before they build their prototypes to test on the track.

. . . .

Strategy Steps

Use the following eight steps to help you implement the Peer Critiquing strategy.

1. Identify the task students must complete and review, as well as the criteria to assess the quality of the task.

2. Design a Peer Critiquing worksheet appropriate for the age level of your students. Younger students (preK–3) might need more checklists with graphics to circle to assess the level of quality; upper elementary and secondary students can record evidence for their critique. For these students, provide a section to record constructive feedback. Consider terming this section *Stars and Wishes* or *Medals and Missions*. In the Stars or Medals box, students would record specific positive qualities, and in the Wishes or Missions section they would list explicit ways to improve. Visit **go.SolutionTree.com /instruction** to find online reproducible versions of these worksheets.

3. Model the peer-review process for students. Make sure the class has a clear understanding of the assessment criteria and the task. Teach students how to make comments. Peer feedback should have compliments and suggestions for improvement. Feedback should be specific ("Could you edit the graphics on the first page to match the title?") versus vague ("Could you edit the graphics?"). Feedback should also be helpful and kind. Students should understand the importance of providing considerate and constructive feedback.

4. Use an anonymous example for training and have students practice giving feedback so you can confirm they have reliable scoring and understand the process.

5. After students complete their own assignment, create peer-review groups and distribute a Peer Critiquing task sheet. Individually, students should mark the sheet.

6. Instruct students to share their feedback with their peer-review partner. They should discuss any questions the reader had. You may consider providing students with sentence starters using the TAG protocol so they can effectively articulate their thoughts in the comments section (see figure 6.3). The *TAG protocol* has students provide feedback by: (1) stating a positive

---

Tell Something You Like

- I really like the way you _____.
- I enjoyed _____.

Ask a Question

- I am wondering _____.
- Why did you _____?
- I'm a little confused about _____.

Give a Suggestion

- Can you write or develop a little more _____?
- Do you need help with _____?
- Maybe you can come up with a better way to _____.
- How do you feel about adding _____?

Figure 6.3: TAG sentence stems.

Visit **go.SolutionTree.com/instruction** *for a free reproducible version of this figure.*

remark, (2) asking a question about the work, and (3) giving a positive suggestion.

7. Allow time for students to revise their work based on peer feedback. How much time you should provide depends on the nature of the assignment.

8. Students should submit the Peer Critiquing form and the final copy of their assignment. They should highlight the changes they made based on the peer review, so it is evident how they used the feedback to improve their work.

Variations

You can use the following variations in association with this strategy.

- Have students provide feedback online through a class blog, class website, or online forms like Google Forms (www.google.com/forms/about). Many productivity applications, including Google Docs and Microsoft Word, have a version history feature that allows you to see how a document changes over time. In addition, try using the free digital tool, Kaizena (www .kaizena.com), as a way to allow students (and you) to provide both text and audio feedback.

- To structure the feedback for younger learners, students use stars (what is good) and steps (what to do next) or wishes (what could improve the work). Another option is for students to fill the

expression on the smiley face (unsure, smiley, or excited) to indicate their evaluation (see figure 6.4, page 88).

- You can adapt this strategy for the purposes of self-assessment instead of for peer critique. In John Hattie's (2012) research on 138 variables, students' rating of their own knowledge gain had one of the highest average effect sizes—over three times larger than the other variables. Hattie (2012) termed this *self-report grades*. As students self-assess their work, they can learn to set goals for improvement. After reminding students of the learning target at the end of class, students can use a peer critique worksheet (or a worksheet you adapt specifically for this purpose) to self-assess whether they met the learning target.

Additional Content-Area Examples

This section provides examples of some ways you can connect this strategy to your teaching in different content areas.

- A language arts teacher has students use an assignment checklist or rubric detailing assignment expectations (such as focus, organization, idea development, language and vocabulary, or conventions) to determine if another student's informative essay has any missing or unclear parts.

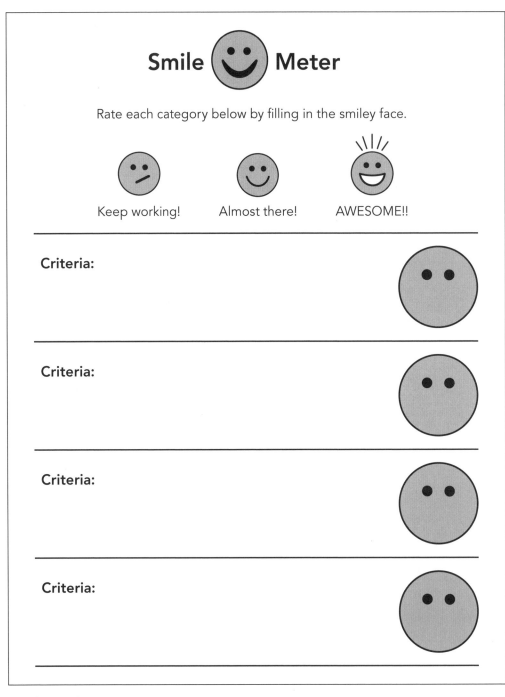

Source: Adapted from Fink, 2010.

Figure 6.4: Smile meter in a peer-review template.

Visit **go.SolutionTree.com/instruction** *for a free reproducible version of this figure.*

- A science teacher instructs students to craft a scientific (labeled) drawing of a plant. The teacher then has students use the "Peer Critiquing With Medals and Missions Worksheet" (visit **go.SolutionTree.com /instruction**) to evaluate whether the other student met each indicator. Upon finishing, students pass the student work and peer-review sheet to the next peer reviewer.

- A mathematics teacher directs students to evaluate each other's work on a complex mathematics problem using the "Peer Critiquing With Stars and Wishes Worksheet" to provide feedback (visit **go.SolutionTree.com/instruction**).

- A social studies teacher instructs students to practice for an oral presentation with a partner. The teacher directs students to use an oral-presentation rubric to evaluate each other's presentations and provide feedback (see figure 6.5). This rubric allows students to mark their ratings after watching the presentation and share with their peer two key strengths and one way to improve.

- A physical education teacher instructs students to self-assess their in-class performance. The teacher has students use the self-assessment form in figure 6.6 (page 90) to assess how well they met each component for the current quarter.

- A band teacher instructs students to create a video or audio recording of a piece they are playing in preparation for a concert performance. The teacher provides students a rubric to evaluate themselves and their section individually. Students must assess whether they are meeting expectations and what they must do to improve before the final performance.

Consider each requirement for the presentation and determine (by circling the smiley face) if your friend could improve in that area, met the expectation (good), or went beyond what was expected (brilliant).			
	Could Be Better	**Good**	**Brilliant**
Speaks loudly and clearly	😕	🙂	😃
Speaks with good expression	😕	🙂	😃
Uses eye contact	😕	🙂	😃
Uses hand motions	😕	🙂	😃
Uses visual aids	😕	🙂	😃
Describe two strengths of this presentation.	1. _____ _____ 2. _____ _____		
Describe one way to improve this presentation.			

Figure 6.5: Oral-presentation rubric.

*Visit **go.SolutionTree.com/instruction** for a free reproducible version of this figure.*

Self-assess your performance in class. Provide evidence of how you met each component this quarter.	
Components	**Comments**
Follows directions, demonstrates sportsmanship qualities, and makes positive contributions	
Consistently demonstrates effort regardless of activity	
Consistently prepared for class	

Figure 6.6: Physical education self-assessment.

*Visit **go.SolutionTree.com/instruction** for a free reproducible version of this figure.*

Strategy 33: Evaluate Around the Circle Jigsaw

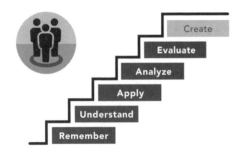

Often, information has bias or underlying assumptions that students must be capable of identifying to determine if the source is credible. In a world in which every conceivable source of information exists online, materials often provide less-than-credible information. This is why being able to evaluate information is key to the Analyze and Evaluate levels of Bloom's taxonomy revised (Anderson & Karthwohl, 2001). Author and inspirational speaker Lee Watanabe-Crockett (2019) goes even further, highlighting these skills as essential for *information fluency*. To be information fluent requires students to use what Watanabe-Crockett (2019) calls the *five As*: (1) ask meaningful questions, (2) acquire background information, (3) analyze that information for relevance and credibility, (4) apply that information to their work, and (5) assess the effectiveness of that application. Using the *Evaluate Around the Circle Jigsaw* strategy, you can help students prepare to evaluate the quality of information they review, and whether that information comes from online sources, their friends and family, or even their teachers.

• •

CLASSROOM EXAMPLE

A teacher has students watch a commercial and review materials related to the marketing for a weight-loss program. The teacher assigns students to numbered, expert groups of four, with each group assigned to investigate a question assessing the credibility of the program. After completing the research, the teacher redistributes students into new, home groups in which each member acts as a representative of their expert group. Each member then shares his or her question and research findings. Finally, as a whole class, students debate whether this weight-loss program is credible.

• •

Strategy Steps

Use the following seven steps to help you implement the Evaluate Around the Circle Jigsaw strategy.

1. Identify a text, website, or media students can evaluate for quality and credibility.

2. Based on the skill level of your students and the number of groups you want, select three or more of the following questions for students to consider. (Each group will take one of these questions.) Prepare a handout with a numbered list of these questions and provide space for students to record evidence.

   • Does the author or speaker accomplish their objective in this piece or effectively address the point at issue?

- Is information logical, relevant, and well-supported?

- Does the author reach appropriate conclusions based on reasoning? Are his or her interpretations accurate?

- Are the underlying assumptions logical?

- What other perspectives on this issue should you consider?

- What other ways could you examine this information? (Nosich, 2008)

3. Have students read or watch the source.

4. Have students number off into expert groups (basing the number of groups on how many questions you are using). For example, if you selected four questions, there should be four groups. Each student with the same number is a member of that group.

5. Instruct each expert group to discuss their question. Students should compile evidence to support or contradict the source's credibility and have that evidence ready to share with the other students.

6. When the expert groups have completed their research, form home groups to discuss all the questions. Each home group should have a representative from each of the expert groups.

Students hold up their question number with their fingers and keep standing until each home group has a representative from each expert group. When the groups have representatives from each expert group, each group member shares his or her thoughts about each question and discusses the questions. Students should take notes on the ideas.

7. As a whole class, have students debate whether the source is credible.

Variations

You can use the following variations in association with this strategy.

- Require the expert groups to prepare a unique question related to their topic to ask each member of their home group.

- Instead of using the questions from the Strategy Steps section, have groups use questions, like those in figure 6.7, which is based on the RADCAB (reliability, appropriateness, detail, currency, authority, bias) method, to analyze a specific aspect of the source's credibility.

Additional Content-Area Examples

This section provides examples of some ways you can connect this strategy to your teaching in different content areas.

Reliability	Appropriateness
• Is the information verifiable from another source? • Is the information reasonable and believable?	• Do I understand what the source is saying? • Is the resource age-appropriate for me, and does it align with my values?
Detail	**Currency**
• Is the information detailed and in depth? • Does it correctly cite other credible resources? • Are all the facts and figures either cited or directly from the author's own work?	• When was it published? • Have any major events related to this topic occurred since it was last updated?
Authority	**Bias**
• Who is the author? • What are the author's credentials, and are they relevant to the topic? • Who is the resource's publisher?	• Is the writing factual and opinion free? • Is the author or publisher trying to sell you something? • What are your own biases on this topic? • Does the author acknowledge dissenting opinions and counter them?

Source: Christensson, n.d.

Figure 6.7: Effective questions to gauge credibility.

- A language arts teacher instructs students to examine two persuasive issue websites and evaluate the credibility of each to assess their ability to analyze arguments with claims, reasons, and evidence.

- A science teacher instructs students to examine a lab report and evaluate whether the conclusions are accurate. The teacher assigns students to expert groups to review each specific conclusion, and then puts them to work in home groups to make their final assessments.

- A mathematics teacher instructs students to look at a mathematical engineering solution. The teacher puts students in expert groups to assess either the given solution or one of several alternate solutions. In home groups, students discuss their findings and reach a conclusion as to which solution is best.

- A social studies teacher works with students to select a political speech from the American Revolution and examine it for credibility. The teacher forms expert groups to address each question. Then, instead of forming home groups, each expert group shares its thinking with the class and then the class votes on whether the source is credible.

- A music teacher instructs students to examine two websites on the composer Stephen Foster. Students work in expert groups to evaluate a different aspect of each site's credibility and then form home groups to share their conclusions.

Strategy 34: Investigation

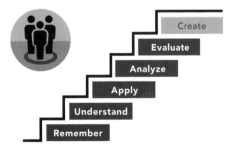

The *Investigation* strategy involves students examining a topic in detail. Investigations can be rather short, as students find relevant information and draw conclusions during the class period, or they may be longer and more complex. Often, the best investigations start with a question. In *The Power of Questioning*, elementary-level science teachers Julie V. McGough and Lisa M. Nyberg (2015) detail how powerful questions lend themselves to knowledge-building investigations. For example, investigations could explore the causes or effects of a situation by asking a simple question such as, What are the reasons for bullying in our school? Students could make predictions with questions like, What would happen if . . . ? An Investigation might involve defining a concept (Senn & Marzano, 2015). For example, ask, "What does conservation mean to our community?" Additionally, an Investigation could focus on probing questions like, Why is it important that students collaborate?, or it could focus on pros and cons issues with questions such as, Should we add extra recess time to our school schedule?

To initiate the Investigation strategy, you must give students a question to investigate and access to several informational sources. From there, students must develop a claim that answers the question, investigate it, and formulate a conclusion based on their research findings.

CLASSROOM EXAMPLE

On the board, a teacher writes: *Were all of the body features of ancient dinosaurs important for their survival?* The teacher then explains that in the Investigation process, students need to develop a claim that answers this question. The students suggest a claim drawn from the question: Body features are key for an animal's survival.

The teacher explains that students should research to find relevant information to confirm or dispute their claim. The teacher cautions that students might find contradictions or points of confusion. After discussing some of these points of confusion as a class, the class suggests several conclusions they could draw related to the claim; for example, "Adaptations generally occur over a long period of time, helping animals to survive."

With the process modeled, the teacher gives students several other information sources and a graphic organizer to collect their notes. They work individually to compile their research and formulate their conclusions. After students complete their organizer, they form groups, discuss points of contradiction or confusion, and collaborate to refine their conclusions.

· ·

Strategy Steps

Use the following six steps to help you implement the Investigation strategy.

1. Choose a question for students to investigate and then model the four-step investigative process you want them to use: (1) determine a claim, (2) research pertinent information, (3) pinpoint contradictions, points of confusion, or logical errors in the source or sources, and (4) cultivate a conclusion responding to the claim, evidence collected, and any confusing or conflicting information.

2. Select and provide students with the stimulating prompt. Make sure the prompt requires students to think beyond the facts. If students can find information that directly answers the question and summarize those facts, then it would be at an Understand level of Bloom's taxonomy revised rather than at the target Evaluate level (Anderson & Krathwohl, 2001). Some prompt stems include the following (Senn & Marzano, 2015).

- Why did this happen?
- Take a position on . . .
- What would happen if . . . ?
- What are the defining characteristics of . . . ?

3. In groups, have students brainstorm possible claims related to the prompt and select the best claim.

4. Students should then utilize appropriate resources to investigate and support the claim. For elementary students, you might need to provide several options of research material. You can allow secondary students more freedom to locate sources on their own. As students work, circulate the room to ensure they are adequately supporting claims with sufficient evidence and recording notes in a graphic organizer like the one in figure 6.8.

5. After students complete the graphic organizer, have them discuss in groups any points of confusion and contradiction in the research materials.

6. With their group, instruct students to refine their conclusions to explain why they believe they can support or disprove the claim based on their research. Be careful to avoid supporting students too much as they craft their conclusions because students may just record your ideas rather than form their own.

Claim	
Research	
Contradictions or Confusions	
Conclusion	

Figure 6.8: Investigation graphic organizer.

Visit **go.SolutionTree.com/instruction** *for a free reproducible version of this figure.*

Variation

You can use the following variations in association with this strategy.

- Instead of having students conduct an investigation over the course of a single class or week, have students select their own, more complex and deeper investigation that they can complete over an entire semester or course. Their investigation should speak to an overarching theme for the class.

- Have students use a digital form like Google Forms (www.google.com/forms/about) to submit their claims, research, contradictions, and conclusions for formative feedback from you. You could also have students share a digital document like Google Docs (www.google.com/docs/about) to allow other groups to insert comments with feedback.

Additional Content-Area Examples

This section provides examples of some ways you can connect this strategy to your teaching in different content areas.

- A language arts teacher asks students, "Do all stories have a hero?" The teacher instructs students to adopt a claim on this question and conduct the research necessary to support or contradict their claim.

- A science teacher asks students, "What would happen if a racing team replaced the tires on a race car with smoother ones?" The teacher then instructs students to adopt a claim on this question and conduct the research necessary to support or contradict their claim.

- A mathematics teacher poses the question of whether ancient mathematicians could teach high school–level mathematics. The teacher then instructs students to adopt a claim on this question and conduct the research necessary to support or contradict their claim.

- A social studies teacher asks students, "What are the defining characteristics of our community?" The teacher then instructs students to adopt a claim on this question and conduct the research necessary to support or contradict their claim.

- A music teacher asks students whether all music includes the musical elements of form, melody, harmony, timbre, tempo, rhythm, and texture. The teacher then instructs students to adopt a claim on this question and conduct the research necessary to support or contradict their claim.

Strategy 35: Evaluate an Author's Reasoning

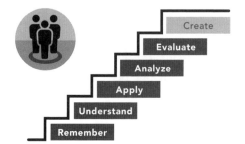

In Bloom's (1956) taxonomy, the attributing cognitive process at the Analyze level focuses on identifying bias, points of view, and assumptions. *Evaluate an Author's Reasoning* helps students analyze the veracity of the source by addressing questions about its perspective. To ensure students have an equal opportunity to share aloud, you should randomly call a number and have students with that number stand and share their thinking.

• •

CLASSROOM EXAMPLE

Students read the article, "Existence of Manifest Destiny Today?" (txxinblog, 2016). The teacher then puts students in equal-size, small groups with each group member assigned a number from one to four. Students use a graphic organizer to identify the purpose, question, information, concepts, assumptions, inference or conclusions, and point of view of the article. After groups finish discussing and completing their graphic organizer, the teacher randomly selects a number from one to four and asks the students in each group with that number to stand and share their group's thinking about the article's purpose. After these students share their thinking with the class, the teacher selects another number and repeats this process until the class discusses all the sections in the graphic organizer.

• •

Strategy Steps

Use the following four steps to help you implement the Evaluate an Author's Reasoning strategy.

1. Select a text where the author has a point of view, bias, or assumptions.

2. Have students read the text and work in equal-size groups to complete a graphic organizer to analyze the author's reasoning. You can use the organizer in figure 6.9 with elementary students, while the organizer in figure 6.10 (page 96) offers more challenges suitable for secondary learners to more deeply examine texts.

3. Assign a number to each member in each small group. For example, if each group has four members, have students number off from one to four.

4. Randomly call a number. Students with that number stand. Ask these students to share their group's thinking with the class about the first section of the graphic organizer (claim or purpose). Repeat this process to share the thinking on the other sections, moving from group to group.

Variations

You can use the following variations in association with this strategy.

- Have students compare the reading to a second source to identify differences between the texts.

- Have students use similar methods to analyze media clips, such as news segments, interviews, or documentaries.

- Instruct students to use their notes recorded in their graphic organizer to write an essay on the validity of the sources.

- Instead of having individual students express their ideas in step four, conduct a classroom debate on the validity of the source.

Additional Content-Area Examples

This section provides examples of some ways you can connect this strategy to your teaching in different content areas.

- A language arts teacher instructs students to read an editorial about proposed renovations to the local park and assess the author's reasoning using a graphic organizer.

- A science teacher instructs students to read an article about alternative theories to the big bang

List all group members:	
Name of the article you read:	
Claim	What is the author's claim?
Reasons and evidence	What reasons and evidence support the claim?
Convincing	Is the argument convincing? Why or why not?

Source: Adapted from Elder & Paul, 2007.

Figure 6.9: Evaluating an author's reasoning using an elementary-level graphic organizer.

List all group members:	
Name of the article you read:	
Purpose	What is the author's purpose?
Question	• What question does the text answer? • Is the question unbiased? How so?
Information	• What is the most important information presented? • Is the information relevant to the question and accurate? How so?
Concepts	• What are the fundamental concepts supporting the author's reasoning? • Does the author clarify ideas when necessary?
Assumptions	• What are the author's assumptions? • How does the author acknowledge that those are assumptions? • Does the author state any questionable assumptions?
Inference or conclusions	• What are the important inferences or conclusions the author states? • Do the inferences or conclusions clearly link to information presented? Why or why not?
Point of view	• How does the author acknowledge alternative points of view? • How does the author address potential objections from alternative points of view?

Source: Adapted from Elder & Paul, 2007.

Figure 6.10: Evaluating an author's reasoning using a secondary-level graphic organizer.

and evaluate the author's reasoning using a graphic organizer.

- A mathematics teacher instructs students to read a peer's opinion piece on memorizing formulas rather than using a calculator and evaluate the peer's reasoning using a graphic organizer.

- A social studies teacher instructs students to read an article about whether America was justified in going to war with Mexico in 1846. The teacher tells students to evaluate the author's reasoning using a graphic organizer.

- A humanities teacher instructs students to read a review about a recent performance in the community. The teacher instructs students to evaluate the reviewer's reasoning using a graphic organizer.

Strategy 36: Media Analysis

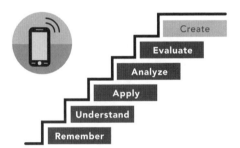

Analyzing media can be difficult for students. Through the *Media Analysis* protocol, students learn to be discriminating consumers of media. Teachers should utilize probing questions that allow students to make meaning (Scheibe & Rogow, 2012). It starts with presenting students with a rich media document and providing sufficient background knowledge to spark discussion. You will ask students questions about authorship, interpretations, and credibility, which align with the checking cognitive process at the Evaluate level. At this level, students are judging the credibility of information and questioning interpretations, assumptions, and beliefs.

. . . .

CLASSROOM EXAMPLE

While learning about *persuasion* as a form of author's purpose, students view a political cartoon from a recent election. The teacher starts the discussion by asking students probing questions and then allows

the discussion to continue by asking questions about students' responses.

. . . .

Strategy Steps

Use the following six steps to help you implement the Media Analysis strategy.

1. Begin with a rich media document with video, audio, or other elements that engage viewers, and that is appropriate for the age of your students and relates to your instructional goals. Limit the number of documents you select, as it is more beneficial for students to gain a deep understanding of a few video clips or documents than a superficial analysis of lots of media.

2. Take time to identify background information and probing questions to associate with this document. Answer this question: What background information will students need to know to decode the documents? Plan thoughtful questions students can use to analyze the media and connect it to the learning goals. For example, you might ask students, "What are your impressions from what you see (just saw, just heard)? Who wants to comment first? What is the message about?" Another option is to begin with some media literacy questions such as, Who do you think made this (produced this)? What was their purpose? and Who's the target audience? Figure 6.11 (page 98) has examples of additional media questions you might ask.

3. Provide students a context for the media. Point out the focus of the activity.

4. Have students examine the media by utilizing your questions to begin the decoding discussion. Instruct students to provide evidence to support their statements. Ask them, "What specific evidence have you observed, heard, or read in the media that supports your thinking?"

5. As appropriate, continue to ask students probing questions to reveal key content points and perspectives. Provide additional questions to expand, interpret, reveal, and clarify students' perspectives. To facilitate this, consider the following examples.

Audience and authorship	Authorship	• "Who made this message?"
	Purpose	• "Why was this made?" • "Who was the target audience? (and how do you know?)"
	Economics	• "Who paid for this?"
	Impact	• "Who might benefit from this message?" • "Who might be harmed by this message?" • "Why might this message matter to me?"
	Response	• "What kinds of actions can I take in response to this message?"
Messages and meaning	Content	• "What is this all about? What makes you think that?" • "What ideas, values, information, or points of view are overt? What are implied?" • "What is left out of this message that might be important to know?"
	Techniques	• "What techniques are used?" • "Why were those techniques used?" • "How do they communicate the message?"
	Interpretations	• "How might different people understand this message?" • "What is my interpretation of this, and what do I learn about myself from my reaction or interpretation?"
Representations and reality	Content	• "When was this made?" • "Where and how was it shared with the public?"
	Credibility	• "Is this fact, opinion, or something else?" • "How credible is this? What makes you think that?" • "What are other sources of the information, ideas, or assertions?"

Source: Project Look Sharp & Rogow, 2017.

Figure 6.11: Key questions to ask when analyzing media messages.

- *Expansion*—"Tell me more about that. What do you mean by _____?"

- *Interpretation*—"What words might you use to describe _____? How does this make you feel?"

- *Perspectives*—"Is there only one viewpoint on that? Why might someone say _____?"

- *Clarification*—"So, you're saying _____? Do you mean _____?"

6. Summarize what students say and provide positive feedback while inviting others to join the discussion. Ask questions like the following.

- "Anyone else? What else? Does anyone else have a different interpretation?"

- "I'm going to go around and have each of you say one word that describes _____."

Variations

You can use the following variations in association with this strategy.

- Promote student discussion in step four by having students work in pairs. Provide groups with a copy of figure 6.11 and have them select ten of the questions to answer with at least two from each of the main categories.

- Using figure 6.11 as a guide, students could lead discussion about the source with students posing questions to each other.

Additional Content-Area Examples

This section provides examples of some ways you can connect this strategy to your teaching in different content areas.

- A language arts teacher instructs students to review images and videos based on the theme, *Crime doesn't pay.* The teacher provides students with specific questions designed to help them determine and express the theme's portrayal.

- A science teacher instructs students to read an opinion blog about mountaintop removal. The teacher instructs students to answer key questions to determine the purpose and source of the writing, the pictures, and any embedded video content. Students examine this media for inherent biases in the writing and then decide their opinion on the topic.

- A mathematics teacher instructs students to read an online opinion article about students' calculator use. After examining the viewpoints and evidence presented in the article and answering questions from the teacher, students present an argument for or against the use of calculators in class based on the article and their own personal experiences.

- A social studies teacher instructs students to watch three separate TED Talks of their choosing on democracy. Students answer two key questions about analyzing media and then describe how: (1) the talks are similar and (2) whether they agree with the speakers' premise. To support their assertions, the teacher instructs students to cite textual evidence.

- A music teacher instructs students to watch a video of composer Eric Whitacre's Virtual Choir on the musical pieces "Lux Aurumque" (Whitacre, n.d.a) or "Sleep" (Whitacre, n.d.b). The teacher asks students what they think the main goals of this composer were when he wrote the music, whether he was effective, and who his target audience was for this project.

Strategy 37: ReQuest

ReQuest is a teaching strategy that incorporates the elements of reciprocal learning, which teaches students to pose and answer questions while they read (Manzo, 1969). Using this strategy, you divide a text into smaller chunks of reading. After reading the initial text chunk, students prepare higher-level-thinking questions for the teacher. After reading the next section, the roles reverse and the teacher asks the class thoughtful questions. Through this process, students are actively engaged in the text through a sound, proven inquiry approach to reading (Kuhlthau, Maniotes, & Caspari, 2015).

CLASSROOM EXAMPLE

Students silently read the first few paragraphs of the article "We Still Don't Really Know Where Dogs Came From" by Sara Chodosh (2017). The teacher poses some thoughtful questions, including, "How did migration affect the domestication of dogs?" and "What traits are people looking for in dogs?" Students discuss each question in their groups, and then the teacher selects a few students to share their thinking. The class reads the next section of text. This time the process is reversed as the students develop thoughtful questions based on the reading to stump the teacher. To aid students, the teacher provides them with a list of question stems. Visit **go.Solution Tree.com/instruction** to access a list of sample question stems for a variety of thinking levels.

Strategy Steps

Use the following eight steps to help you implement the ReQuest strategy.

1. Select reading materials and critical points in the text to pause and ask students questions.

2. Organize students in small groups.

3. Instruct students to silently read a section of the text.

4. Ask students to work in groups to discuss your specific critical-thinking questions about this section of text. You should use these questions as a model to reinforce what constitutes thoughtful questioning. After the group discussion, select a few students to share their thoughts with the class.

5. Instruct students to silently read the next section of the text.

6. Have students work in groups to develop thoughtful questions. Encourage them to use open-ended questions for you about the text. Use question stems to support their question development.

7. Groups should determine their most thoughtful questions and pose them to you.

8. Repeat steps three through seven as needed until the class has addressed each section of the reading.

Variations

You can use the following variations in association with this strategy.

- Use this strategy to have students analyze a picture or media, with students absorbing and considering just one section or aspect of it at a time.

- Have students record their answers to your questions before discussing them with a group and then have students refine their answers as they hear others' thinking.

- Instead of reading silently, read the text aloud yourself.

- Instead of exchanging questions between you and your students, have them identify stopping points and create questions for a partner to answer. Students can then share their questions and provide feedback to their partner as to whether they correctly answered the question. Then the partners exchange roles with the other partner asking questions (Frey, 2011).

Additional Content-Area Examples

This section provides examples of some ways you can connect this strategy to your teaching in different content areas.

- A language arts teacher instructs students to read the *New York Times* article "Oxford Comma Dispute Is Settled as Maine Drivers Get $5 Million" (Victor, 2018). After reading the title, students make predictions about how the Oxford comma could win someone $5 million. Students read the first half of the article and answer questions the teacher poses. Students then finish reading and construct five thoughtful questions about the importance of the Oxford comma.

- A science teacher instructs students to read an online news article titled, "Robots Will Control Everything You Eat" (Bell, 2018). After students read the first section, the teacher asks questions including, "What could be benefits of using robots in agriculture?" and "What could be negative aspects of using robots?" After group and classroom discussions, students create questions for the teacher about the next part of the reading.

- A mathematics teacher gives students a multistep problem about shopping for school supplies on a budget but instructs them to only read the first portion. Groups of students then ask questions about solving the problem before reading the next portion (or portions) of the scenario and continuing the process. Students must consider the budget, taxes, needs and wants, sales discounts, and so on.

- A social studies teacher instructs students to read a paragraph of *Thomas Paine's Common Sense* (Paine, 1976). The teacher asks, "What does Paine mean in this section? What is his purpose for saying this?" After the group and classroom discussions, students read the next text section and design astute questions to continue discussion with the teacher.

- A music teacher instructs students to listen to "The Four Seasons: Spring" (Vivaldi, 1949). The teacher then asks, "What do you think the composer intended for the listener to picture upon hearing this section of the music? Explain your reasoning." After the discussion, students listen to another selection from one of the other three movements and develop their own questions for the teacher.

Strategy 38: Find the Fiction

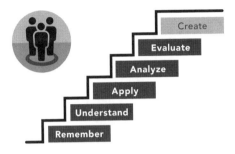

To expose misunderstandings or misconceptions, *Find the Fiction* challenges students to scrutinize information to identify incorrect statements (Kagan & Kagan, 1998). Using this strategy, students use a reading, media clip, or another stimulus to craft two truthful statements and one fictional statement. The correct statements should be accurate inferences, and the fiction statement should be an incorrect statement—a potential misconception, misunderstanding, or illogical inference. In doing so, they engage in thinking at the Evaluate level as they are assessing the credibility of information.

. . . .

CLASSROOM EXAMPLE

After watching "10 Amazing Science Tricks Using Liquid!" (brusspup, 2015), students write down two logical inferences and one illogical inference. In groups, students share their statements and try to ascertain which statement is false.

. . . .

Strategy Steps

Use the following eight steps to help you implement the Find the Fiction strategy.

1. Identify a topic, reading, video clip, political cartoon, or another stimulus.

2. Group students into teams of five.

3. Each group writes down two true statements and one false statement drawn from the topic or stimulus. The true statement should be accurate inferences, whereas the fiction statements are potential misconceptions, misunderstandings, or illogical inferences.

4. One student in each group stands up and shares the group's three statements.

5. Other groups discuss and reach consensus on what they believe is the false statement.

6. The student who is standing reveals the false statement.

7. If the other groups correctly identified the inaccurate statement, then the presenting group applauds the other groups. If the statement from the presenting group is incorrect, the other groups clap for the presenting group. The presenting group then explains why the statement is incorrect.

8. One student from another group stands and presents its statements and so on until all groups have presented.

Variations

You can use the following variations in association with this strategy.

- Instead of working in groups, have students individually write their own fact and fiction statements and then share their statements with a small group.

- After developing their two fact and one fiction statements, have group members mingle around the room and meet other group members with each trying to guess the fiction statement. When finished, groups should split up and find another person to pair with that was not in their original group.

Additional Content-Area Examples

This section provides examples of some ways you can connect this strategy to your teaching in different content areas.

- A language arts teacher instructs students to read the autobiographical essay, "The Unauthorized Biography of Me," by Sherman Alexie (2008) and record true and false statements of what life was like on a Native American reservation. Students then work in groups to test each other using their true and false statements. The teacher uses this opportunity to dispel myths about Native American culture.

- A science teacher instructs students to watch a video of a Hawaiian volcano eruption. Students record logical and illogical inferences based on what they know about the explosion and, in groups, test each using a series of true and false statements based on those inferences.

- A mathematics teacher instructs students to analyze a graph of numerical data that shows the attendance statistics for the last four football games. Students record logical and illogical inferences based on the data and, in groups, test each other on their knowledge.

- A social studies teacher instructs students to examine a map of India. The students record logical and illogical inferences about the map and how the country's terrain might affect its culture. Students then work in groups to test each other on their knowledge.

- A business teacher instructs students to read an article on budgeting practices for a small business. The students then write down three true statements on sound budgeting and one false statement. Students then work in groups to test each other using their true and false statements.

Strategy 39: Quads

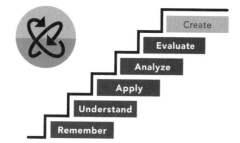

Quads is a strategy focused on evaluating the correctness of information. In this strategy, after learning a section of content, students develop four thought-provoking questions. They must then trade questions with another student, and each student then answers one of the other's questions. Students move around the classroom finding three other students to answer the other questions while providing answers to a question from those students. After all their questions are answered, students read the responses and evaluate

them for accuracy. When students are appraising the correctness of information, they are working with the checking cognitive process at the Evaluate level. Considering the wealth of information our society produces, it is imperative that students can evaluate the credibility of information.

CLASSROOM EXAMPLE

After learning some basics of statistics through using dot plots, histograms, and box plots, students each develop four questions about the topic. Some questions include: How could this be used in basketball? How are histograms and box plots similar? How could we use this to plot the number of siblings each student has in our class? How are a bar chart and a histogram different? and When would it be best to use a dot plot, histogram, or box plot?

After creating four questions, each student finds four students to answer his or her questions, while also providing an answer to one of each other student's questions. After all their questions are answered, students return to their seat to evaluate the answers, checking them for completeness and correctness. In a whole-class discussion, students share some of the best questions and answers along with any misunderstandings they encountered.

Strategy Steps

Use the following five steps to help you implement the Quads strategy.

1. Instruct students to each write four thoughtful questions about the lesson content. Tell them to write questions that spark thinking.

2. When students have finished writing questions, have them stand up and find one other student also standing. These students should exchange papers and each answer one of the questions on the other's paper.

3. Have students repeat the process for step two three more times, finding three other students to exchange papers, so all questions are answered.

4. Have students return to their seats to evaluate the answers they received to their questions. Instruct them to consider the following criteria.

    • Are there any misunderstandings or inaccurate information in the answers? If so, students should make any necessary corrections. Students should use appropriate resources to verify the information.

    • Are the answers complete? If not, students should add additional information to fully answer the question.

5. In a full-class discussion, invite students to share one of their thoughtful questions along with the most exceptional response they received. Without sharing the names of the responders, ask students what misunderstandings they noticed in the answers they received.

Variations

You can use the following variations in association with this strategy.

• Provide the same four thoughtful questions to the class and then have students meet individually with four peers to collect answers.

• In step five, have students post misunderstandings on the board or a digital wall, such as Padlet (https://padlet.com). Those misunderstandings then become the discussion's focus.

Additional Content-Area Examples

This section provides examples of some ways you can connect this strategy to your teaching in different content areas.

• A language arts teacher instructs students to read a chapter of *Holes* by Louis Sachar (2000) and write four questions: (1) one about the plot, (2) one about character development, (3) one about the setting, and (4) one about the vocabulary. Students must then use the Quads strategy to get answers to their questions.

• A science teacher instructs students to create four questions about using simple machines for everyday tasks. Students use the Quads strategy to get answers to their questions and evaluate the answers.

• A mathematics teacher displays survey results on a graph of students' favorite foods, showing the class, grade level, and school results. Students create four questions on what they could mathematically solve based only on the given information. Students engage in the Quads strategy to obtain answers to their questions and check accuracy.

• A social studies teacher instructs students to create four thoughtful questions about the five themes of geography and the impact they have on their community. Students use the Quads strategy to get answers to their questions.

• After teaching students musical elements basics, a music teacher instructs them to create four questions about how these musical elements are present in the music they listen to. Students use the Quads strategy to collect answers and evaluate information.

Strategy 40: Claims, Evidence, Reasons

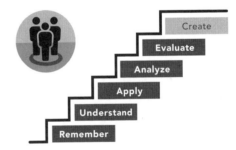

Students often have difficulty writing thoughtful responses. *Claims, Evidence, Reasons* provides a structure to support student writing. If the writing is an argument, a claim is a statement that supports the author's opinion. Evidence is facts that substantiate the claim and could include examples or statistics. Reasons explain the claim and answer the question, Why? The graphic organizer in figure 6.12 (page 104), which is based on the following Classroom Example, is an excellent tool for this purpose. At the Evaluate level, students appraise evidence and information from all angles and also question unsubstantiated claims. With this strategy, students peer review other students' claims, evidence, and reasons to determine if the claim is substantiated or disproved.

Opinion: *Many animals benefit from living in groups.*		
Claim one: *Working in groups, animals can get food.*	Claim two: *Staying in groups helps some animals better defend themselves.*	Claim three: *Animals that live in groups support each other.*
Evidence: *Killer whales work as a group to create large waves that lead to washing seals off the ice and ultimately into their bellies.*	Evidence: *When meerkats eat, one meerkat stands guard. If the meerkat guard notices danger, it alerts the group so they can run for safety.*	Evidence: *Elephants are intelligent and caring animals. If any member of their herd is injured or sick, the others will attempt to pick the member up with their trunks. Elephants also express sadness if another elephant in the herd dies.*
Reason: *Many animals work together in groups to isolate their prey or be stronger, such as when hunting as a group.*	Reason: *Smaller animals are often prey for larger animals, but in groups they can defend themselves better.*	Reason: *Animals can show expressions of caring for one another by helping another animal that is sick or dying.*

Figure 6.12: Claims, Evidence, Reasons graphic organizer.

Visit **go.SolutionTree.com/instruction** *for a free reproducible version of this figure.*

. . . .

CLASSROOM EXAMPLE

The teacher asks students to respond to the following prompt: "Do animals need to live in groups to survive?" Students use a graphic organizer to organize their claims, evidence, and reasons (see figure 6.12). Students exchange graphic organizers and evaluate if the claims are substantiated or disproven.

. . . .

Strategy Steps

Use the following three steps to help you implement the Claims, Evidence, Reasons strategy.

1. Develop a higher-level-thinking prompt that makes it possible for students to establish at least three claims they can support with evidence and provide reasons for.

2. Give the prompt and a graphic organizer like the one in figure 6.12 to students. Instruct them to develop an opinion statement that begins with establishing three claims and goes on to provide the evidence for those claims and the reasons they are true.

3. Instruct students to exchange their graphic organizer with another student and evaluate the writing. Students should use a clear rubric like the one in figure 6.13.

Variations

You can use the following variations in association with this strategy.

- If students are using this writing strategy for the first time, it can be helpful for them to work in groups. Also consider modeling the strategy for students to help them get comfortable.

- A variation of this strategy is the *Debate Team Carousel* strategy, which supports students as they develop evidence and reasons. First, students record their opinion and evidence on a graphic organizer similar to figure 6.14 and then they pass it to another student to add additional evidence. Then, the third student provides reasons against the idea. Finally, students return the paper to its original author to review the thoughts of others and develop all the ideas into a well-written paragraph (Himmele & Himmele, 2011). Students can use a graphic organizer with the following sections to organize their thinking with the following sections: opinion, evidence, additional evidence, and opposing viewpoint.

- After using a graphic organizer to plan their writing, have students develop each set of claims, evidence, and reasons into an essay. Have students use the essay's introductory paragraph to establish their opinions and subsequent

	Revision Needed	Approaching Standard	Meeting Standard
Claim	Claim is inaccurate or not a statement	States an accurate but unclear or incomplete claim	States an accurate and complete claim
Evidence	Evidence is not given or inappropriate	Presents appropriate but insufficient evidence to support claim; may include some inappropriate evidence	Presents appropriate and sufficient evidence to support the claim
Reasons	Reasons are not given or do not connect to claim	Repeats evidence or does not provide sufficient evidence to the claim	Specifies accurate and complete reasoning that links evidence to the claim

Source: Adapted from Meacham, 2017.

Figure 6.13: Rubric for the Claims, Evidence, Reasons strategy.

*Visit **go.SolutionTree.com/instruction** for a free reproducible version of this figure.*

Opinion:	Global warming is a threat to all life on this planet.
Evidence:	Global temperatures have increased by more than one full degree Celsius, with models showing four degree increases or more in the next fifty to one hundred years.
Reasons in favor of:	The amount of carbon particles in the air has not been this high since humans became the planet's predominant species, and they continue to rise.
Reasons against:	Humans are developing technology to remove carbon from the air.
Your reason:	Although there are promising carbon-removal technologies, they are not sufficient to counteract the amount of carbon humans put into the air each year, let alone the amount already contributed.

Figure 6.14: Debate Team Carousel organizer.

*Visit **go.SolutionTree.com/instruction** for a free reproducible version of this figure.*

paragraphs to establish the evidence and reasons. To help facilitate this, provide students with a second graphic organizer, one geared toward a persuasive essay, like the one in figure 6.15 (page 106).

- Access an elementary version for a Claims, Evidence, Reasons graphic online at https://bit .ly/2sCd5Y5 (Mrs. Bayna's Class Resources, n.d.).

Additional Content-Area Examples

This section provides examples of some ways you can connect this strategy to your teaching in different content areas.

- A language arts teacher instructs students to establish three claims regarding the author's purpose in the book *Wonder* (Palacio, 2012). Students use a graphic organizer to establish

their claims, supporting evidence, and reasons for each claim's accuracy.

- A science teacher asks students to establish three claims on how the environment affects genetic traits. Students use a graphic organizer to establish their claims, supporting evidence, and reasons for each claim's accuracy.

- A mathematics teacher asks students to use their knowledge of surface area, volume, and rates to establish three claims on how the size of the ice cubes in a drink affects how cold it gets. Students must use evidence and reasons to evaluate their claims and determine which size keeps the drink the coldest.

- A social studies teacher asks students if their school is organized on democratic principles. Students use a graphic organizer to establish

Introduction	Introduce issue or topic to capture the reader's attention:
	Thesis statement:
First body paragraph	First argument:
	Evidence one:
	Evidence two:
	Evidence three:
Second body paragraph	Second argument:
	Evidence one:
	Evidence two:
	Evidence three:
Third body paragraph	Counterargument:
	Reasons for their position:
	Evidence for their argument:
	Evidence that counters their argument:
	Restatement of position:
Fourth body paragraph	Third and most powerful argument:
	Evidence one:
	Evidence two:
Conclusion paragraph	Summary of reasons:
	Clincher (call to action or powerful statement):

Figure 6.15: Graphic organizer for a persuasive essay.

*Visit **go.SolutionTree.com/instruction** for a free reproducible version of this figure.*

their claims, supporting evidence, and reasons for each claim's accuracy.

- A music teacher asks students what the composer's message and purpose are for the song "Four Minutes, Thirty-Three Seconds" (Cage, 1974). Students use a graphic organizer to establish their claims, supporting evidence, and reasons for each claim's accuracy.

Strategy 41: Color-Coded Critical Feedback

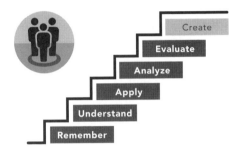

The *Color-Coded Critical Feedback* strategy has students analyze writing by highlighting ineffective and effective parts (or key parts), such as sources, inferences, and reasons. When peers provide color-coded feedback, it simplifies the process and makes it interesting. The colors also can increase student focus and teachers can use color to improve student writing (Mack, 2013), because by scanning the colors, an author can quickly assess which are strengths and weaknesses in their work.

. . . .

CLASSROOM EXAMPLE

In groups, students examine police data from their state to determine if their city's officers are using excessive force. Students use a word processor to form and defend their opinion in a paragraph citing the reviewed statistics. Students share their files with another student in the classroom, and they examine each other's work based on using a rubric that evaluates for *accurate calculations of central tendency* and *clear and correct conclusions*. The peer reviewers use the word processor's toolset to highlight in red statements that needed major improvements; in orange, some improvement needed; and in green, criteria met. Students then return the feedback to the author to revise before the final submission.

. . . .

Strategy Steps

Use the following five steps to help you implement the Color-Coded Critical Feedback strategy.

1. Identify a writing topic or prompt that asks students to critically think about or analyze information.

2. Select a color-coding system for students to use when providing peer feedback. You could use any of the following.

   - Facts (green); sources (pink); inferences (red); judgments (blue); reasons (yellow)

   - Author assumptions (red); contradictions, inconsistencies, or omissions (green); inferences (blue); examples of clear writing (yellow); confusing statements (pink)

   - Areas for major improvement (red); some improvement needed (orange); criteria met or exemplary work (green)

   - Clear writing (green); minor revision necessary (yellow); major revision necessary (pink); or needs proofreading (gray)

3. Provide students with a rubric or checklist you create to help them further delineate each category in the color-coding system.

4. Either with highlighters or digitally on a computer, have students review another student's writing and apply the color-coding system to provide clear and specific feedback.

5. After students return the writing to its author, conduct a whole-class discussion or have students individually reflect on ways they can use this peer feedback to improve their writing.

Variations

You can use the following variations in association with this strategy.

- Teachers can also use the color-coded system to provide feedback to students. Just make sure students are aware of the coding system you are using.

- Based on feedback from peers in step five, have students develop a plan to improve on the challenging area. For example, you could provide additional modules to support students struggling in a certain area.

Additional Content-Area Examples

This section provides examples of some ways you can connect this strategy to your teaching in different content areas.

- A language arts teacher instructs students to write an opinion piece about the amount of recess or outside time they get during a school day. Using the color-coding system, students trade their writing pieces and identify author assumptions (red); contradictions, inconsistencies, or omissions (green); inferences (blue); examples of clear writing (yellow); and confusing statements (pink).

- After testing the size and shapes of magnets, a science teacher instructs students to write laboratory reports. After trading lab reports with another student, students peer review each other's reports by marking facts (green), sources (pink), inferences (red), judgments (blue), and reasons (yellow).

- A mathematics teacher instructs students to write an explanation for their calculations from a real-world problem—calculating the area and perimeter of their school garden. Students exchange papers to identify clear writing (green), minor revisions (yellow), major revisions (pink), and areas that need proofreading (gray).

- A social studies teacher instructs students to write a performance critique about a historic musical or theater performance. Before they write their papers, the teacher gives students a rubric to help them understand how their peers are to analyze their writing using the color-coding system. Students exchange papers to identify clear writing (green), minor revisions (yellow), major revisions (pink), and areas that need further proofreading (gray).

- A business teacher leads the class in a critical feedback session examining their business plans and instructs students to share digital copies of the plans with a peer, using the online highlighting tools to identify clear writing (green), minor revisions (yellow), major revisions (pink), and areas that need further proofreading (gray).

Strategy 42: Rank, Talk, Write

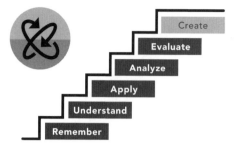

Rank, Talk, Write is similar to *Pause, Star, Rank* (Himmele & Himmele, 2011), which encourages students to prioritize and summarize information. After reading, students record important concepts and develop summary statements for each. Students rank the importance of their statements from most important to least important. In groups, students then share their rankings and summaries and select the most important concept and summary to present to the whole class. This strategy features the critiquing cognitive process because it involves using set criteria to evaluate the various options, including the most important concept in the reading and the best summary statement.

• •

CLASSROOM EXAMPLE

Students read a passage that answers the question, What is an Artist? They individually record key terms in the reading like *art*, *artist*, and *painter*. For each term, students write a summary sentence and then rank which summary sentence is the most important for the passage based on the criteria. Students then join small groups to share their terms and summary statements. After discussion, the group selects the most important concept in the reading and the best summary statement and records them on chart paper. Students walk around and view statements from other groups to see how they are similar or different.

• •

Strategy Steps

Use the following six steps to help you implement the Rank, Talk, Write strategy.

1. After conducting a reading related to your lesson or learning topic, instruct students to identify the key concepts or ideas from that

reading. Students should write a summary sentence for each concept or idea they identify.

2. Instruct students to rank the elements they identified in order from most important to least important based on four criteria: (1) the most important ideas, (2) conciseness, (3) accuracy, and (4) objectivity.

3. Have students work in small groups to share their summary sentences and the reasoning for their rankings.

4. Groups should determine which concept is most important and identify the best summary statement in the group considering the four criteria. Each group records its most important concept and best summary statement on chart paper and posts them on the wall.

5. Groups walk around and review the ideas from the other groups.

6. Conduct a whole-group discussion on what students observed and how each group's analysis was different or similar.

Variations

You can use the following variations in association with this strategy.

- Instead of having students identify multiple aspects of one reading, have them summarize one unique aspect of multiple, related readings. Then have them work in groups to determine which reading is the most important.

- Instead of the group activity, have students post their statements on a digital wall and use a polling technology like Poll Everywhere (www.polleverywhere.com) to determine what all students believe is the best statement.

Additional Content-Area Examples

This section provides examples of some ways you can connect this strategy to your teaching in different content areas.

- A language arts teacher has students read an article on the latest iPhone release and construct a list of summary statements or key aspects. Students work in groups to determine the most

important of these, post the list in the classroom, and then review the postings from other groups.

- A science teacher instructs students to read an article about mudslides in California and make a list of key terms with a summary statement for each. Students work in groups to determine the most important of these, post the list in the classroom, and then review the postings from other groups.

- A mathematics teacher instructs students to read an article about currency inflation and make a list of key terms with a summary statement for each. Students work in groups to determine the most important of these, post the list in the classroom, and then review the postings from other groups.

- A social studies teacher instructs students to read the preamble to the U.S. Constitution and identify key concepts with a summary statement for each. Students work in groups to determine the most important of these, post the list in the classroom, and then review the postings from other groups.

- A music teacher instructs students to read an article about the impact the Beatles had on American rock-and-roll culture and identify key ideas with a summary statement for each. Students work in groups to determine the most important of these, post the list in the classroom, and then review the postings from other groups.

Strategy 43: Affirm and Challenge Quotes

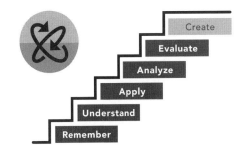

An internet-connected society bombards students daily with information from a multitude of sources—news outlets, blogs, social media, family, friends, and more. The information students see and search out is not always accurate, making it critical for students to understand how to determine a source's credibility before accepting it as valid (Watanabe-Crockett, 2019). With the checking cognitive process, students examine the credibility of statements, beliefs, opinions, or accounts to assess the strength of the logic. Socrates was known for questioning all things, especially his own biases (History.com Editors, 2018). Students need to learn to assess the relevance and validity of information.

Using *Affirm and Challenge Quotes*, students evaluate a text by selecting quotes they agree with and ones they challenge (Brookfield, 2012). In groups, students utilize other sources to evaluate the credibility of the statements they selected. They then post the quotes for other groups to examine. Another benefit of this strategy is that it engages students in metacognition (or thinking about their thinking). Sousa (2017) defines *metacognition* as the "higher-order thinking where an individual has conscious control over the cognitive processes *while* learning" (p. 30).

. . . .

CLASSROOM EXAMPLE

A teacher instructs students to read an article on the safety of nuclear power. Students select one quote they would like to affirm because it provides an example, key information, or a new idea they agree with. They also identify one quote they believe is confusing, biased, contradictory, unethical, or makes inferential leaps to challenge. In small groups, students disclose their quotes and provide an explanation for selecting those quotes. While discussing the quotes, the group selects one quote to affirm and another quote to challenge using research to substantiate or disprove the statement. Students then share the quotes with the class, recording them on chart paper. Each group then views the ideas from other groups, recording on the chart paper additional reasons or comments about the quotes.

. . . .

Strategy Steps

Use the following eight steps to help you implement the Affirm and Challenge Quotes strategy.

1. Select a text with statements, beliefs, and opinions students can debate.

2. After reading the text, instruct students to identify one quote they want to affirm. The students might like the phrasing, a new insight it presents, key information, or a distinct and memorable example.

3. Have students select one quote from the text that is confusing, biased, contradictory, unethical, or makes inferential leaps.

4. Form students into groups of three to five to share both quotes and to discuss the reasons for their selections.

5. Groups should identify the most thought-provoking affirmation quote and challenge quote from the group and share them with the whole class. With the challenge quote, the group should conduct research to provide evidence about the validity of the statement.

6. Have each group record its quotes and reasons for them on a sheet of chart paper and post them around the room.

7. Have groups choose another group's quotes and move to their chart paper. After reviewing the quotes and reasoning, the group adds additional reasons why the quote is important and poses questions related to whether the quote is biased, contradictory, unethical, credible, or unsupported. Students rotate around the room viewing and adding comments to all the other posted quotes as time allows.

8. Have students individually reflect on the experience by having them answer the following questions.

   - What was your initial reason for choosing your two quotes?

   - Would you change the two quotes you initially selected if you could do this again? Why or why not?

   - Through this process, what did you learn about your thinking on this topic?

Variations

You can use the following variations in association with this strategy.

- Instead of conducting a reading, have students examine a website, video clip, or song lyrics. These forms of media are often biased and provide rich opportunities to evaluate credibility.

- Instead of having students choose both affirming and challenging quotes, have them engage with a difficult binary question (like a mathematics proof) to gauge where it is correct or incorrect.

Additional Content-Area Examples

This section provides examples of some ways you can connect this strategy to your teaching in different content areas.

- A language arts teacher leads groups to select one slam poem on a social issue. Students record a quote they agree with and another they challenge. In groups, students share their quotes and select one set to record on chart paper for classmates to scrutinize. Each group examines the other posted quotes and inserts thoughts and questions.

- A science teacher asks students to review a controversial documentary on animal testing and identify a quote they support and a quote they dispute, along with their reasons for each. Students work in groups to share their quote pairs and choose one set to post for the class. Each group rotates among the posted quotes and adds its thoughts to the posted quotes.

- A mathematics teacher instructs students to review a previous student's work on a difficult mathematics problem and note whether the work is correct or incorrect. Students work in groups to share their conclusions and then join a class discussion as to whether the previous student correctly solved the problem.

- A social studies teacher instructs students to watch a news segment or feature on a world government. Students must write down a quote they affirm and a quote they challenge. Students work in groups to share their quote pairs and choose one set to post for the class. Each group rotates among the posted quotes and adds thoughts to the posted quotes.

- A music teacher instructs students to examine the lyrics to the song, "What Are You Fighting For?" (Ochs, 1976) in relation to the Vietnam War in the 1960s. The teacher instructs students to choose a lyric to affirm and one to challenge. Students work in groups to share their lyric pairs and choose one set to post for the class. Each group rotates among the posted lyrics and adds thoughts to the posted lyrics.

Discussion Questions

As you reflect on this chapter, consider the following five questions.

1. Which strategies in this chapter already align with your existing instructional practices? What small changes could you make to improve these practices to enhance student thinking for evaluation?

2. What are two strategies you could use within the next month to build Evaluate-level skills?

3. What is your favorite collaboration strategy from this chapter? What makes it a great fit for your students?

4. What variation can you come up with to enhance a strategy in this chapter that you intend to adopt?

5. What are some ways you can tailor a strategy from this chapter for your specific curriculum?

Take Action

Use the following three activities to put this chapter's concepts to work in your own classroom.

1. Pick just one strategy that you want to use with your students and create a plan for it specific to the content you teach.

2. After using a strategy you've adopted with your students, ask them whether they enjoyed the strategy and how you can improve it for next time.

3. Observe another teacher who uses critical-thinking strategies that develop evaluation skills. Write down your reflections and ideas about what you noticed and how you could adopt them into your own teaching.

CHAPTER 7

Implementing Strategies for Create-Level Thinking

The goal of education is not to increase the amount of knowledge but to create the possibilities for a child to invent and discover, to create men who are capable of doing new things.
—Jean Piaget

In this chapter, you will find seven instructional strategies that focus on learning at the Create level of Bloom's taxonomy revised (Anderson & Krathwohl, 2001). Each of the following instructional strategies requires Create-level cognitive applications like generating, planning, or producing content. By their nature, Create-level strategies invoke multiple lower-thinking levels. Icons with each strategy indicate which steps (levels) of the taxonomy the activity touches as well as its primary tool for engagement (movement, collaboration, or media literacy).

Within each strategy, you will find a brief introduction that explains its concept and purpose, a classroom example, a series of steps for implementing the strategy, a list of variations you can choose to implement, and a section detailing additional classroom examples based on different content areas.

Strategy 44: Affinity Diagram

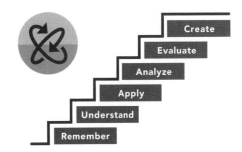

An *Affinity Diagram* is an analytical tool students utilize to classify ideas with common attributes into subgroups. The Affinity Diagram strategy is an effective brainstorming technique students use to creatively generate new ideas and reveal patterns as they examine relationships between various terms and group similar ideas. Using this strategy, you will pose to students a topic or issue and have them brainstorm ideas about it and record those ideas on sticky notes. Students then classify similar ideas together and create labels for each grouping. This process promotes creative thinking and brainstorming about ways to, for example, address a community problem, explore options a historical leader could have chosen to address a problem, or identify ways to test a scientific theory.

CLASSROOM EXAMPLE

At the end of the unit on dance styles, a teacher has students brainstorm ideas for creating their own dance. In groups, students record each new idea on a sticky note. After brainstorming, students group similar ideas together and identify a category heading.

Strategy Steps

Use the following five steps to help you implement the Affinity Diagram strategy.

1. Pose the topic for students to focus on.

2. Provide sticky notes for students and explain they should use a separate note for each new idea. Students should accomplish this step independently without discussing it with other group members. Challenge each student to submit at least five notes.

3. Group students and have them post their notes so all can view the ideas. Groups should discuss the ideas and use a large table or chart paper to organize and group similar ideas together.

4. For each cluster of sticky notes, have student groups agree on a category title that uniquely identifies the ideas in each category.

5. Each group should present its category ideas to the class.

Variations

You can use the following variations in association with this strategy.

- Give students a blue, red, and yellow colored dot, and instruct them to place the blue dot on the sticky note they feel is the best solution, the red dot on the second-best solution, and the yellow dot on the third-best solution.

- After students present their diagrams, have each group discuss similarities or differences between the diagrams and further refine their thinking.

Additional Content-Area Examples

This section provides examples of some ways you can connect this strategy to your teaching in different content areas.

- A language arts teacher instructs students to brainstorm topics for a short story they will write and then group similar ideas to determine the best idea.

- A science teacher instructs students to brainstorm characteristics of a new super animal that could thrive in arctic climates.

- A mathematics teacher instructs students to brainstorm ways to geometrically construct a new park in their neighborhood and group similar ideas together.

- A social studies teacher instructs students to brainstorm topics for a new law they could propose in their mock congress.

- A music teacher instructs students to brainstorm characteristics for a new music piece they will compose and perform at the school assembly. Students group similar ideas together.

Strategy 45: Problem Solving

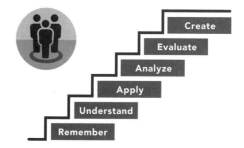

The ability to work to break down and solve a problem is a critical skill for students coming of age in the 21st century (Watanabe-Crockett, 2016a), and a full 96 percent of educators agree, ranking problem solving as a *very important* or *important* skill for career success (Greenberg & Nilssen, 2014). The *Problem Solving* strategy provides a systematic process students can use to identify and solve problems, and involves three key parts: (1) obtaining information about the problem, (2) generating new ideas, and (3) making a decision. Students often enjoy high levels of engagement in projects that involve addressing authentic problems because they can make a difference by impacting the school, larger community, or world.

CLASSROOM EXAMPLE

A teacher asks students to examine the problem: How can we increase the number of healthy lunches students eat? Students then work in groups to identify issues related to the number of healthy lunches students eat and the reasons students eat unhealthy lunches. The groups brainstorm possible solutions, including making weekly school television segments on why healthy eating is cool and creating visual models in the front hall of how much fat is in each type of food.

One group chooses to create a sample video segment and a visual model. The group asks ten students to watch the segment, look at the model, and complete a survey to determine which idea was more persuasive in encouraging them to eat healthier. Using the student-gathered data, the group lists the positive and negative aspects of each idea and, as a result, chooses to create multiple television segments to show on the school's weekly news program. After creating and showing their segments to the student body, the group asks classmates to complete a short survey assessing the effect of the segments on their eating behaviors. Finally, the group creates a presentation sharing its project and the results to the class.

Strategy Steps

Use the following six steps to help you implement the Problem Solving strategy.

1. Identify the problem or obstacle. Some potential prompts include the following (Senn & Marzano, 2015).

   - How would you overcome . . . ?
   - What solution do you think will work best?
   - How would you determine if . . .?
   - Develop a strategy to . . .

2. Based on the problem you chose, assign one or more of the following tasks to help students understand the problem.

   - Paraphrase the problem.
   - List the known information.
   - List what is unknown.
   - Identify issues surrounding the problem.
   - Describe the cause of the problem.

3. Instruct students to work in groups to brainstorm potential solutions. To improve the quality of the brainstorming process, students could use any of the following strategies.

   - Create an image of the solution to help visualize it. For example, if students want to improve the school's environmental impact, they could draw several ideas for classroom recycling bins.
   - Use manipulatives. For example, if students were looking for ways to improve community health, they could create a model for a community playground.
   - Engage in a trial-and-error approach by trying out an idea. For example, if students are trying to address school funding shortfalls, they could sell a few holiday-themed items to see if a holiday store would be a good fund-raiser.
   - Create a table or graphic to organize the data relevant to the problem. For example, students could create a table adding up the number of fruits and vegetables discarded each lunch period.

4. Instruct student groups to try out a few of the best solutions. Make sure to consider what resources students will need for this step and if there are any limits during the testing process. Some suggestions you can offer students include the following.

   - Record predictions, data, and conclusions with each trial to keep records of the success.
   - Evaluate options by generating pros and cons for each solution.

5. Have students evaluate their results. Some questions each group could ask itself include the following.

   - Are you satisfied with the results you obtained?

- Why do you believe this is an appropriate response to the problem?

- How is your final solution similar or different to the original ideas brainstormed?

- What is the best final solution? What evidence supports that conclusion?

6. Provide time for students to share their results. Students might show their problem-solving process in a digital presentation, video, text, or another creative product.

Variations

You can use the following variations in association with this strategy.

- In a Shark Tank–style manner, have students pitch their best solutions to the class. Classmates can provide feedback on how students can refine their own ideas.

- To monitor progress on the process, use a large chart to display the name of each group. When groups finish a step in the process, have them mark it on the chart. Using the chart, you can quickly gauge where students are in the process of completing the problem-solving strategy.

Additional Content-Area Examples

This section provides examples of some ways you can connect this strategy to your teaching in different content areas.

- In a language arts class, students are discussing their disagreement with the administration over censorship of the school newspaper. The teacher uses this to create an assignment in which students work in groups to formulate a plan to fairly resolve the issue.

- A science teacher instructs students to work in groups to investigate how they can reduce the community's carbon footprint and what positive effects their solution would have.

- A mathematics teacher instructs students to work in groups to explore the basketball statistics for the upcoming rival team, come up with tactics to defeat it, and create a presentation for the coach to convey their ideas.

- A social studies teacher asks students, "How can America protect the privacy rights of individuals while still adequately protecting the public?" The teacher instructs students to work in groups to research the problem, develop a solution, and present the solution to the class.

- In a humanities class, students voice their disagreement with the administration over cutting school arts programs. The teacher uses this discussion to have students work in groups to formulate a plan to demonstrate the importance of the arts programs in school and identify an alternative means to cut school expenses and save the arts programs. The teacher instructs students to create a presentation that highlights their conclusions.

Strategy 46: Carousel Brainstorming

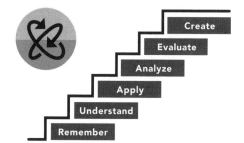

Carousel Brainstorming (Kagan, 1994) is a group activity designed to brainstorm ideas for Create-level projects. Specifically, it is an activity for the generating-level cognitive process. In small groups, students record ideas on chart paper and subsequently rotate around the classroom to view other groups' brainstorming ideas and then add new ideas. After viewing all the other groups' ideas, teams return to their original chart and review the suggestions of other groups. Groups can refine their ideas based on the thoughts given by other groups or add on ideas they gained while rotating around to the various brainstorming stations. Students can use the best idea selected from the brainstorming process (a generating cognitive process) to create an outline or model (a planning cognitive process), and finally complete the project with a finished product (a producing cognitive process).

CLASSROOM EXAMPLE

A teacher instructs students to work in teams to select one of the following science standards as a basis for their science investigation.

1. "Plan an investigation to provide evidence that the change in an object's motion depends on the sum of the forces on the object and the mass of the object" (MS-PS2-2 Motion and Stability: Forces and Interactions; NGSS Lead States, 2013, p. 59).

2. "Plan an investigation to determine the relationships among the energy transferred, the type of matter, the mass, and the change in the average kinetic energy of the particles as measured by the temperature of the sample" (MS-PS3-4 Energy; NGSS Lead States, 2013, p. 217).

Teams post their selected standard and initial ideas on chart paper. They then rotate around the room to view the other groups' ideas and provide suggestions and feedback. The teams return to their original chart paper and examine the ideas and refine their thinking for their investigation.

Strategy Steps

Use the following nine steps to help you implement the Carousel Brainstorming strategy.

1. Decide on a topic, problem, project, or challenge for students to explore.

2. Organize spaces around the classroom for groups to rotate to and view each group's chart paper. Post chart paper for each group in different sections of the room.

3. Provide resources for students to obtain background information on the topic, problem, project, or challenge.

4. Give each group a unique color marker to identify which group contributed each idea.

5. In home teams, have students generate their initial ideas to approach the project, problem, or situation and record those on chart paper.

This could be in words or using visual representations, such as sketches.

6. At a designated time, instruct teams to move to the next station, rotating clockwise. At the new station, students should read all the ideas from the home group for that station and add other thoughts to improve the idea or ask questions.

7. Have teams continue to circulate until they have contributed ideas at all the stations.

8. When teams return to their home stations, instruct them to review the ideas they received from other groups, add any new ideas that emerge as a result of this review, and identify key points or ideas they want to share with the class.

9. Have each home team share a summary of its ideas with the whole class.

Variations

You can use the following variations in association with this strategy.

*   Use this strategy at the beginning of a lesson or unit to stimulate students' prior knowledge and establish an intent for learning. Or, use it as a review for the lesson or unit, with students brainstorming concepts about different topics listed around the room. Using the strategy in this way operates at the Remember, Understand, or both levels of Bloom's taxonomy revised (Anderson & Krathwohl, 2001).

*   Instead of brainstorming, groups can use this strategy to engage in reflection. Assign different reflection topics to each group. To help groups as they rotate among the stations, each home group should identify its topic at the top of the chart paper.

Additional Content-Area Examples

This section provides examples of some ways you can connect this strategy to your teaching in different content areas.

*   A language arts teacher instructs students to work in groups to write a potential thesis statement on greenhouse gases, along with their supporting reasons on chart paper. The teacher

instructs groups to rotate around to give feedback and write any questions they have about their peers' work. When students return to their home station, they use this feedback to revise their work and share their key points with the class.

- A science teacher instructs students to brainstorm and write down the best ways to document weather or erosion in their community. The teacher instructs groups to rotate around to give feedback and write any questions they have about their peers' work. When students return to their home station, they use this feedback to revise their work and share new knowledge about weather effects with this class.

- A mathematics teacher asks students to use their knowledge of unit rates to work in groups to brainstorm the best way to determine which business has the best deal on different types of pizza. The teacher instructs groups to rotate around to give feedback and write any questions they have about their peers' work. When students return to their home station, they use this feedback to revise their work and determine the best deals.

- A social studies teacher asks students to work in groups to identify a current economic issue that affects their family and brainstorm various solutions and their impact on various societal groups. The teacher instructs groups to rotate around to give feedback and write any questions they have about their peers' work. When students return to their home station, they use this feedback to revise their work and share their key points with the class.

- A humanities teacher asks students to work in groups to brainstorm the best ways to create a fund-raiser event for a school arts program. The teacher instructs groups to rotate around to give feedback and write any questions they have about their peers' work. When students return to their home station, they use this feedback to revise their work and share their key points with the class.

Strategy 47: SCAMPER

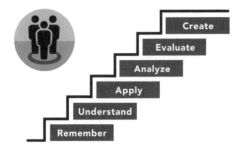

SCAMPER is a brainstorming technique that enables students to consider alternative ideas through a seven-step process: (1) substitute, (2) combine, (3) adapt, (4) modify or magnify, (5) put to other uses, (6) eliminate or minify, and (7) rearrange or reverse. This is useful because many tasks that are complex require students to design unique solutions. To bolster this creative process, SCAMPER assists students by helping them to consider multiple alternatives and develop a variety of ideas which is the generating cognitive process within the Create level. This is an ideal process for students to use when brainstorming topics for a research paper, poem, experiment, or project.

. . . .

CLASSROOM EXAMPLE

A teacher assigns students to small groups and instructs them to agree on an idea for a new product to sell. Students then share their ideas, with each group selecting what they feel is the best idea and then using the SCAMPER process to consider ways to improve the idea. One such group decides to sell slime and uses the following criteria to refine its idea.

- **Substitute:** Could we substitute any of the ingredients to make it more cost efficient?

- **Combine:** Could we sell slime and snacks to attract more people?

- **Adapt:** Do we anticipate problems that will cause us to adapt our business model?

- **Modify or magnify:** Could we make a special slime with school colors?

- **Put to other uses:** Can our slime be marketed to minimize student stress levels?

- **Eliminate or minify:** Could we eliminate any ingredients in our slime to lessen the cost?

- **Rearrange or reverse:** Would changing the order of our ingredients improve our recipe?

. . . .

Strategy Steps

Use the following three steps to help you implement the SCAMPER strategy.

1. Identify the idea or a range of ideas groups can choose from.

2. Assign students to small groups and instruct them to think about the idea for their group following the SCAMPER process. Students can use a graphic organizer, such as the one in figure 7.1, to record new ideas.

3. Instruct groups to evaluate all the creative suggestions and refine their idea.

Variations

You can use the following variations in association with this strategy.

- Consider breaking up the steps in the SCAMPER strategy and instead have groups all focus on one topic, with each group focusing on just one of the SCAMPER categories.

- Introduce students to SCAMPER one element at a time. This gives students time to consider and refine their ideas before you introduce the next SCAMPER element.

- Instead of having groups work on a single idea, have each individual student choose his or her concept and then use the SCAMPER strategy in groups to get peer feedback to refine the concept.

Additional Content-Area Examples

This section provides examples of some ways you can connect this strategy to your teaching in different content areas.

- A language arts teacher instructs students to establish an idea for a short story and then work in groups to pitch their idea. Groups should use the SCAMPER strategy to help each other revise the concept before they write.

	Term	Key Ideas to Keep in Mind	New Ideas
S	Substitute	Who else? What else? When else? Where else? Change components, venue, setting, context.	
C	Combine	Join together, blend, synthesize; merge audiences, markets, purposes.	
A	Adapt	Alter, modernize, put into a new situation, employ a new purpose, add a constraint.	
M	Modify or magnify	Change size, color, fabric, material, direction, length, meaning; make smaller or larger.	
P	Put to other uses	Find unusual ways of using, other places to use, new ways to use, emergency uses.	
E	Eliminate or minify	Take pieces away, remove, eradicate.	
R	Rearrange or reverse	Put together in a different order or sequence; change layout, design, or pattern; change direction or values; invert.	

Source: Boyes & Watts, 2009, p. 221.

Figure 7.1: SCAMPER graphic organizer.

- A science teacher instructs students to establish a project idea for the science fair. Students must then work in groups to share their ideas and use the SCAMPER process to gather suggestions for their ideas before they finalize them.

- A mathematics teacher instructs students to work in groups to create plans for a new cafeteria design at the school. Based on ideas of symmetry, groups must use the SCAMPER method to create a design that is practical and appealing.

- A social studies teacher instructs students to work in groups to propose an idea for a new American flag. Groups must use the SCAMPER process to evaluate their options and come up with a final design.

- A visual arts teacher instructs students to propose an idea for creating a piece of art similar to Dale Chihuly's work (www.chihuly.com). Through the SCAMPER process, students work in groups to gain feedback from peers to revise their design ideas before creating the various pieces.

Strategy 48: Hits and Spots

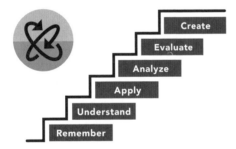

Hits and Spots is a tool for focusing brainstorming to help students identify the best ideas or questions. It works by having students choose, analyze, and evaluate a variety of different ideas and then select those ideas worthy of further evaluation. This can then lead naturally into Create-level thinking as students work to create projects from the ideas they chose.

CLASSROOM EXAMPLE

After reading a blog, students brainstorm ideas for a new blog about using their scientific knowledge to positively impact their community. Each student works in a group to choose some ideas, with each one going on a sticky note for the group to post in the classroom for others to see. Students then examine all the ideas before them, and each puts a dot on three sticky notes that he or she feels describe the best idea for a blog. The students then return to their groups to select those sticky notes with several *hits* (dots), categorizing them into broad groupings (*spots*) to identify the ideas that they should evaluate further.

Strategy Steps

Use the following five steps to help you implement the Hits and Spots strategy.

1. Instruct students, individually or in small groups, to use sticky notes to generate a wide variety of ideas related to a major topic, problem, or key question. Each sticky note should represent a new idea.

2. Have students work in small groups to review the ideas on each sticky note.

3. Using round label stickers or a marker, each student puts a dot on three sticky notes with the most promising ideas. These are the hits.

4. Groups select the sticky notes with the most hits (the most dots) and group them into similar categories (spots).

5. In small groups, students discuss what conclusions about the topic can be drawn from this activity. Instruct groups to examine the spot categories and work to perfect their idea.

Variations

You can use the following variations in association with this strategy.

- Have the class generate ideas and then post five or more ideas around the room. Give each student three dots for him or her to place on any ideas.

- Have students individually brainstorm ideas on a topic, record them on a sticky note, and place it on the classroom board. The class could then view all the ideas.

Additional Content-Area Examples

This section provides examples of some ways you can connect this strategy to your teaching in different content areas.

- After reading the book *Wonder* by R.J. Palacio (2012), a language arts teacher instructs students to work in groups to generate a list of questions they want to ask the main character. Each question goes on its own sticky note, and students then use the Hits and Spots strategy to determine the most popular questions.

- After reviewing a video of an explosion, a science teacher instructs students to brainstorm theories about what happened. Each theory goes on its own sticky note, and students then use the Hits and Spots strategy to determine the most popular theories.

- A mathematics teacher instructs students to read a scenario about constructing a new racetrack that involves using mathematical formulas, such as the Pythagorean theorem or those for determining circumference or arc length. The teacher instructs students to brainstorm the best approaches or ideas, record them on sticky notes, and use the Hits and Spots strategy to determine the most popular approaches.

- A social studies teacher instructs students to brainstorm ways to get involved in the local election. Students work in groups to share their ideas, record them on sticky notes, and use the Hits and Spots strategy to determine the most popular ideas.

- After reading an article about a composer or artist, a humanities teacher instructs students to work in groups to generate questions they would like to ask. Each question goes on its own sticky note, and students then use the Hits and Spots strategy to determine the best questions.

Strategy 49: Six Thinking Hats

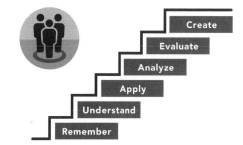

Psychologist and brain-training pioneer Edward de Bono (1985) establishes a method for examining information through multiple angles or hats. His *Six Thinking Hats* strategy helps students work in groups of six, with each member representing a color that focuses on the following: (1) thinking process (leader), (2) facts (thinking), (3) feelings, (4) creative ideas, (5) benefits, and (6) cautions (de Bono, 1985). By considering multiple, assigned viewpoints, students examine an issue or decision from different perspectives to arrive at a comprehensive analysis or a better understanding of a problem or issue. This strategy helps students avoid making quick decisions without considering emotional responses, negative aspects, or creative options. The hats include the following.

- **The leader (blue) hat:** The wearer of this hat is the leader of the group who seeks help from different-color thinking hats when necessary to spur the thinking process.

- **The thinking (white) hat:** The wearer of this hat focuses on examining available data and information to gain a comprehensive knowledge base about the facts of a topic or issue.

- **The feeling (red) hat:** The wearer of this hat considers how others might react emotionally to a decision or information by using intuition and gut reactions.

- **The creativity (green) hat:** The wearer of this hat proposes innovative solutions to a problem.

- **The positivity (yellow) hat:** The wearer of this hat identifies the benefits and value in an idea.

- **The cautious (black) hat:** The wearer of this hat carefully considers the potentially negative impacts of an idea and its weak elements or what might not work, thereby helping the group eliminate or change plans to address these concerns.

You can summarize this list for students by giving them role expectation cards, like the ones in figure 7.2.

This strategy encompasses several levels of thinking with the leader (blue) hat overseeing the full scope of the process. The thinking (white) hat provides the information necessary to solve the problem (the Understand level). The feeling (red) hat is considering how others might react to the information or idea (the Analyze level). The creativity (green) hat proposes unique solutions (the Create level). Finally, the positivity (yellow) and cautious (black) hats identify strengths and weakness in the ideas (Evaluate level).

· ·

CLASSROOM EXAMPLE

Students read an article about the lack of citizen participation in their government and consider ways to increase citizen participation. The teacher assigns a hat role to each student in the group, and students

Leader (Blue) Hat	• Process control • Focus • Big picture • Agenda • Summary • Time management	Questions to ask: • What thinking is needed? • What have we done so far? • What do we do next?
Thinking (White) Hat	• Information • Figures • Facts • Data	Questions to ask: • What are the facts? • What information do we have? • What information do we need?
Feeling (Red) Hat	• Fears • Impact on others • Feelings • Intuition	Questions to ask: • How does this make me feel? • What do I like about the idea? • What don't I like about this?
Creativity (Green) Hat	• Creative thinking • Alternative solutions • Refine • Develop ideas	Questions to ask: • What new ideas are possible? • What is my suggestion? • Can I create something new? • Is there an alternative plan?
Positivity (Yellow) Hat	• Best scenario • Benefits • Positive thinking • Optimism	Questions to ask: • What are the good points? • Why does this work? • What are the strengths? • How will this help us?
Cautious (Black) Hat	• Risks • Potential problems • Obstacles • Downsides • Weaknesses	Questions to ask: • What is wrong with this? • Will this work? • Is it safe?

Source: Adapted from de Bono, 1985.

Figure 7.2: Six Thinking Hats strategy's role expectation cards.

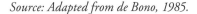

*Visit **go.SolutionTree.com/instruction** for a free reproducible version of this figure.*

review their role expectation card (see figure 7.2) and prepare for the group discussion. The leader (blue hat) invites the spokesperson (white hat) to summarize the information about the topic. The feeling representative (red hat) shares why citizens might not be participating in government. The creativity student (green hat) suggests ideas to increase citizen participation in government. The cautious representative (black hat) offers negative aspects on the proposed ideas. The positivity student (yellow hat) suggests some positive aspects of the proposed ideas. The leader (blue hat) then allows any of the representatives to continue to discuss to solidify the best ideas to increase citizen participation in government.

· ·

Strategy Steps

Use the following five steps to help you implement the Six Thinking Hats strategy.

1. Identify a topic or problem that could effectively integrate the Six Thinking Hats protocol.

2. Create groups of six students and assign or allow each group to determine who will assume each hat profile during this activity. Provide each student a hat description card corresponding to his or her assigned hat (see figure 7.2).

3. Distribute information about the topic or problem and have students analyze the information from their hat's perspective.

4. Instruct the blue hat student to facilitate a small-group discussion, with the white hat person sharing first, followed by the red hat, green hat, black hat, and yellow hat. After all students have spoken, the blue hat can invite others to add more to the discussion.

5. Have students reflect on the process by asking the following questions.

   - "How did analyzing the topic through the lens of the six hats improve your thinking about the topic?"

   - "How did your thinking about the topic change?"

   - "What new ideas emerged and were refined through this process that you could create?"

Variations

You can use the following variations in association with this strategy.

- You could adapt this process to have students give feedback on the work or presentations of their peers. The leader (blue) hat would lead the conversation, while the thinking (white) hat would summarize how the student met the assignment objectives, the feeling (red) hat would describe their feelings or opinions about the work, the creativity (green) hat would propose suggestions for improvement, the cautious (black) hat would identify the main challenge or area that needs to be revised, and the positivity (yellow) hat would identify the positive aspects of the project.

- deBono for Schools (n.d.) has a free card game students can use to practice thinking about issues using the six hats.

Additional Content-Area Examples

This section provides examples of some ways you can connect this strategy to your teaching in different content areas.

- A language arts teacher asks students to consider the school policy on what books are not allowed in the library. Students form groups of six to conduct a discussion, with each assuming a specific role (hat).

- A science teacher asks students to consider how the local high school can use more renewable resources and decrease their use of nonrenewable resources. Students form groups of six to conduct a discussion, with each assuming a specific role (hat).

- The school wants to build a garden proportional in size to their playground. A mathematics teacher asks students how they can effectively accomplish this task while also being budget friendly. Students form groups of six to conduct a discussion, with each assuming a specific role (hat).

- A social studies teacher asks, "How can the community increase voter registration?" Students form groups of six to conduct a discussion, with each assuming a specific role (hat).

- A business teacher asks students to consider ways to boost sales at the school store. Students form groups of six to conduct a discussion, with each assuming a specific role (hat).

Strategy 50: Inferential Ladder

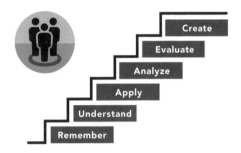

Inferential Ladder is a strategy that provides a mental pathway of increasing abstraction through reasoning. The first step involves perceiving information from the environment through the five senses. Second, students focus on important pieces of information and try to make meaning. As learners establish meaning, they build in both assumptions and conclusions. Finally, based on these conclusions, they take action (Brookfield, 2012). Together, the four rungs consist of the following: (1) senses, (2) meaning, (3) assumptions and conclusions, and (4) actions. The senses and meaning rungs build knowledge at the Understand level. As students make assumptions and conclusions, they begin to think at the Analyze level. At the actions rung, tasks are structured to be at the Create level. For example, students can design solutions to real-world tasks, create novel artwork, or write original works.

- -
CLASSROOM EXAMPLE

A teacher dresses up as Hester Prynne from *The Scarlet Letter* (Hawthorne, 1998). She delivers a monologue from the story and, staying in character, encourages students to ask questions that start at the first rung of the Inferential Ladder strategy and proceed up to the second rung. Students then make assumptions and draw conclusions about the novel based on their interactions (the third rung). Only after completing this discussion do they read the story and then write a monologue from the perspective of Hester Prynne or Pearl ten years after Dimmesdale's death (the fourth rung).

- -

Strategy Steps

Use the following four steps to help you implement the Inferential Ladder strategy.

1. Identify a thoughtful topic for discussion.

2. Draw a ladder on the board with four rungs: (1) senses, (2) meaning, (3) assumptions and conclusions, and (4) actions, and explain its purpose to your students.

3. Conduct a whole-class discussion on the topic. As students hear comments that fit into one of the four categories, one student gets up and writes the statement on the appropriate rung of the ladder.

4. To reach the fourth rung of the ladder (identify the product), students can write, present, or create a product. Identify ways students can apply and transfer their learning as they think at high levels.

Variations

You can use the following variations in association with this strategy.

- Have students work through the ladder in small groups or pairs before combining their information through whole-group discussion.

- Instead of you identifying the action product at the fourth rung of the inferential ladder, have students brainstorm ways to take action on the topic.

Additional Content-Area Examples

This section provides examples of some ways you can connect this strategy to your teaching in different content areas.

- A language arts teacher instructs students to examine images, videos, and artifacts from the Great Depression and participate in a class discussion assigning information to each of the Inferential Ladder strategy's three rungs before reading (the fourth rung) *Of Mice and Men* (Steinbeck, 1994). After reading, students address one of the following essential questions in an essay: How important in life are hopes and dreams? Who in society has power? Is mercy killing ever justified?

- A science teacher instructs students to observe a digital, online simulation that demonstrates the effect of heat on different molecules. Groups use the Inferential Ladder strategy to focus on important information, make conclusions, and follow up by designing a hands-on experiment.

- A mathematics teacher instructs students to analyze a local roadway in need of an overhead sign design. Students follow the Inferential Ladder strategy process to analyze the roadway, use their analysis to make conclusions about what is needed, and design a sign based on appropriate calculations and desired scale.

- A social studies teacher instructs students to examine a photograph of the Appalachian Mountain range in eastern Kentucky. Students use the Inferential Ladder strategy to discuss the possibility of mountaintop removal, its effects, and how local community organizations can take action to support or prevent it.

- An art teacher instructs students to examine a painting about the blues era (1870s). The teacher and students pose questions and make inferences about the artwork to understand the meaning. Students then create a plan to design a painting based on the ideas of the 1870s blues by representing an aspect of their community.

Discussion Questions

As you reflect on this chapter, consider the following five questions.

1. Which strategies in this chapter already align with your existing instructional practices?

What small changes could you make to improve these practices to enhance creative thinking?

2. What are two strategies for building creation skills that you could use within the next month?

3. What are some ways you could involve movement, collaboration, and media literacy within the scope of a Create-level project?

4. What variation can you come up with to enhance a strategy in this chapter that you intend to adopt?

5. What are some ways you can tailor a strategy from this chapter for your specific curriculum?

Take Action

Use the following three activities to put this chapter's concepts to work in your own classroom.

1. Pick just one strategy that you want to use with your students and create a plan for it specific to the content you teach. Use a rubric to help you gauge the level of critical thinking your students are displaying in their work. Washington State University (2001) provides a useful rubric for this purpose.

2. After using a strategy you've adopted with your students, ask them whether they enjoyed the strategy and how you can improve it for next time.

3. Observe another teacher who uses critical-thinking strategies that result in creative products. Write down your reflections and ideas about what you noticed and how you could adopt them into your own teaching.

CHAPTER 8

Cementing a Culture of Thinking

A tree falls the way it leans. Be careful which way you lean.
—The Lorax

Utilizing effective instructional strategies can spur students' critical-thinking skills; however, there are other elements in a classroom environment that can foster a thinking culture. In other words, a teacher may use variations of learning strategies and critical-thinking tasks, but without a culture of thinking to cement it all together, students cannot reach their optimal potential. Reflect on your classroom and school. How does your classroom and school environment promote a thinking culture? Does your classroom *lean into* thinking? Consider the following questions.

- Do you model real-time thinking and utilize thinking norms?

- Do you empower and engage students during learning?

- Do student tasks provide an appropriate level of challenge and nurture student confidence and understanding of the content?

- Do tasks consistently and routinely include real-world applications?

- Do you provide clear, impactful feedback?

- Do you provide opportunities for practice and transfer critical-thinking skills to new situations?

- Does the organization of physical space in your classroom encourage learner-centered instruction?

This chapter examines several aspects of classroom environment, practices, and instruction that impact a thinking culture. But first, let's quickly review the traits of the student-centered thinking classroom as compared to the traditional teacher-centered classroom.

Upon entering a thinking classroom, you might not immediately notice the teacher, as students are working in groups with a great deal of autonomy. Students are challenged to think divergently about probing questions and various ways to solve a problem. The focus is on the learning process and developing deep understanding through authentic tasks. Students have plenty of time to research and refine their thinking about content, analyze content from various perspectives, and create products for a real-world audience. Furthermore, teachers make conscious decisions about how students are learning based on their needs, while also celebrating students' growth. Table 8.1 (page 128) summarizes the differences between traditional and thinking classrooms.

Table 8.1: Traditional Versus Thinking Classrooms

Traditional Classroom	Thinking Classroom
Is teacher-centered	Is learner-centered
Demonstrates a culture of work	Demonstrates a culture of learning
Teacher dispenses information and content via lecturing.	Students ask probing questions.
Focuses on the teacher's knowledge	Focuses on intellectually demanding tasks for students to gain understanding
Features student dependence	Features student independence
Presents problems with one right answer or method	Presents problems that emphasize divergent thinking, with multiple possible resolutions
Focuses on the grades	Focuses on the learning process
Encourages speedy answers	Encourages research and analysis to answer questions with time for feedback, reflection, and revision to incorporate new information and thinking
Features limited student discussion with focus on the teacher	Features students routinely discussing diverse ideas and solutions
Fosters fixed mindsets	Fosters growth mindsets
Features work and assignments designed for the teacher	Features authentic intellectual work and assignments that reflect real-world issues
Follows set curriculum with a fixed schedule	Adapts and is responsive to students' needs

The fifty strategies you've read about in this book will go a long way toward establishing these traits in your classroom, but the content in this chapter will help you finish the job by sustaining your culture of thinking and ensuring that your students reap the benefits. This chapter covers the following ten topics.

1. Understanding the teacher's role

2. Adjusting task difficulty

3. Modeling thinking skills

4. Empowering students

5. Establishing norms for thinking

6. Designing real-world applications

7. Developing a thinking vocabulary and common language

8. Creating opportunities for practice

9. Providing feedback

10. Organizing the physical space

Understanding the Teacher's Role

When creating a thinking classroom, a teacher's role is to mediate the intellectual development of students by becoming a learning coach who promotes agency in students. To inculcate higher-level-thinking skills, teachers need to be supportive, but not provide too much guidance to the point where it decreases students' thinking levels. Never lose sight of the fact that learner-centered practices focus on increasing student capacity.

According to research, teachers speak nearly 70 percent of the time in a typical classroom environment, with the rate rising in classrooms with low-achieving students (Hattie, 2012). You have read about plenty of methods for making better use of instructional time in this book. To combat this tendency to speak, some teachers time themselves and allocate eight minutes to give directions or key information, then provide students with work time (Ritchhart, 2015). The Singapore Ministry of Education has an initiative called Teach Less, Learn More (Yng & Sreedharan, 2012), which focuses on increasing student learning through decreasing teacher talk.

As teachers design instruction, it should be from the lens of learning instead of work or completing tasks. Instead of telling students "Start working," a culture of thinking has teachers replace that language with "Start learning." Frame all tasks around the learning instead of the assignment's logistics. Center conversations on "What are you learning now?" instead of "What are you doing?" These subtle shifts in verbiage honor what is most valuable—*learning*.

Adjusting Task Difficulty

When learning, students perform at optimum levels when the task difficulty increases as their own skill level increases. Hence, it's critical for teachers to take the pulse of what their students can do and adjust task difficulty accordingly. (This could be up or down.) This sweet spot for instruction is often termed *flow*. Psychologist Mihaly Csikszentmihalyi says *flow* is:

> Being completely involved in an activity for its own sake. The ego falls away. Time flies. Every action, movement, and thought follows inevitably from the previous one, like playing jazz. Your whole being is involved, and you're using your skills to the utmost. (as cited in Geirland, 1996)

There are three psychological triggers to establishing flow: (1) clear goals, (2) immediate feedback, and (3) a balanced challenge-to-skills ratio. If students show signs of being overwhelmed due to task difficulty, make the task more manageable so they re-enter flow and remain motivated. When tasks are too easy and students show signs of boredom, increase the challenge. Figure 8.1 illustrates the flow concept.

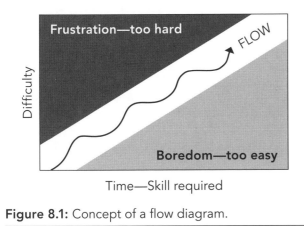

Figure 8.1: Concept of a flow diagram.

To find flow in your classroom, target the difficulty of tasks at a level just beyond what students can do already on their own (Ritchhart, 2015). Psychologist Lev S. Vygotsky (1978) asserts in his preeminent theory of the zone of proximal development that, with complex tasks, students might need support from a partner at first until becoming more competent. Sustained student engagement and perceived learning are most present in learning environments with challenge and support (Shernoff, Csikszentmihalyi, Shneider, & Shernoff, 2003).

As you plan instruction, do so with students' existing performance level in mind. As learners achieve success, raise the level of challenge. This means differentiating and providing scaffolded support, which might include a student working with a partner or the teacher giving additional resources with challenging tasks. For example, you could provide students with graphic organizers or thinking maps, less complex text or graphics, or checklists of steps to complete. Through these appropriate-level tasks, you can nurture students' confidence and build their understanding of the content. To provide more challenge, select higher-level-thinking tasks that are more open-ended, with less explicit instructions. Press for thinking by pushing and challenging students, and by not allowing simplistic answers or answers without reason or evidence (Ritchhart, 2015).

Modeling Thinking Skills

Humans naturally learn better when they see others demonstrate new skills and concepts. Thinking aloud originally emerged from Bloom's (Anderson & Krathwohl, 2001) work and received support from later research (Barell, 1991; Bloom & Broder, 1950; Davey, 1983). Through real-time modeling, the teacher's thinking becomes visible to students. In addition, students can share their process audibly to reveal their thinking as they question, offer suggestions, connect to personal experiences, and make judgments. This slows down the thinking process, granting students time to monitor their understanding and reflect on their thinking (metacognition). Wilhelm (2001) finds that inferencing skills improve with thinking aloud, because students then connect information to their lives and text, thus acquiring deeper understandings and critical-analysis skills as they consider what information is important and relevant. Thinking aloud has also been shown to be particularly helpful with students with disabilities and those who are learning English as a second language (Migyanka, Policastro, & Lui, 2005).

As teachers and students model critical thinking by explaining their thinking aloud, other students can understand the process to effective thinking. When modeling thinking strategies, it is important to showcase the decision-making aspect of the process. This process involves a scaffolded approach, moving from modeling to coaching so students can independently replicate the process on their own. For example, if a teacher asks students to select a contemporary painting and compare it to the Revolutionary War, he or she might say:

> When I look at the Sunset on the Lake painting, I see an empty boat in the middle of the water. It makes me think about how the Continental Army, without foreign support, felt alone much of the time. The black colors closing in around the edges of the painting make me think of how the Continental Army probably felt like everything was closing in on them as they lacked supplies, training, money, and transportation.

After the teacher explains the example, he or she then challenges students to think of other comparisons that are different from his or her ideas.

Empowering Students

To nurture a culture of thinking, students need a voice to propose unique ideas, perspectives, and interpretations. When you empower students to be independent thinkers, it gives them independence while creating an educated citizenry. Students then move from being consumers of information to producers of their own messages (Naiditch, 2017). Leading educational performers in Shanghai, Singapore, and Finland have altered their focus from teaching facts to teaching deeper learning, which gives students some autonomy to personalize learning choices (OECD, 2012).

When building a culture of thinking, teachers should be *nondirective*. This means sharing power regarding classroom decisions, encouraging student voices, and

reinforcing to students that their ideas and contributions matter (Ritchhart, 2015). You can ensure students feel listened to and encouraged with statements like, "I never thought of that," "I'm glad you brought that up," and, "I'm not sure; let's find out." Educators and authors Roxann Rose-Duckworth and Karin Ramer (2009) state, "Independent learners are internally motivated to be reflective, resourceful, and effective as they strive to accomplish worthwhile endeavors when working in isolation or with others—even when challenges arise, they persevere" (p. 2). This type of classroom environment promotes a sense of shared expertise.

To motivate students and support their autonomy, students need for tasks to present them with choices. When they feel encouraged to be independent learners and have some control over their learning, students are more likely to engage in critical thinking with improved outcomes (Anderson, 2016; Mathews & Lowe, 2011; Stupnisky, Renaud, Daniels, Haynes, & Perry, 2008). A study of high school students finds increased engagement and enjoyment when teachers challenge students at appropriate levels, give students choices in how they spend their time, and assign students tasks related to their own interests (Shernoff et al., 2003).

Ask the students for their ideas on exciting ways to study a topic; for example, "This is our class, how would you like to learn about poetry?" Authors William Carbonaro and Adam Gamoran (2002) posit:

> By inviting students to become more equal partners in classroom discourse, expectations for students as thinkers and learners are elevated, and students are encouraged to become engaged in their studies. In addition, when students are allowed to choose their own readings, they are likely to become more deeply engaged in their academic work. (p. 805)

The ability for voice and choice extends to learning topics, assessment, and technology. Brains thrive on explorations and self-directed learning—true inquiry (Kohn, 2015). With more student freedom, teachers and students can develop learning contracts or learning agreements. Through this process, students learn to manage tasks, organize information and meetings, keep records, and generally manage freedom.

Establishing Norms for Thinking

Classrooms that promote thinking have norms that encourage thinking. Such norms can include considering all viewpoints and ideas, learning from mistakes, celebrating others' successes, and treating others with respect.

Open discussions should value diverse viewpoints, making it safe to share different ways of thinking. When students engage in difficult tasks, they must feel safe to make mistakes. As students feel that others value their thoughts, they will be more likely to ask questions and engage in discussion. Research reveals 39 percent of learners comment that students encourage one another (Fisher et al., 2018). When classrooms are emotionally safe places to explore new ideas, make mistakes, and take risks, students are more willing to consider divergent perspectives and alternate ways of thinking. This is important because 33 percent of students report that giving them the freedom to make mistakes, ask questions, and correct mistakes is key to the learning process (Stengel & Weems, 2010).

Some teachers use the term *a mulligan*, which is often connected to golf where players can replay a stroke (a shot) without penalty. In essence, it is a second chance to perform an action after a mistake. In classrooms, allowing students to call a mulligan on a statement or idea allows them to change their minds (Arter, 2015). As a teacher, calling your own mulligans promotes the idea that everyone is a learner, including you. Encourage students to notice errors in their thinking and adjust their understanding.

When setting classroom community rules, identify some non-negotiables, but leave the students options for establishing other rules. Students should also agree on some expectations for activities like group discussions to promote healthy dialogue. For example, some teachers use the equation: "Call a Classmate + No Hogs, No Logs = No Need for Hands Up" (Ritchhart, 2015, p. 212). This means the teacher will randomly call on students, but the students can seek help from a classmate if they are unsure about something. During discussions, students are equal, thus no one is monopolizing (hogging) the discussion or not participating (acting like logs). With this equation, there is no need to raise a hand because all students are participating and monitoring their behavior. In a thinking classroom, student collaboration is pervasive.

Often, collaborative tasks are unsuccessful due to students not understanding requisite behaviors for working in a group. If you perceive students struggling to work together during group work, play a video for them that highlights good teamwork and identify behaviors necessary for effective teams. With this knowledge, students can self-assess their abilities to demonstrate good collaborative behaviors and hold each other accountable. To facilitate more effective discussions, distribute statement and question stems to students (see figure 8.2). Students can use these stems to help frame their comments and questions.

Statement Stems	Question Stems
Clarifying	
To be clear, you're saying that _____.	Can you give us an example of _____?
I'm confused when you say _____. Can you elaborate?	Where in the story _____?
So, you're saying that _____.	What would be a good reason for _____?
Is it fair to say that you believe _____?	What is some evidence for _____?
I hear you saying that _____.	That's a good point. What about _____?
	What do you mean by _____?
	Will you explain _____ again?
	I have a question about _____?

Source: Adapted from Heick, 2018.

Figure 8.2: Classroom discussion statement and question stems.

continued →

Agreeing	
I agree because _____. Her point about _____ was important because _____. The evidence for _____ is overwhelming when you consider _____. She and I are coming from the same position about _____. Despite disagreeing about _____, I agree with him that _____. I agree with _____ that _____. I share your point of view about _____. My thinking is similar in that _____.	What evidence supports your perspective or ideas? What are some other examples?
Disagreeing	
I see it differently because _____. The evidence I've seen suggests something different than _____. Some of _____ is fact, but some of it is opinion as well. I agree that _____, but we also have to consider that _____. We see _____ differently because _____. I disagree a little. To me _____.	Why do you think _____? What evidence disputes your perspective or ideas? What is another way to think about _____?
Summarizing	
Overall, what I'm trying to say is _____. My whole point in one sentence is _____.	So what you are saying is that _____? If I understand you correctly, your opinion is that _____.
Building On	
They mentioned that _____. Yes—and furthermore, _____. The author's claim that _____ is interesting because _____. Adding to what he said _____. If we change her position just a little, we can see that _____.	What do you think? What are your thoughts? We haven't heard from you yet; do you agree?

*Visit **go.SolutionTree.com/instruction** for a free reproducible version of this figure.*

Designing Real-World Applications

To prime student motivation and create more rigorous responsibilities, classroom tasks should simulate a real-world problem or be an authentic problem and situation. A great place to begin is to connect tasks to students' personal lives and interests while engaging them in problem solving. When students are engaged and relate learning to their personal lives, they are fourteen times more likely to be educationally motivated

(Fisher et al., 2018). Similarly, in another study, students could either summarize or connect their learning to their personal lives. Students in the second group, particularly those with the lowest probability of doing well, scored higher on average and expressed more interest in the subject area (O'Keefe, 2014).

When you design work that is authentic and intellectually challenging, it compels students to persist and increases their feelings of satisfaction upon success (Shernoff, 2013). In short, it makes learning powerful. Ritchhart (2015) defines *powerful learning opportunities* as those that require "novel application, meaningful inquiry, effective communication, and perceived worth" (p. 163). In essence, as students transfer knowledge and skills to new contexts, they are able to develop and demonstrate mastery by justifying their thinking and ideas to produce something.

To establish this sense of purpose and importance, identify a problem in your classroom, school, community, state, nation, or world. Then assess how students can use content knowledge to solve the problem. The following are examples of teacher instructions for projects you could present to students.

- With the end of the school year approaching, the school's Spirit Store has lots of inventory left. Design a plan to liquidate this inventory while achieving the greatest profit margin. Develop a presentation for this plan you can pitch to the principal.

- With your team of four students, you will act as scientists to design and conduct an experiment to show natural selection. Determine a focus for your investigation (such as traits). Design the experiment, including the research question, procedures, and materials you require to carry it out. Conduct your experiment and synthesize and analyze the data. Your science team will present your findings to parents and community members.

- You were just hired at Nat's Sports store. A new tennis shoe has just been released, and your boss is contemplating how many shoes to buy in each size. With your partner, collect data on shoe sizes and sales for similar products and create a report displaying the data, including a box-and-whisker plot, histogram, line graph, and frequency table. For each chart, explain the implications of the data you collected. Summarize your findings and prepare an informative presentation for your boss to use when making a decision.

Examine figure 8.3. Notice how the authentic experiences are directly tied to deep cognitive learning. Where are you on this continuum of critical-thinking implementation?

Entry	Developing	Approaching	Ideal or Target
Teacher directs student interaction with content at Bloom's Remember, Understand, or Apply level.	Teacher directs student interaction with the content at Bloom's Understand or Apply level.	Teacher directs student interaction with content at Bloom's Analyze, Evaluate, or Create level. Teacher incorporates problem- and project-based learning with open-ended learning experiences.	Students generate questions or projects at Bloom's Analyze, Evaluate, or Create level. Students engage in complex thinking like a content expert designing real-world solutions to problems.

Source: Adapted from Maxwell, Stobaugh, & Tassell, 2016.

Figure 8.3: Critical-thinking levels of implementation.

Developing a Thinking Vocabulary and Common Language

Marzano (2009) stresses the importance of establishing a common language as a framework to talk about instruction across the entire school. For example, do all teachers and students agree on what it means for students to *evaluate* content? Walsh and Sattes (2017) state, "A language of thinking promotes exactness and precision in expressing cognitive processing" (p. 144). When schools establish common understandings of critical-thinking vocabulary, then students can receive consistent reinforcement to demonstrate these skills. The following list offers some common critical-thinking criteria teachers use when assigning and defining tasks at the Analyze, Evaluate, and Create taxonomy levels (Stobaugh, 2013).

- **Analyze:**
  - Distinguishing relevant from the irrelevant information to draw logical conclusions
  - Recognizing biases, assumptions, intentions, or points of view

- **Evaluate:**
  - Pursuing unsubstantiated claims, questioning ideas, and demanding validation for arguments, interpretations, assumptions, or beliefs
  - Decision making through identifying the problem or situation, securing relevant information, defining criteria for evaluation, exploring options, and prioritizing alternatives

- **Create:**
  - Exploring various hypotheses or ideas to address a novel or ill-defined problem
  - Designing and carrying out a solution that is entirely different from the original source's

When you model the use of clear and specific thinking terminology, it encourages students to use similar terms. It's even better if this modeling occurs at the school level, so the student experience is consistent across the board. Faculties should work together to brainstorm ways to teach key words and definitions to students. Figure 8.4 showcases some common phrases teachers

Instead of Saying . . .	Use Thinking Terminology
"Let's look at these two items to see how alike they are."	"Let's **compare and contrast** these two items."
"Let's find the problem."	"Let's **analyze** this problem."
"What might happen next?"	"What do you **infer** to happen next?"
"How did you feel about this text?"	"What **conclusions** did you draw from this text?"
"What might happen using this approach?"	"**Predict** some of the **consequences** of using this approach."
"How will you judge your work?"	"What **criteria** will you use to **evaluate** your work?"
"What makes you say this is true?"	"What **evidence** do you have to support your assertion?"

Source: Adapted from Swartz et al., 2008.

Figure 8.4: Critical-thinking terminology substitutions.

use and some suggestions for changing these phrases to emphasize more accurate and appropriate critical-thinking terminology.

Creating Opportunities for Practice

To be a good thinker, students need multiple opportunities to practice. In a competition between kindergarteners and Harvard MBA graduate students to construct the tallest tower using spaghetti, string, tape, and a marshmallow within a time limit, MBA students used their time to plan while kindergartners constructed many more prototypes and then redesigned when they were unsuccessful. The kindergartners' end product was the tallest, reinforcing that effective thinkers make many tries and many fails (Wujec, 2010). Thus, mistakes produce innovative ideas.

In order for students to think critically, teachers must expose them to new material that they read and examine to create meaning. Design tasks and assignments to elicit student thinking and transfer of learning to new situations. To provide new opportunities for students to apply their learning, give them text-based materials like claims, passages, quotes, or reports. Students could also respond to graphics like charts, graphs, tables, maps, pictures, models, diagrams, drawings, or spreadsheets.

One common mistake I see teachers make is to reuse examples from learning materials on summative assessments. This lowers the thinking level students require for the assessment. Design assessment items or questions to use the same concepts but different content to allow students to demonstrate a deeper understanding of concepts.

School-improvement expert Mike Schmoker (2009) suggests replacing low-level tasks common to traditional classrooms with opportunities to engage in intellectually demanding work is the single most effective and cost-efficient strategy to boost student achievement. For most teachers, this means examining current tasks and ratcheting up the thinking levels by connecting with authentic audiences, providing student choice, and increasing the open-endedness of tasks. With more choice, creativity, and challenge, students can strengthen their abilities.

As instruction shifts to higher levels of thinking, students cannot produce immediate answers to dilemmas, challenges, and questions. In fact, if students can produce an answer within the typical wait time, the question is most likely lower level, requires a memorized answer, or students are trying to guess what the teacher thinks is the answer. Higher-level questions are best when students can review them several times, discuss ideas with a partner, and conduct research before producing an answer. In a thinking classroom, faster isn't better. Students need time to think and reflect. During that reflection time, students might even change their mind based on new evidence.

Avoid immediately correcting students' answers and instead seek to understand their reasoning. For example, you might say, "Please share your reasoning" or "Please provide reasons for your ideas." Let the discussion flow from there while avoiding a ping-pong match (questions and answers bouncing from the teacher to the students and back to the teacher). Instead, picture a sort of basketball game, with many students participating and extending on others' ideas (McIntosh, 2012).

Providing Feedback

In Hattie's (2009) review of the factors impacting student achievement, teacher-student relationships are among the key practices affecting learning. The teacher-student relationship impacts achievement, ranking twelfth of 150 variables influencing K–12 student learning (Hattie, 2012). Strong teacher-student relationships not only positively impact student achievement but also particularly develop critical-thinking skills (Pianta, Hamre, & Allen, 2012). Cofounder of What Kids Can Do (www.whatkidscando.org/index.html) Kathleen Cushman (2005) notes the types of teacher-student relations that promote a culture of thinking: "Remind us often that you expect our best," "Encourage our efforts even if we are having trouble," "Give helpful feedback and expect us to revise," "Don't compare us to other students," and "Stick with us" (pp. 64–65, 67).

Coaching and providing effective feedback can propel learning and create momentum. Feedback should focus on the growth of the learner and provide the learner with actionable information to guide future learning (Hattie & Timperley, 2007). Feedback should provide specific, descriptive guidance to learners. Teachers should notice good thinking and then provide specific reinforcement (Ritchhart, 2015). Teachers often say, "Practice makes progress, not perfect." Thinking critically is a growth process.

Feedback that centers on a growth mindset includes comments like: "You are really challenging yourself" and "You worked exceptionally hard on this project" (Dweck, 2006). To prompt students to analyze their work, ask them, "How do you feel about it?" and "Is there something else you can add?" For an example of a teacher modeling how to use effective feedback, watch the online video "Austin's Butterfly: Building Excellence in Student Work" (Berger, 2012).

Organizing the Physical Space

Physical environments convey the ideals or principles of those who use the space (Curtis & Carter, 2015). In other words, the physical environment signals to students what is important when they occupy that space. How does your classroom space promote learner-centered instruction? Does it instead convey or promote student passivity and compliance?

A thinking classroom might look radically different from a traditional classroom, particularly when it's arranged to promote students interacting. For example, seating arrangements in small groups, a horseshoe, or other configurations promote student discussion. Allowing for multiple arrangements also facilitates a variety of thoughtful interactions. Figure 8.5 shows examples of a classroom with multiple spaces for different groups of students to collaborate.

Author and consultant David Thornburg (2014) defines three different spaces teachers need in their classrooms: (1) campfires (the classroom is arranged around a central, sage-like figure who imparts wisdom), (2) waterholes (small group spaces for peers to collaborate), and (3) caves (spaces where students can individually reflect and study). Thus, a classroom might have different learning zones for different types of activities (Ritchhart, 2015). Other flexible seating options include student lounge areas, makerspaces, cafes, moveable stations, and indoor-outdoor spaces. To encourage thinking about the best use of classroom space, consider involving students in designing arrangements that best work for them.

You might also consider flexible learning spaces, where students have various seating options, like exercise balls, standing desks, yoga mats, stools, sitting on the floor, lying on the floor, standing desks, or standing with no desk at all.

In addition to the arrangement of the learning space, thinking classrooms include quotes, probing questions, and displays that visually draw students into thinking. Quotes, like the epigraphs at the start of each chapter in this book, can spur students' thinking. You might also sprinkle in displays of student work from previous tasks to showcase various stages of completion (the learning progression).

Music and light are also useful tools, like playing popular music during social tasks and classical, jazz, or wordless music during individual tasks. Consider dimming the lights for deeper discussions.

Finally, thinking classrooms vary group work to better support student learning. For example, use ability groups based on preassessment data to group students who need support or additional challenge, or to allow students strong in a specific topic to work with

Source: © 2018 Amanda Rupsch. Used with permission.

Figure 8.5: Engaging classroom environments.

students who need help with that topic. Center rotations are another way to use ability groups fluidly. Students can move between centers while working with like-level students, or they can work heterogeneously while the teacher works with ability groups on certain tasks. You can form cooperative groups based on students' interests and include different ability levels. Use an interest inventory (survey) to help form appropriate groups for this approach.

Douglas Fisher and colleagues (2018) comment on the value of group work: "It is easier to tell whether students are cognitively engaged when the classroom is filled with discussion and dialogue. As students interact with each other and their teachers, their thinking becomes evident" (p. 5).

Sustaining Your Culture of Thinking

A thinking-centered classroom is an energizing place where everyone is collaborating and contributing to the learning. The culture extends beyond the classroom and must become an intentional and planned schoolwide effort. It is the responsibility of all to open the minds of students and guide them to receive the ideas and thinking of others. Administrators set the tone, providing support, professional development, and resources to the teachers. Teachers model appropriate thinking practices and provide a supportive environment with multiple thinking opportunities. Teaching students to become effective critical thinkers takes time, energy, knowledge, and effort from all stakeholders—students, teachers, administrators, and parents. What small changes can you make in your classroom or school to positively impact the thinking culture?

Discussion Questions

As you reflect on this chapter, consider the following five questions.

1. Reflect on the epigraph at the start of the chapter. In what way is this true of your classroom? In which direction does the culture of your classroom lean?

2. How can you establish a classroom culture that promotes thoughtful engagement?

3. If you visit a classroom that promotes thinking, what do you see or hear?

4. What would your students and colleagues say about how you promote a culture of thinking in your classroom?

5. What ideas in the chapter can you use to improve the thinking in your classroom?

Take Action

Use the following five activities to put this chapter's concepts to work in your own classroom.

1. Assign students to engage in a collaborative task and, upon its completion, provide them with a rubric that supports self-assessment. You can use one of the grade-appropriate rubrics from the Buck Institute for Education (2013a, 2013b, 2013c).

2. Distribute a rubric to your students, such as the one in figure 8.6 (page 138), to learn more about their perceptions of the culture of thinking in your classroom. Analyze the data you receive to find areas of agreement. From this, determine how you can better promote a culture of thinking in your classroom.

3. Self-assess your level of developing a culture of thinking in your classroom. What are your strengths and areas for improvement? Share your thinking with a colleague to evaluate the best course of action to improve.

4. Have an administrator or colleague observe your class and use figure 8.7 (page 139) to assess its culture of thinking. Analyze the feedback you receive to identify areas for improvement.

5. Post an "Observe Me" sign on your door and invite other educators to observe you for one day. Identify on your sign how you are specifically working on developing a culture of thinking and what your colleagues' feedback should focus on.

Date: _____ Class Period: _____ Subject: _____	

Rank your choices 1, 2, and 3.

1—is what the class spent the most time doing, 2—for the next most, and then 3.

In this class period, we spent **MOST** of our time . . .

	Looking closely at things, describing them, noticing details, or detecting patterns
	Building our own explanations, theories, hypotheses, or interpretations
	Reasoning with evidence and supporting our ideas with facts and reasons
	Wondering, raising issues, and showing curiosity about what we are studying
	Making connections between different things, to the world, or to our own lives
	Looking at things from different perspectives and points of view to see things in a new way
	Identifying the central or core ideas, forming conclusions, or capturing the essence of things
	Digging deeply into a topic to uncover mysteries, complexities, and challenges
	Organizing and pulling together ideas, information, notes, and experiences to make sense of them
	Reflecting on where we are at in our learning and understanding to determine where to go next
	Using and applying what we have been learning to solve new problems or create something original
	Reviewing and going over information from the readings or previous class work
	Reading, listening, or getting new information about the topic we are studying
	Practicing the skills and procedures the class has already learned

In this class, I was really pushed to think (*Circle one.*)

           Not at all   A little   Some   A lot

As a learner, it would have helped me if **I** had . . .

As a learner, it would have helped me if the **teacher** had . . .

Source: Ritchhart, 2015, p. 307.

Figure 8.6: Rubric for reflecting on in-class learning activities.

Administrators or colleagues can use this evaluation to provide feedback on the level of critical thinking in a classroom.

Critical-Thinking Evaluation		
	Observed	Not Observed
Teacher		
Poses questions and comments that are thought provoking		
States an alternate, creative, or controversial position to spark discussion		
Respectfully challenges students to provide evidence or support for their position		
Encourages peers to carefully consider opinions and ideas of others		
Provides tasks at an appropriate level of challenge		
Models real-time thinking		
Promotes thinking norms to encourage critical thinking		
Connects to real-world topics and applications of knowledge		
Provides clear, impactful feedback		
Offers multiple opportunities for students to engage in critical thinking		
Utilizes classroom space to promote thinking		
Provides multiple opportunities to engage in critical thinking		
Students		
Pose questions and comments that are thought provoking and related		
State comments that are precise and accurate		
Demonstrate depth of analysis through comments		
Respond to or build logically on comments from others		
Support positions and comments with evidence indicating critical reasoning, modes of analysis, synthesis, and judgment		
Tie thoughts to previous instruction or other writings and information about the topic at hand		
Respectfully challenge others to provide evidence or support for their position		
Approach the discussion or problem in a creative manner		
Approach the discussion or problem in a thoughtful, reasoned manner		
Show tolerance toward opposing beliefs, ideas, or opinions		
Encourage peers not to dismiss out of hand the opinions and ideas of others		

Source: Adapted from U.S. Army, 2013.

Figure 8.7: Critical-thinking evaluation.

Visit **go.SolutionTree.com/instruction** *for a free reproducible version of this figure.*

References and Resources

Adobe Systems. (2018). *Creative problem solving: Essential skills today's students need for jobs in tomorrow's age of automation* [Infographic]. Accessed at http://cps.adobeeducate.com/US-Infographic on September 6, 2018.

Aesop. (2014). The north wind and the sun. In D. L. Ashliman (Ed.), *Aesop's fables*. New York: Penguin.

Alexie, S. (2008). *The unauthorized biography of me* [Blog post]. Accessed at http://bibliosity.blogspot.com /2008/11/unauthorized-autobiography-of-me.html on January 23, 2019.

Anderson, L. W., & Krathwohl, D. R. (Eds.). (2001). *A taxonomy for learning, teaching, and assessing: A revision of Bloom's taxonomy of educational objectives* (Complete ed.). New York: Longman.

Anderson, M. (2016). *Learning to choose, choosing to learn: The key to student motivation and achievement*. Alexandria, VA: Association for Supervision and Curriculum Development.

Antonetti, J. V., & Garver, J. R. (2015). *17,000 classroom visits can't be wrong: Strategies that engage students, promote active learning, and boost achievement*. Alexandria, VA: Association for Supervision and Curriculum Development.

Arter, L. (2015). Road tested / calling mulligan! Two rules for dynamic discourse. *Education Update, 57*(2). Accessed at www.ascd.org/publications/newsletters /education-update/feb15/vol57/num02/Calling -Mulligan!-Two-Rules-for-Dynamic-Discourse.aspx on September 6, 2018.

Azzam, A. M. (2009). Why creativity now? A conversation with Sir Ken Robinson. *Educational Leadership, 67*(1), 22–26.

Bandura, A. (1986). *Social foundations of thought and action: A social cognitive theory*. Englewood Cliffs, NJ: Prentice Hall.

Barell, J. (1991). *Teaching for thoughtfulness: Classroom strategies to enhance intellectual development*. New York: Longman.

Bell, T. (2018, January 25). Robots will control everything you eat. *Science News for Students*. Accessed at https://sciencenewsforstudents.org/article/robots-will-control -everything-you-eat on September 6, 2018.

Berger, R. (2012, March 9). *Austin's butterfly: Building excellence in student work* [Video file]. Accessed at https://vimeo.com/38247060 on September 6, 2018.

Berger, W. (2014). *A more beautiful question: The power of inquiry to spark breakthrough ideas*. New York: Bloomsbury.

Bernard, B. (2007). Cupid shuffle [Recorded by Cupid]. On *Time for a change* [Digital download]. New York: Asylum Atlantic.

Bloom, B. S. (Ed.). (1956). *Taxonomy of educational objectives: The classification of educational goals*. New York: Longmans, Green.

Bloom, B. S., & Broder, L. J. (1950). Problem-solving processes of college students: An exploratory investigation. *American Journal of Education, 58*(9), 558–560.

Boyes, K., & Watts, G. (2009). *Developing habits of mind in secondary schools*. Alexandria, VA: Association for Supervision and Curriculum Development.

BrainyQuote. (n.d.). *Gustave Flaubert quotes*. Accessed at https://brainyquote.com/quotes/gustave_flaubert _119642 on October 1, 2018.

Brinckloe, J. (1986). *Fireflies*. New York: Aladdin Books.

Brislin, T. (1999). *Integrating active learning, critical thinking and multicultural education in teaching media ethics across the curriculum.* Paper presented at the annual meeting of the Association for Education in Journalism and Mass Communication, New Orleans, LA. Accessed at https://files.eric.ed.gov/fulltext /ED434371.pdf on September 6, 2018.

Brookfield, S. D. (2012). *Teaching for critical thinking: Tools and techniques to help students question their assumptions.* San Francisco: Jossey-Bass.

brusspup. (2015). *10 amazing science tricks using liquid!* [Video file]. Accessed at www.youtube.com/watch ?v=HQx5Be9g16U on January 23, 2019.

Bryant, F., & Bryant, B. (1967). Rocky top [Recorded by the Osborne Brothers]. On *Rocky Top* [Vinyl]. London: Decca.

Buck Institute for Education. (2013a). *Collaboration rubric for PBL (for grades 6–12).* Accessed at https://bie.org /object/document/6_12_collaboration_rubric_non _ccss on September 6, 2018.

Buck Institute for Education. (2013b). *Collaboration rubric for PBL: Individual performance (for grades 3–5).* Accessed at https://bie.org/object/document/3_5 _collaboration_rubric_non_ccss on September 6, 2018.

Buck Institute for Education. (2013c). *Teamwork rubric for PBL (for grades K–2).* Accessed at https://bie.org /object/document/k_2_teamwork_rubric on September 6, 2018.

Cage, J. (1974). *4'33".* On *John Cage* [Vinyl]. Italy: Cramps Records.

Cameron, J., Landau, J. (Producers), & Cameron, J. (Director). (1997). *Titanic* (Motion picture). United States: Paramount Pictures.

Carbonaro, W. J., & Gamoran, A. (2002). The production of achievement inequality in high school English. *American Educational Research Journal, 39*(4), 801–827.

Carpenter, R., Sweet, C., & Blythe, H. (2012). *Introduction to applied creative thinking: Taking control of your future.* Stillwater, OK: New Forums Press.

Chen, D.-T., Wu, J., & Wang, Y.-M. (2011). Unpacking new media literacy. *Journal of Systemics, Cybernetics and Informatics, 9*(2), 84–88. Accessed at www.iiisci .org/journal/sci/FullText.asp?var=&id=OL508KRA on September 6, 2018.

Chodosh, S. (2017, July 19). We still don't really know where dogs came from. *Popular Science.* Accessed at www.popsci.com/dog-evolution-single-origin -controversy on September 6, 2018.

Chopin, K. (1993). *The awakening.* Mineola, NY: Dover.

Chouinard, M. M., Harris, P. L., & Maratsos, M. P. (2007). Children's questions: A mechanism for cognitive development. *Monographs of the Society for Research in Child Development, 72*(1), 1–129.

Christensson, K. M. (n.d.). *RADCAB: Your vehicle for information evaluation.* Accessed at www.radcab.com on January 25, 2019.

Chung, R., Kasprian, G., Brugger, P. C., & Prayer, D. (2009). The current state and future of fetal imaging. *Clinics in Perinatology, 36*(3), 685–699.

Church, R. B., & Goldin-Meadow, S. (1986). The mismatch between gesture and speech as an index of transitional knowledge. *Cognition, 23*(1), 43–71.

Collins, M. F. (2005). ESL preschoolers' English vocabulary acquisition from storybook reading. *Reading Research Quarterly, 40*(4), 406–408.

Connell, G. (2014, October 16). *Use popular music to improve reading and inspire writing* [Blog post]. Accessed at www.scholastic.com/teachers/blog -posts/genia-connell/use-popular-music-improve -reading-and-inspire-writing on September 6, 2018.

Cook-Harvey, C. M., Darling-Hammond, L., Lam, L., Mercer, C., & Roc, M. (2016). *Equity and ESSA: Leveraging educational opportunity through the Every Student Succeeds Act.* Washington, DC: Learning Policy Institute. Accessed at www.hunt-institute .org/wp-content/uploads/2016/11/ESSA-Summary _11.10.16.pdf on September 6, 2018.

Crow, S., & Trott, J. (2017). Roller skate [Recorded by S. Crow]. On *Be myself* [MP3 file]. Burbank, CA: Wylie Songs, Warner Bros. Records.

Curtis, D., & Carter, M. (2015). *Designs for living and learning: Transforming early childhood environments* (2nd ed.). St. Paul, MN: Redleaf Press.

Cushman, K. (2005). *Fires in the bathroom: Advice for teachers from high school students.* New York: New Press.

Darling-Hammond, L. (2012). *Creating a comprehensive system for evaluating and supporting effective teaching.* Stanford, CA: Stanford Center for Opportunity Policy in Education.

Davey, B. (1983). Think aloud: Modeling the cognitive processes of reading comprehension. *Journal of Reading, 27*(1), 44–47.

Davidson, K. (2016, August 30). Employers find "soft skills" like critical thinking in short supply. *Wall Street Journal.* Accessed at www.wsj.com/articles/employers -find-soft-skills-like-critical-thinking-in-short-supply -1472549400 on October 22, 2018.

de Bono, E. (1985). *Six thinking hats.* Toronto, Ontario, Canada: Key Porter Books.

de Bono for Schools. (n.d.). *Free resource for teachers: Six Thinking Hats classroom activity—card game.* Accessed at https://gagc.org/Resources/Documents/2015%20Convention/Handouts/Hampton/Six_Thinking_Hats_Card_Game_Free_Resource.pdf on January 23, 2019.

de Charms, R. (1976). *Enhancing motivation: Change in the classroom.* Oxford, England: Irvington.

Diamandis, P. H., & Kotler, S. (2015). *Bold: How to go big, create wealth, and impact the world.* New York: Simon & Schuster.

Dillon, J. T. (1988). *Questioning and teaching: A manual of practice.* New York: Teachers College Press.

Drapeau, P. (2014). *Sparking student creativity: Practical ways to promote innovative thinking and problem solving.* Alexandria, VA: Association for Supervision and Curriculum Development.

Dweck, C. S. (2006). *Mindset: The new psychology of success.* New York: Ballantine Books.

Dyer, J., Gregersen, H., & Christensen, C. M. (2011). *The innovator's DNA: Mastering the five skills of disruptive innovators.* Boston: Harvard Business Press.

Elder, L., & Paul, R. (2007). *The thinker's guide to analytic thinking: How to take thinking apart and what to look for when you do* (2nd ed.). Tomales, CA: Foundation for Critical Thinking.

Elofsson, J., Gamson, D., Kurstin, G., & Tamposi, A. (2012). Stronger (what doesn't kill you) [Recorded by K. Clarkson]. On *Stronger* [CD]. Los Angeles: RCA.

Engel, C. (2011). Dictator games: A meta study. *Experimental Economics, 14*(4), 583–610.

Every Student Succeeds Act of 2015, Pub. L. No. 114-95, 20 U.S.C. § 1177 (2015).

Expeditionary Learning. (2013). *Appendix: Protocols and resources.* Accessed at www.engageny.org/sites/default/files/resource/attachments/appendix_protocols_and_resources.pdf on March 12, 2019.

Facione, P. A. (2015). *Critical thinking: What it is and why it counts.* Hermosa Beach, CA: Measured Reasons.

Facione, P. A., & Facione, N. C. (1994). *Holistic critical thinking scoring rubric.* Millbrae, CA: California Academic Press. Accessed at https://teaching.temple.edu/sites/tlc/files/resource/pdf/Holistic%20Critical%20Thinking%20Scoring%20Rubric.v2%20%5BAccessible%5D.pdf on September 6, 2018.

Farrand, P., Hussain, F., & Hennessy, E. (2002). The efficacy of the 'mind map' study technique. *Medical Education, 36*(5), 426–431.

Ferris, J. L. G. (1920). *The landing of William Penn* [Painting]. Washington, DC: Library of Congress.

Feuerstein, M. (1999). Media literacy in support of critical thinking. *Journal of Educational Media, 24*(1), 43–54. doi:10.1080/1358165990240104

Fink, J. (2010, August 31). *New Smile-O-Meter cards* [Blog post]. Accessed at www.pianimation.com/2010/08/31/new-smile-o-meter-cards on September 6, 2018.

Fisher, D., Frey, N., Quaglia, R. J., Smith, D., & Lande, L. L. (2018). *Engagement by design: Creating learning environments where students thrive.* Thousand Oaks, CA: Corwin Press.

Fitzgerald, F. S. (2018). *The great Gatsby.* New York: Scribner.

For the Teachers. (n.d.). *Cube template.* Accessed at www.fortheteachers.org/File%20Cabinet/Cube%20Template.pdf on September 6, 2018.

Frey, N. (2011). *The effective teacher's guide: 50 ways to engage students and promote interactive learning* (2nd ed.). New York: Guilford Press.

Frey, N., Fisher, D., & Everlove, S. (2017). Getting the most out of group work. *ASCD Express, 13*(5). Accessed at www.ascd.org/ascd-express/vol13/1305-fisher.aspx on September 6, 2018.

Fried, S. (2010, January 29). *Differentiated instruction.* Slides presented at the Professional Development Conference at Kulanu Torah Academy, Cedarhurst, NY. Accessed at https://slideshare.net/sholomfried/differentiated-instruction-powerpoint-for-pd-workshop on September 6, 2018.

Geirland, J. (1996, September 1). Go with the flow. *Wired.* Accessed at www.wired.com/1996/09/czik on September 6, 2018.

Gibson, S. (1998). Wide open spaces [Recorded by Dixie Chicks]. On *Dixie Chicks* [Album]. Washington, DC: Monument.

Godfrey, W., Mooradian, G., & Morgan, M. (Producers), & Hardwicke, C. (Director). (2008). *Twilight* [Motion picture]. United States: Summit Entertainment.

GoNoodle. (2017, May 19). *Water cycle—Blazer fresh* [Video file]. Accessed at https://youtube.com/watch?v=KM-59ljA4Bs on September 6, 2018.

Grainger, P. (1927). Homeless blues [Recorded by B. Smith]. Bridgeport, CT: Columbia Phonograph.

Grant, E. (1982). Electric avenue [Recorded by E. Grant]. On *Killer on the rampage* [Record]. London: EMI.

Graphic organizer—Persuasive essay. (n.d.). Accessed at www.pinterest.com/pin/545639311078098030 on September 6, 2018.

Greenberg, A. D., & Nilssen, A. H. (2014). *The role of education in building soft skills: Putting into perspective the priorities and opportunities for teaching collaboration and other soft skills in education.* Duxbury, MA: Wainhouse Research. Accessed at http://cp.wainhouse .com/content/role-education-building-soft-skills on September 6, 2018.

Greene, R. (2012). *Mastery.* New York: Penguin.

Guillaume, A. M., Yopp, R. H., & Yopp, H. K. (2007). *50 strategies for active teaching: Engaging K–12 learners in the classroom.* London: Pearson.

Hanks, T., Rapke, J., Starkey, S., & Zemeckis, R. (Producers), & Zemeckis, R. (Director). (2000). *Cast away* [Motion picture]. United States: ImageMovers.

Hansberry, L. (2004). *A raisin in the sun.* New York: Vintage Books.

Harrison, G. (1966). Taxman [Recorded by the Beatles]. On *Revolver* [Album]. London: EMI Studios.

Hart, B., & Risley, T. R. (2003). The early catastrophe: The 30 million word gap by age 3. *American Educator, 27*(1), 4–9.

Hart Research Associates. (2013). *It takes more than a major: Employer priorities for college learning and student success—Overview and key findings.* Washington, DC: Association of American Colleges and Universitites.

Hattie, J. (2009). *Visible learning: A synthesis of over 800 meta-analyses relating to achievement.* London: Routledge.

Hattie, J. (2012). *Visible learning for teachers: Maximizing impact on learning.* New York: Routledge.

Hattie, J., & Timperley, H. (2007). The power of feedback. *Review of Educational Research, 77*(1), 81–112.

Hawthorne, N. (1998). *The scarlet letter.* New York: Oxford University Press.

Heick, T. (2018, April 8). *26 sentence stems for higher-level conversation in the classroom.* Accessed at www.teach thought.com/critical-thinking/sentence-stems-higher -level-conversation-classroom on September 6, 2018.

Heimel, C. (1983). Lower Manhattan survival tactics. *The Village Voice, 13,* 26.

Helgeson, J. (2011). Four simple ways to add movement in daily lessons. *Kappa Delta Pi Record, 47*(2), 80–84.

Henry, O. (2005). *The gift of the magi* [Short story]. Accessed at www.gutenberg.org/files/7256 /7256-h/7256-h.htm on September 6, 2018.

Hewes, B. (2012, October 17). *Feedback, feed-forward, peer-assessment and project-based learning* [Blog post]. Accessed at https://biancahewes.wordpress.com/2012 /10/17/feedback-feed-forward-peer-assessment-and -project-based-learning on September 6, 2018.

Himmele, P., & Himmele, W. (2011). *Total participation techniques: Making every student an active learner* (2nd ed.). Alexandria, VA: Association for Supervision and Curriculum Development.

History.com Editors. (2018). *Socrates.* Accessed at www .history.com/topics/ancient-history/socrates on January 23, 2019.

Hoberman, D., & Lieberman, T. (Producers), & Condon, B. (Director). (2017). *Beauty and the beast* [Motion picture]. United States: Walt Disney Pictures.

Hofman, P., Goodwin, B., & Kahl, S. (2015). *Re-balancing assessment: Placing formative and performance assessment at the heart of learning and accountability.* Denver, CO: McREL International.

Honigsfeld, A., & Dunn, R. (2009). Learning-style responsive approaches for teaching typically performing and at-risk adolescents. *Clearing House, 82*(5), 220–224.

Hughes, L. (1990). *Selected poems of Langston Hughes.* New York: Random House.

Jensen, E. (2019). *Poor students, rich teaching: Seven high-impact mindsets for students from poverty* (Rev. ed.). Bloomington, IN: Solution Tree Press.

Jeong, S. H., Cho, H., & Hwang, Y. (2012). Media literacy interventions: A meta-analytic review. *Journal of Communication, 62*(3), 454–472.

John, E., & Taupin, B. (1972). Rocket man [Recorded by E. John]. On *Honky Château* [Vinyl]. London: DJM Records.

Johnson, D. W., & Johnson, R. T. (1999). Making cooperative learning work. *Theory Into Practice, 38*(2), 67–73.

Johnson, S. (2010). *Where good ideas come from: The natural history of innovation.* New York: Riverhead Books.

Kagan, S. (1994). *Cooperative learning.* San Clemente, CA: Kagan Cooperative Learning.

Kagan, S., & Kagan, M. (1998). *Multiple intelligences: The complete MI book.* San Clemente, CA: Kagan Cooperative Learning.

Kendon, A. (1988). How gestures can become like words. In F. Poyatos (Ed.), *Cross-cultural perspectives in nonverbal communication* (pp. 131–141). Toronto, Ontario, Canada: Hogrefe.

Kinberg, S., Scott, R., Schaefer, M., Sood, A., & Huffam (Producers), & Scott, R. (Director). (2015). *The martian* [Motion picture]. United States: Scott Free Productions.

King, M. L., Jr. (1963). *I have a dream* [Speech]. Accessed at https://archives.gov/files/press/exhibits/dream-speech.pdf on September 6, 2018.

Klem, A. M., & Connell, J. P. (2004). Relationships matter: Linking teacher support to student engagement and achievement. *Journal of School Health, 74*(7), 262–273.

Knowles, B., & Nash, T. (2011). Run the world (girls). [Recorded by B. Knowles]. On *4* [Studio album]. New York: Jungle City Studios.

Koenig, R. (2010). *Learning for keeps: Teaching the strategies essential for creating independent learners.* Alexandria, VA: Association for Supervision and Curriculum Development.

Kohn, D. (2015, May 16). Let the kids learn through play. *New York Times.* Accessed at www.nytimes.com/2015/05/17/opinion/sunday/let-the-kids-learn-through-play.html on September 6, 2018.

Kuhlthau, C. C., Maniotes, L. K., & Caspari, A. K. (2015). *Guided inquiry: Learning in the 21st century* (2nd ed.). Santa Barbara, CA: Libraries Unlimited.

Lee, H. (1989). *To kill a mockingbird.* New York: Grand Central.

Lickona, T. (1991). *Educating for character: How our schools can teach respect and responsibility.* New York: Bantam Books.

Lionni, L. (1960). *Inch by inch.* New York: HarperCollins.

Livingston, N. (1983). Electric boogie [Recorded by Marcia Griffiths]. On *Electric Boogie* [Vinyl]. London: Mango.

Lynch, R., McNamara, P. M., & Seery, N. (2012, January 23). Promoting deep learning in a teacher education programme through self- and peer-assessment and feedback. *European Journal of Teacher Education, 35*(2), 179–197. Accessed at www.tandfonline.com/doi/abs/10.1080/02619768.2011.643396?src=recsys&journalCode=cete20 on October 1, 2018.

Mack, N. (2013). Colorful revision: Color-coded comments connected to instruction. *Teaching English in the Two-Year College, 40*(3), 248–256.

Manzo, A. V. (1969). Reading and questioning: The request procedure. *Journal of Reading, 13*(2), 123–126.

Marzano, R. J. (2004). *Building background knowledge for academic achievement: Research on what works in schools.* Alexandria, VA: Association for Supervision and Curriculum Development.

Marzano, R. J. (2009). Setting the record straight on "high-yield" strategies. *Phi Delta Kappan, 91*(1), 30–37.

Marzano, R. J. (2010). The art and science of teaching / teaching inference. *Educational Leadership, 67*(7), 80–81. Accessed at www.ascd.org/publications/educational-leadership/apr10/vol67/num07/Teaching-Inference.aspx on September 27, 2018.

Marzano, R. J., & Pickering, D. J. (2011). *The highly engaged classroom.* Bloomington, IN: Marzano Resources.

Marzano, R. J., & Toth, M. D. (2014). *Teaching for rigor: A call for a critical instructional shift.* West Palm Beach, FL: Learning Sciences International. Accessed at https://marzanocenter.com/wp-content/uploads/2018/10/MC05-01-Teaching-for-Rigor-Paper-05-20-14-Digital-1.pdf on October 23, 2018.

Mathews, S. R., & Lowe, K. (2011). Classroom environments that foster a disposition for critical thinking. *Learning Environments Research, 14*(1), 59–73.

Maxwell, M., Stobaugh, R., & Tassell, J. L. (2016). *Real-world learning framework for secondary schools: Digital tools and practical strategies for successful implementation.* Bloomington, IN: Solution Tree Press.

McCombs, B. (2015). *Developing responsible and autonomous learners: A key to motivating students* [Teacher's modules]. Accessed at www.apa.org/education/k12/learners.aspx on September 6, 2018.

McGough, J. V., & Nyberg, L. M. (2015). *The power of questioning: Guiding student investigations.* Arlington, VA: National Science Teachers Association Press.

McIntosh, E. (2012, February 8). *Stop ping pong questioning. Try basketball instead* [Blog post]. Accessed at http://edu.blogs.com/edublogs/2012/02/stop-ping-pong-questioning-try-basketball-instead.html on September 6, 2018.

Meacham, B. (2017, February 13). Implementing the claim, evidence, reasoning framework in the chemistry classroom. *ChemEd X.* Accessed at https://chemedx.org/article/implementing-claim-evidence-reasoning-framework-chemistry-classroom on September 6, 2018.

Mercury, F. (1975). Bohemian rhapsody [Recorded by Queen]. On *A night at the opera* [MP3 file]. London: EMI Records.

Migyanka, J., Policastro, C., & Lui, G. (2005). Using a Think-Aloud with diverse students: Three primary grade students experience *Chrysanthemum. Early Childhood Education Journal, 33*(3), 171–177.

Miller, S. (1976). Take the money and run [Recorded by Steve Miller Band]. On *Fly like an eagle* [Album]. Los Angeles: Capitol.

Mrs. Bayna's Class Resources. (n.d.). *Argumentative writing graphic organizer.* Accessed at https://dbayna.com/uploads/4/2/0/9/4209638/argumentative_writing_-_graphic_organizer_copy.jpg on September 6, 2018.

Mualem, R., Leisman, G., Zbedat, Y., Ganem, S., Mualem, O., Amaria, M., et al. Ornai, A. (2018). The effect of movement on cognitive performance. *Frontiers in Public Health, 6*(100), 1–6.

Naiditch, F. (Ed.). (2017). *Developing critical thinking: From theory to classroom practice.* Lanham, MD: Rowman & Littlefield.

National Center for Education Statistics. (2006). *The condition of education 2006: Section 1, participation in education* (NCES No. 2006-071). Washington, DC: U.S. Government Printing Office. Accessed at https://nces.ed.gov/pubs2006/2006071_1.pdf on September 6, 2018.

National Council for the Social Studies. (2016). Media literacy [Position statement]. *Social Education, 80*(3), 183–185. Accessed at https://socialstudies.org/publications/socialeducation/may-june2016/media-literacy on January 4, 2019.

Nesbit, J. C., & Adesope, O. O. (2006). Learning with concept and knowledge maps: A meta-analysis. *Review of Educational Research, 76*(3), 413–448. Accessed at http://cmapspublic2.ihmc.us/rid=1J61L9C8Y-GCMY3Z-W9P/nesbit2006.pdf on September 27, 2018.

Nessel, D. D., & Graham, J. M. (2007). *Thinking strategies for student achievement: Improving learning across the curriculum, K–12* (2nd ed.). Thousand Oaks, CA: Corwin Press.

Nettles, J., Bush, K., Griffin, K., & Carter, S. (2010). Stuck like glue [Recorded by Sugarland]. On *The incredible machine* [Digital download]. Nashville, TN: Mercury.

NGSS Lead States. (2013). *Next Generation Science Standards: For states, by states.* Washington, DC: National Academies Press.

Nosich, G. M. (2008). *Learning to think things through: A guide to critical thinking across the curriculum* (3rd ed.). London: Prentice Hall.

Ochs, P. (1976). What are you fighting for? [Recorded by P. Ochs]. On *Sings for Broadside* [Vinyl]. New York: Folkways Records.

O'Keefe, P. A. (2014, September 5). Liking work really matters. *New York Times.* Accessed at https://nytimes.com/2014/09/07/opinion/sunday/go-with-the-flow.html on September 6, 2018.

Olejnik, S., & Algina, J. (2000). Measures of effect size for comparative studies: Applications, interpretations, and limitations. *Contemporary Educational Psychology, 25*(3), 241–286.

Organisation for Economic Co-operation and Development. (n.d.). *Preparing our youth for an inclusive and sustainable world: The OECD PISA global competence framework.* Accessed at www.oecd.org/pisa/Handbook-PISA-2018-Global-Competence.pdf on January 17, 2019.

Organisation for Economic Co-operation and Development. (2012). *Programme for International Student Assessment (PISA): Results from PISA 2012—United States.* Accessed at www.oecd.org/pisa/keyfindings/PISA-2012-results-US.pdf on September 6, 2018.

Ostroff, W. L. (2016). *Cultivating curiosity in K–12 classrooms: How to promote and sustain deep learning.* Alexandria, VA: Association for Supervision and Curriculum Development.

Paine, T. (1976). *Thomas Paine's common sense: The call to independence.* Woodbury, NY: Barron's Educational Series.

Paivio, A. (1991). Dual coding theory: Retrospect and current status. *Canadian Journal of Psychology, 45*(3), 255–287.

Palacio, R. J. (2012). *Wonder.* New York: Random House.

Pappano, L. (2014, February 5). Learning to think outside the box. *New York Times.* Accessed at https://nytimes.com/2014/02/09/education/edlife/creativity-becomes-an-academic-discipline.html?hp&_r=0 on September 6, 2018.

Paul, R., & Elder, L. (2007). *Consequential validity: Using assessment to drive instruction* [White paper]. Tomales, CA: Foundation for Critical Thinking. Accessed at www.criticalthinking.org/pages/consequential-validity-using-assessment-to-drive-instruction/790 on September 6, 2018.

Penn, J. L. G. (1932). *The landing of William Penn* [Painting]. Cleveland, OH: Foundation Press.

Peretti, H., Creatore, L., & Weiss, G. D. (1961). Can't help falling in love [Recorded by E. Presley]. On *Blue Hawaii* [Album]. Hollywood, CA: RCA Victor.

Perry, K., Eriksen, M. S., Hermansen, T. E., Wilhelm, S., & Dean, E. (2010). Firework [Recorded by K. Perry]. On *Teenage dream* [Album]. Los Angeles: Capitol.

Piaget, J. (n.d.). *Jean Piaget quotes.* Accessed at www.brainyquote.com/quotes/jean_piaget_751077 on January 25, 2019.

Piaget, J. (1959). *The language and thought of the child.* London: Routledge & Kegan Paul.

Pianta, R. C., Belsky, J., Houts, R., & Morrison, F. (2007). *Opportunities to learn in America's elementary classrooms.* Accessed at http://science.sciencemag.org/content/315/5820/1795 on September 6, 2018.

Pianta, R. C., Hamre, B. K., & Allen, J. P. (2012). Teacher-student relationships and engagement: Conceptualizing, measuring, and improving the capacity of classroom interactions. In S. L. Christenson, A. L. Reschly, & C. Wylie (Eds.), *Handbook of research on student engagement* (pp. 365–386). New York: Springer.

Potts, B. (1994). Strategies for teaching critical thinking. *Practical Assessment, Research and Evaluation, 4*(3). Accessed at www.pareonline.net/getvn.asp?v=4&n=3 on September 6, 2018.

Prince, M., & Felder, R. (2007, February 15). The many faces of inductive teaching and learning. *NSTA WebNews Digest.* Accessed at www.nsta.org /publications/news/story.aspx?id=53403 on September 28, 2018.

Project Look Sharp, & Rogow, F. (2017). *Developing habits of inquiry: Key questions to ask when analyzing media messages.* Accessed at www.projectlooksharp.org /Resources%202/keyquestions.pdf on September 6, 2018.

Redford, J., Thiede, K. W., Wiley, J., & Griffin, T. (2012). Concept mapping improves metacomprehension accuracy among 7th graders. *Learning and Instruction, 22*(4), 262–270. Accessed at https://scholarworks .boisestate.edu/cifs_facpubs/93 on September 27, 2018.

Reeves, D. (2015). *Inspiring creativity and innovation in K–12.* Bloomington, IN: Solution Tree Press.

Ritchhart, R. (2015). *Creating cultures of thinking: The eight forces we must master to truly transform our schools.* San Francisco: Jossey-Bass.

Ritchhart, R., Church, M., & Morrison, K. (2011). *Making thinking visible: How to promote engagement, understanding, and independence for all learners.* San Francisco: Jossey-Bass.

Robaton, A. (2015, June 6). *What will you be doing in 2022? Hottest jobs for grads.* Accessed at https://cnbc .com/2015/06/06/what-will-you-be-doing-in-2022 -hottest-jobs-for-grads.html?view=story&%24DEVICE %24=native-android-tablet on September 6, 2018.

Rose-Duckworth, R., & Ramer, K. (2009). *Fostering learner independence: An essential guide for K–6 educators.* Thousand Oaks, CA: Corwin Press.

Roth, W.-M. (2001). Gestures: Their role in teaching and learning. *Review of Educational Research, 71*(3), 365–392.

Rothstein, D., & Santana, L. (2015). *Make just one change: Teach students to ask their own questions* (6th ed.). Cambridge, MA: Harvard Education Press.

Sachar, L. (2000). *Holes.* New York: Yearling.

Scheibe, C., & Rogow, F. (2012). *The teachers' guide to media literacy: Critical thinking in a multimedia world.* Thousand Oaks, CA: Corwin Press.

Schmoker, M. (2009). What money can't buy: Powerful, overlooked opportunities for learning. *Phi Delta Kappan, 90*(7), 524–527.

Schroeder, C. M., Scott, T. P., Tolson, H., Huang, T.-Y., & Lee, Y.-H. (2007). A meta-analysis of national research: Effects of teaching strategies on student achievement in science in the United States. *Journal of Research in Science Teaching, 44*(10), 1436–1460.

Senn, D., & Marzano, R. J. (2015). *Engaging in cognitively complex tasks: Classroom techniques to help students generate and test hypotheses across disciplines.* West Palm Beach, FL: Learning Sciences International.

Shakespeare, W. (1935). *The tragedy of Romeo and Juliet.* New York: Heritage Press.

Shernoff, D. J. (2013). *Optimal learning environments to promote student engagement.* New York: Springer.

Shernoff, D. J., Csikszentmihalyi, M., Shneider, B., & Shernoff, E. (2003). Student engagement in high school classrooms from the perspective of flow theory. *School Psychology Quarterly, 18*(2), 158–176. doi:10.1521 /scpq.18.2.158.21860

Silver, H. F., Strong, R. W., & Perini, M. J. (2007). *The strategic teacher: Selecting the right research-based strategy for every lesson.* Alexandria, VA: Association for Supervision and Curriculum Development.

Silverstein, S. (n.d.). "Smart" [Poem]. Accessed at https:// poemhunter.com/poem/smart-7 on September 6, 2018.

Simon, C. A. (n.d.). *Strategy guide: Brainstorming and reviewing using the carousel strategy.* Urbana, IL: National Council of Teachers of English. Accessed at www.readwritethink.org/professional-development /strategyguides/brainstorming-reviewing -usingcarousel-30630.html on September 6, 2018.

Smith, T., Baker, W., Hattie, J., & Bond, L. (2008). A validity study of the certification system of the National Board for Professional Teaching Standards. In L. Ingvarson & J. Hattie (Eds.), *Assessing teachers for professional certification: The first decade of the National Board for Professional Teaching Standards* (pp. 345–380). Bingley, England: Emerald Group.

Sousa, D. A. (2011). *How the brain learns* (4th ed.). Thousand Oaks, CA: Corwin Press.

Sousa, D. A. (2017). *How the brain learns* (5th ed.). Thousand Oaks, CA: Corwin Press.

Stauffer, R. G. (1975). *Directing the reading-thinking process.* New York: Harper & Row.

Steinbeck, J. (1994). *Of mice and men*. New York: Penguin Books.

Stengel, B., & Weems, L. (2010). Questioning safe space: An introduction. *Studies in Philosophy and Education, 29*(6), 505–507.

Stewart, J. (2012). *The life and work of Kierkegaard as the "Socratic task"* [Video file]. Accessed at www.coursera .org/learn/kierkegaard#syllabus on September 6, 2018.

Stobaugh, R. (2013). *Assessing critical thinking in middle and high schools: Meeting the Common Core*. Larchmont, NY: Eye on Education.

Stobaugh, R. (2016). *Sparking student questioning* [White paper]. Tyler, TX: Mentoring Minds. Accessed at https://mentoringminds.com/downloads /white-papers/Sparking-Student-Questioning.pdf on September 6, 2018.

Stobaugh, R., & Love, S. (2015). *Fusing critical thinking with kinesthetic learning* [White paper]. Tyler, TX: Mentoring Minds. Accessed at https://mentoringminds .com/learn/white-papers/fusing-critical-thinking -kinesthetic-learning on September 6, 2018.

Strauss, V. (2017, December 20). The surprising thing Google learned about its employees—and what it means for today's students. *Washington Post*. Accessed at https://washingtonpost.com/news/answer-sheet /wp/2017/12/20/the-surprising-thing-google -learned-about-its-employees-and-what-it-means -for-todays-students/?utm_term=.cb8565261663 on September 6, 2018.

Stupnisky, R. H., Renaud, R. D., Daniels, L. M., Haynes, T. L., & Perry, R. P. (2008). The interrelation of first-year college students' critical thinking disposition, perceived academic control, and academic achievement. *Research in Higher Education, 49*(6), 513–530.

Summer, D., & Omartian, M. (1983). She works hard for the money [Recorded by D. Summer]. On *She works hard for the money* [Album]. Chicago: Mercury Records.

Sutton, B. (2009, February 10). *Reward success and failure, punish inaction* [Blog post]. Accessed at http:// bobsutton.typepad.com/my_weblog/2009/02 /reward-success-and-failure-punish-inaction.html on September 6, 2018.

Swartz, R. J., Costa, A. L., Beyer, B. K., Reagan, R., & Kallick, B. (2008). *Thinking-based learning: Promoting quality student achievement in the 21st century*. New York: Teachers College Press.

SWOT analysis. (n.d.). In *Wikipedia*. Accessed at https://en.wikipedia.org/wiki/SWOT_analysis on December 13, 2018.

Swift, J. (1996). *A modest proposal and other satirical works*. Mineola, NY: Dover.

Swift, T. (2006). I'm only me when I'm with you [Recorded by T. Swift]. On *Taylor Swift* [Studio album]. Nashville, TN: Big Machine Records.

Swift, T. (2008). Love story [Recorded by T. Swift]. On *Fearless* [Studio album]. Nashville, TN: Big Machine Records.

Swift, T., Martin, M., & Shellback. (2012). We are never ever getting back together [Recorded by T. Swift]. On *Red* [Studio album]. Nashville, TN: Big Machine Records.

SWOT analysis. (n.d.). In *Wikipedia*. Accessed at https://en.wikipedia.org/wiki/SWOT_analysis on October 2, 2018.

Tchaikovsky, P. I. (n.d.). *Dance of the sugar plum fairy* [Audio file]. Accessed at www.free-stock-music.com /tchaikovsky-dance-of-the-sugar-plum-fairy.html.

The Teacher Toolkit. (n.d.). *Consensogram* [Online lesson]. Accessed at www.theteachertoolkit.com/index.php /tool/consensogram on September 6, 2018.

TeacherVision. (n.d.). *Directed Reading-Thinking Activity*. Accessed at www.teachervision.com/directed-reading -thinking-activity on January 23, 2019.

TeachRock. (n.d.). Beatlemania [Online lesson]. In *Book 2: Teenage rebellion*. Accessed at http://teachrock.org /lesson/beatlemania on September 6, 2018.

Thornburg, D. (2014). *From the campfire to the holodeck: Creating engaging and powerful 21st century learning environments*. San Francisco: Jossey-Bass.

Treffinger, D. J., Schoonover, P. F., & Selby, E. C. (2013). *Educating for creativity and innovation: A comprehensive guide for research-based practice*. Waco, TX: Prufrock Press.

Tsirkunova, S. A. (2013). Conceptual metaphor as a means for teaching critical thinking skills. *International Journal of Humanities and Social Science, 3*(16), 44–48.

txxinblog. (2016, November 30). *Existence of manifest destiny today?* [Blog post]. Accessed at https://txxinblog .wordpress.com/2016/11/30/existence-of-manifest -destiny-today on September 6, 2018.

U.S. Army. (2013). *TRADOC pamphlet 350–70–7*. Fort Eustis, VA: Author.

U.S. Chamber of Commerce Foundation. (n.d.). *Bridging the soft skills gap: How the business and education sectors are partnering to prepare students for the 21st century workforce*. Accessed at https://uschamberfoundation .org/sites/default/files/Bridging%20The%20 Soft%20Skills%20Gap_White%20Paper%20 FINAL_11.2.17%20.pdf on September 6, 2018.

van de Vall, T. (2013). *Fishbone diagram.* Accessed at www.timvandevall.com/wp-content/uploads/Blank -Fishbone-Diagram.pdf on October 29, 2018.

Vecchione, J., & Else, J. (1990). *Eyes on the prize* [Television series]. Arlington, VA: PBS.

Victor, D. (2018, February 9). Oxford comma dispute is settled as Maine drivers get $5 million. *New York Times.* Accessed at https://nytimes.com/2018/02/09/us /oxford-comma-maine.html on September 6, 2018.

Viorst, J. (1987). *Alexander, who used to be rich last Sunday.* New York: Atheneum Books for Young Readers.

Vivaldi, A. (1949). *Concerti delle stagioni (the four seasons).* New York: Concert Hall Society.

Vygotsky, L. S. (1978). *Mind in society: The development of higher psychological processes* (M. Cole, Ed.). Cambridge, MA: Harvard University Press.

Walsh, J. A., & Sattes, B. D. (2017). *Quality questioning: Research-based practice to engage every learner* (2nd ed.). Thousand Oaks, CA: Corwin Press.

Washington State University. (2001). *Washington State University critical thinking project: Resource guide.* Accessed at https://assessment.trinity.duke.edu/sites /assessment.trinity.duke.edu/files/page-attachments /WashingtonStateUniversityCriticalThinking ProjectResource Guide_000.pdf on September 6, 2018.

Watanabe-Crockett, L. (2016a, August 2). *The critical 21st century skills every student needs and why* [Blog post]. Accessed at https://globaldigitalcitizen.org/21st -century-skills-every-student-needs on October 2, 2018.

Watanabe-Crockett, L. (2016b, December 12). *The critical thinking skills cheatsheet* [Blog post]. Accessed at https:// globaldigitalcitizen.org/critical-thinking-skills -cheatsheet-infographic on September 6, 2018.

Watanabe-Crockett, L. (2019). *Future-focused learning: Ten essential shifts of everyday practice.* Bloomington, IN: Solution Tree Press.

Webb, T., & Martin, K. (2012). Evaluation of a US school-based media literacy violence prevention curriculum on changes in knowledge and critical thinking among adolescents. *Journal of Children and Media, 6*(4), 430–449.

Wendover Productions. (2017, December 5). *India's geography problem* [Video file]. Accessed at https:// youtube.com/watch?v=6mDsa-AqNcQ on November 15, 2018.

Wenglinsky, H. (2004). Closing the racial achievement gap: The role of reforming instructional practices. *Education Policy Analysis Archives, 12*(64), 1–24.

Whitacre, E. (n.d.a). *Virtual choir 1: Sleep.* Accessed at https://ericwhitacre.com/the-virtual-choir/history/vc1 -luxaurumque on December 13, 2018.

Whitacre, E. (n.d.b). *Virtual choir 2: Sleep.* Accessed at https://ericwhitacre.com/the-virtual-choir/history/vc2 -sleep on December 13, 2018.

Wilhelm, J. D. (2001). Think-alouds: Boost reading comprehension. *Instructor, 111*(4), 26–28.

Wineburg, S., McGrew, S., Breakstone, J., & Ortega, T. (2016). *Evaluating information: The cornerstone of civic online reasoning.* Accessed at https://purl.stanford.edu /fv751yt5934 on September 6, 2018.

Wing, N. (2005). *The night before first grade.* New York: Grosset & Dunlap.

World Economic Forum. (2016). *The future of jobs report.* Accessed at http://reports.weforum.org/future-of-jobs -2016 on September 6, 2018.

Wujec, T. (2010). *Build a tower, build a team* [Video file]. Accessed at www.ted.com/talks/tom_wujec_build_a _tower on January 23, 2019.

Yenawine, P. (2013). *Visual thinking strategies: Using art to deepen learning across school disciplines.* Cambridge, MA: Harvard Education Press.

Yng, N. J., & Sreedharan, S. (2012, August 24). Teach less, learn more—Have we achieved it? *Today.* Accessed at https://guanyinmiao.files.wordpress.com/2012/08 /teach-less-learn-more-have-we-achieved-it.pdf on September 6, 2018.

Zanuck, R. D., & Brown, D. (Producers), & Spielberg, S. (Director). (1975). *Jaws* [Motion picture]. United States: Zanuck/Brown.

Zhao, Y. (2006, May 9). A pause before plunging through the China looking glass: Why the U.S. race to reform and catch up can wait. *Education Week.* Accessed at www.edweek.org/ew/articles/2006/05/10/36zhao .h25.html on September 6, 2018.

Index

Teaching With the Instructional Cha-Chas
LeAnn Nickelsen and Melissa Dickson

Discover a four-step cycle of instruction—chunk, chew, check, and change—that you can rely on to improve daily teaching, learning, and evaluation. Compatible with any subject area, the book's brain-friendly teaching strategies are designed to help transform students into active learners and independent thinkers.

BKF822

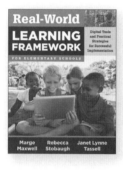

Real-World Learning Framework for Elementary Schools
Marge Maxwell, Rebecca Stobaugh, and Janet Lynne Tassell

Bring about deeper, self-directed learning in elementary school students by exercising cognitive complexity, engagement, and technology integration through real-world project-based instruction. Learn the Create Excellence Framework and take advantage of sample lesson plans from real-world projects to help students partner in their own learning.

BKF753

Real-World Learning Framework for Secondary Schools
Marge Maxwell, Rebecca Stobaugh, and Janet Lynne Tassell

Using the Create Excellence Framework, educators can help students find greater fulfillment in learning, while also meeting the guidelines of curriculum standards. Explore the framework's main components, and understand how to use the framework for classroom, school, and district pursuits.

BKF656

The Quest for Learning
Marie Alcock, Michael Fisher, and Allison Zmuda

This resource dives deep into questing, a customizable pedagogy tailored to a student's interests, needs, and abilities. Learn how to use questing to engross students in emotionally gripping learning experiences, engage them with actionable goals, and promote collaboration in online and physical spaces.

BKF718

EMPOWER Your Students
Lauren Porosoff and Jonathan Weinstein

Discover how to use the elements of EMPOWER—exploration, motivation, participation, openness, willingness, empathy, and resilience—to make school a positive, meaningful experience in your students' lives. This highly practical resource offers engaging classroom activities and strategies for incorporating student values into curriculum.

BKF791

Solution Tree | Press
a division of
Solution Tree

Wait! Your professional development journey doesn't have to end with the last pages of this book.

We realize improving student learning doesn't happen overnight. And your school or district shouldn't be left to puzzle out all the details of this process alone.

No matter where you are on the journey, we're committed to helping you get to the next stage.

Take advantage of everything from **custom workshops** to **keynote presentations** and **interactive web and video conferencing**. We can even help you develop an action plan tailored to fit your specific needs.

Let's get the conversation started.

Call 888.763.9045 today.